Shipwreck Heresies

Gary Gentile

Bellerophon Bookworks

Copyright 2009 by Gary Gentile

All rights reserved. Except for the use of brief quotations embodied in critical articles and reviews, this book may not be reproduced in part or in whole, in any manner (including mechanical, electronic, photographic, and photocopy means), transmitted in any form, or recorded by any data storage and/or retrieval system, without express written permission from the author. Address all queries to:

Bellerophon Bookworks
P.O. Box 57137
Philadelphia, PA 19111

Additional copies of this book may be purchased from the same address by sending a check or money order in the amount of $20 U.S. for each copy (plus $4 shipping per order, not per book). For information about consulting services, workshops, presentations, and a list of available titles that can be ordered online and paid by credit card, visit the GGP website:

http://www.ggentile.com

All uncredited photographs were taken by the author. Front cover top: jars on the *Monitor*, the reverse of a silver coin from *El Cazador*, and the obverse of a gold coin from the *Brother Jonathan*. Front cover bottom: the reverse of a gold coin from the *Brother Jonathan*, the obverse of a silver coin from *El Cazador*, and the docking telegraph on the *Lusitania*. Back cover top: sea lions on a dock in Crescent City, California, and a brass hand wheel on the engine of the *Monitor*. Back cover bottom: hydraulic helm and engine order annunciator in the wheel house wreckage of the *Lusitania*, and a brass revolution counter on the engine of the *Monitor*.

International Standard Book Numbers (ISBN)
1-883056-39-X
978-1-883056-39-1

Second Edition

Printed in the U.S.A.

Contents

On Being a Heretic	4
Gary Gentile: Deep Wreck Diver	6
Gentile on Narcosis	16
Travesty of Justice: Wrongful Passage of the Abandoned Shipwreck Act	20
Murphy's Law: Destroyer Extraordinaire	46
Monitor	
The *Monitor*: America's Socialized Shipwreck	68
The *Monitor* Goes Public	76
The Stellwagen Bank Robbery	79
Cast in Ink: *Hamilton* and *Scourge*	102
Report on Salvage Operations on the *Brother Jonathan*	105
El Cazador - For Lack of a Nail . . .	118
Lusitania	
The *Lusitania* in a Technical Way	130
Lusitania: Historical Sidebar	140
Lusitania Bound	143
Lusitania Turmoil	149
Cast in Bronze: *Lusitania*'s Secret Revealed	154
Forum: the 94 *Lusitania* Expedition - Seductive or Suicidal?	164
Shadow Divers Exposed in Retrospect	189
The Author's Books and Biography	260

Beware the heretic,
for he upsets the order of things.

For all of my adult life I have been branded a heretic. For the most part, I have brought that sentiment upon myself. I refused to be restrained by convention, and I fostered the temerity to ignore the status quo.

I went places where people said I shouldn't go, and I did things that people said couldn't be done. Controversy and unorthodoxy have been my mainstay. In a science fiction novel I paraphrased the *Bible*: "And the meek shall inherit the Earth. The rest of us will have gone to the stars."

In a sense I was obstinate. I did not let people tell me what to do if I felt that the doing was wrong. This attitude of defiance got me into a lot of trouble in the Army. I spent a lot of time on KP, I was court-martialed once, and I was faced with a second court-martial that failed to materialize because it was superseded by a more significant event.

When I worked in construction, I was marked as a troublemaker because I believed that everyone had the right to earn a living, not just the chosen few who were permitted to join the union - this despite the fact that I was a card-carrying member.

As an author, I have never been afraid to tell it like it is. If this penchant for refusing to varnish the facts rubbed a few people the wrong way, so be it. Substance is more important to me than fairy tales. The truth will out.

Looking back, if I had my life to live over again, I would do exactly as I did the first time – but I would do it without equivocation. I have few regrets. Those regrets that I have are the result of omission, not commission. As my e-mail signature reads, "So many shipwrecks, so many mountains, so many rivers, so little time . . . "

On Being a Heretic

I could add "so many books," both to read and to write.

You can't do everything, but you can certainly try!

I have often been asked why I dive on shipwrecks, and particularly on *deep* shipwrecks. The aspects of wreck-diving which appeal to me the most are the challenge of the activity and the exploration of the unknown. I dive in caves for the same reason, but not nearly as often, largely because I got hooked on wreck-diving first.

Diving on reefs is like looking at pretty paintings. While I visit art galleries every once in a while, and dive on reefs every now and again, I prefer rigorous action and adventure to sedentary pastimes. That is why I have climbed mountains, camped in the snow, backpacked in remote areas, and canoed in the wilderness for weeks on end.

Diving on and into deep shipwrecks, where bottom time is short and decompression is long, is admittedly a hazardous pursuit that at first blush doesn't seem worth the effort. As I've written elsewhere:

"A deep dive is like an orgasm: it may not last very long, but duration is not as important as the intensity of the experience and the satisfaction that derives from it."

Shipwreck Heresies is a collection of my shorter works, most of which are heretical in nature. They have seen print in books, magazines, newspapers, courts of law, and on the Internet. Some I have expanded for this collection because space limitations in the original publication precluded me from telling the story in its entirety. Others I have let stand the way they were published, but I have appended annotations either beforehand or afterward. I wrote "Shadow Divers Exposed in Retrospect" exclusively for inclusion in this volume.

There is nothing wrong with being a heretic, as long as you are willing to accept the derision that goes along with the epithet.

Gary Gentile:
Deep Wreck Diver

I have granted hundreds of interviews throughout my life. Authors of books and reporters for newspapers and magazines have found my adventures worthy of recording. Most interviewers paraphrased my words - sometimes unrecognizably so. Michael Menduno, publisher of the first technical diving magazine in the world, AquaCorps: the Journal for Experienced Divers, printed his interview verbatim so that nothing was missed or misinterpreted. The title was his creation.

The following interview was conducted in 1990, after my Monitor expedition (during the first two weeks of July) and before my Ostfriesland dive (on August 10). Production postponements prevented publication for several months. The transcript of the interview was published in the magazine's third issue, dated Winter 1991.

Menduno started the article with a quote from me: "Deep diving is a matter of mind, not physique."

He then did a brief biological sketch in which he wrote that I was "long regarded as one of the crazies," to which I plead guilty.

He also noted, "You can always tell a pioneer from the arrows in his back."

In his preface to the interview, Menduno asked me about my motivation for diving deep. I replied, "It's about freedom, a battle I've been fighting all my life. There will always be people who'll tell you, you shouldn't be doing this. It's dangerous. It can't be done. That's their problem. I just want to live my life the way I want to, and for me, that's what these dives are all about."

I have retained the original spelling and punctuation, even though the punctuation of an interview is decided by the transcriber, and is based upon pauses and inflections in pronunciation. The transcriber is also responsible for breaking the answers into paragraphs.

Usually, when I said "feet," AquaCorps *printed* "fsw," which is shorthand for "feet of seawater."

AquaCorps (AC): Gary, you've been on the cutting edge of wreck diving for 20 years and you were one of the first people to dive the *Andrea Doria* back in '74. Did you take a lot of heat for your diving back then?

Gary Gentile (GG): All my diving career, the local people—the people in dive clubs—looked upon me as a madman. I've gotten back on the boat many times only to have people say to me, "What were you doing down there?" and "Weren't you going anywhere?"

People didn't know anything about decompression dives. And those who did, didn't approve, because I was doing long decompressions. It wasn't that I liked decompression diving; it was that I wanted more bottom time. I was willing to sacrifice for it.

AC: How did you get trained in decompression?

GG: I had the good fortune of falling in with a small group of divers who were doing deep decompression dives. At the time, deep was considered 160, 170 feet. That was the group I first dove the *Doria* with back in '74, and we took a lot of flak for it. People looked at us as crazies because we were doing dives no one else would do.

That's how I picked up most of my early experience in the water—the things I wasn't taught in courses. I studied their techniques and developed my own, just like everybody does. Wreck diving tends to be an evolving sport; everyone who gets into it looks at what other people are doing and adds his own little improvements. I got into that as well. I was really fortunate to get into a group of expert divers.

AC: Would you say that deep wreck diving as practiced today is fairly safe?

GG: Absolutely. It's much safer than it was. Of course, it all depends on your level of expertise. The people that are serious about diving deep wrecks and doing decompression diving are as comfortable with what they're doing—probably more comfortable—than the common tourist reef diver who dives to 25 feet, but only goes to Florida or the Caribbean once a year, and is out of shape.

AC: How many serious wreck divers are there?

GG: I'm finding, as I travel more, that there are many thousands. For example, when I first traveled to the Great Lakes a couple of years ago, I discovered a whole new group of wreck divers I had never known existed. I was astonished at how many good deep wreck divers were there. And that's just one area. The same is true all around the country.

AC: Communication has been a problem, then?

GG: A real problem. Most wreck divers are just doing their own thing. They're not seeking publicity; they're not into it for an ego trip (some are, of course, but most aren't). So there's not a lot of publicity about it.

AC: Would you say it's a competitive field—people looking at what others are doing and wanting to be the "first," wanting to be acknowledged? That's certainly the case in the cave community.

GG: It's funny; when I first got into diving, I thought it was the greatest sport in the world because everyone was working with everyone else, and everyone was trying to see that everybody had a good safe dive—no competition. I very quickly found out that wasn't true.

There were people who wanted to be the first to discover a wreck, or the first to collect an artifact. Artifacts have ruined more friendships than anything I know.

On the other hand, a certain amount of competition is probably good. It means people are interested in exploration and are willing to go out and do something—take action. That helps advance the sport.

AC: It's my impression that the cave diving community is, as a whole, better organized than the wreck diving community, and, I would guess, has a much better safety record. Is this true?

GG: If that's true, I think it's mostly because of better communication among cave divers than among wreck divers—communication of techniques. And that means safety efforts would naturally evolve faster.

But there may be another factor involved in the safety issue. By and large, wreck diving tends to be done in an uncontrolled environment. There are a lot of factors that can compromise safety. Storms can kick up very quickly at sea when divers are in the water; currents can come in when divers are decompressing. A lot of things can go wrong.

It's the changeable conditions that wreck diving necessarily encounters—being out there in the ocean or on a boat—that compromises safety. There are a lot of injuries just on the boat: getting on, getting off—that kind of stuff. All and all, I think it's probably true that the safety record among cave divers is better. But it doesn't have so much to do with the diving as it does with the conditions under which the diving is conducted.

AC: What are the skills and expertise required to be a serious wreck diver?

GG: Number one is awareness. There are a lot of potential hazards in wreck diving that can be created simply by being unaware of them. For example, entanglement in monofilament—fishing nets—is a very serious problem for wreck divers.

After awareness, I would say it comes down to experience. When you talk real wreck diving, you're talking about a combination of penetration, deep diving, and decompression diving. Put all three together and you've got quite a package.

You have to be expert at decompression diving. And you've got to have the proper equipment for each one of those disciplines, including emergency back-ups like decompression reels and ponys.

Equipment is important. That's something you can learn only through experience. Get out there and do it; find out what equipment is necessary for decompression when an anchor line breaks loose, for example. You can't stage bottles like you can in a cave, so you've got a problem there if you want to set up a deep dive. And, like the caves, you can't come right to the surface. So, once you gain awareness and then gather experience, you also need to be properly equipped.

AC: Would you say most wreck divers are well equipped?

GG: The average wreck diver isn't equipped—not for technical diving. But you have to understand that the average wreck diver is still the kind of person who dives on a weekend once or twice a month.

He doesn't get that many dives under his belt. He's under economic constraints and probably won't be buying the top-of-the-line regulator or B.C. He buys equipment he can afford.

Most of these divers are diving wrecks in the 80-100 fsw range, and a few in the 100-130 fsw range. Then there are the people who are diving 130 fsw and beyond. You'll find that their equipment, generally speaking, is far superior to the so-called "tourist divers" running the shallow wrecks.

Shallow wreck diving is essentially the same as reef diving in terms of the kind of expertise that's required. It's when you start doing things—recovering artifacts, inflating lift bags, penetrating the wreck, getting into decompression—then you're talking about a different area. Then you really need the proper equipment.

AC: In your book *Advanced Wreck Diving Guide* you talk a lot about equipment techniques and methods. How did you develop those?

GG: I can't claim to have developed all those techniques. I was part of the wreck diving community when those techniques were being developed. What I *can* claim credit for is setting them down in writing.

Some of the things I worked on myself, but it was an evolutionary process. To make a decompression reel you'd look at what someone had and say, "That's good, but I could add this and make it better." Then someone else would look at it and say, "Yes, but let's do it this way."

I saw the development occurring; I was in the middle of it. I remember one time trying to trace back to who actually developed the idea of making a decompression reel with these disks on the end to prevent the rope from coming out around the pins. No one knew. It had evolved: no one had any conscious awareness of who had done it. It was a group effort, done incrementally.

AC: Do you think recommended procedures and techniques will eventually evolve?

GG: Yes I do. Most of the procedures in *Advanced Wreck Diving Guide*, are now the lowest common denominator. That book is *not* the end result. It's a take-off point for the next generation, and I expect to see evolution coming from that. In fact, the sport is evolving already. Some of the things we're doing now, like using oxygen to add a safety margin in decompression—mostly for deep diving—or using nitrox decompression and custom tables for accelerated decompression times, are still being worked out.

AC: How about mixed gas?

GG: I think mixed-gas diving is going to be the wave of the future in wreck diving, because people are already reaching or exceeding the limits of air diving, and yet they still want to venture further to the deeper wrecks. The only way to do it is with mixed gas; at least it's the only way to do it and remember it!

AC: What do you see as some of the advantages of mixed gas besides remembering what you saw?

GG: I've had a very curious thought about mixed gas. It's clearly the wave of the future, but for some people, I think it may also become an end in itself: becoming proficient in managing the technology. I see people wanting to do mixed-gas diving as much to do the dive as to see the wreck. They want to do something that other people haven't done. That's what the new frontier is all about: to do something that other people haven't done. That's exciting; a real challenge.

AC: How about you?

GG: Personally, I'm a wreck diver. My goals are to be able to use it to get to a wreck, not to gain the expertise in mixed-gas diving itself.

AC: You mentioned that "deep" used to be considered 160 or 170 fsw. What's considered deep today in the serious wreck community?

GG: These days, 200 is not considered deep in the crowd that I dive with. A 200-ft dive...is something you talk about between bites of a sandwich. "Oh, 200? OK." If one of them jumped in the water, and you told him he would be diving 200 feet, he'd say, "Okay," glance at his tables to refresh his mind on what decompression schedules he'd be using, and then go do it. What I'm seeing is deep these days is 250 fsw plus. Now we're talking deep.

AC: You're planning to dive the *Ostfriesland*. Would you talk about it a little?

GG: The *Ostfriesland* is a German battleship that was brought to this country as part of reparations after World War I. The United States Navy did some tests on it and had it sitting in dry dock until Billy Mitchell decided to use it to prove to the Navy that Army bombers could sink Navy capitol ships. So in 1921, the *Ostfriesland* was towed some 70 miles off the Virginia Coast and Billy Mitchell successfully sank it with aerial bombardment.

Its position had been lost since that time; nobody cared about it. But its been relocated, first through historical records, and then by taking the boat out there and checking the various fishermen's LORAN coordinates that coincided with the records. It appears to be in some 380 feet of water, so it's definitely a mixed-gas dive.

We dove another battleship last year: the *Washington*. That was 290 feet. It was sunk in 1924 as a Naval target.

AC: You did it on air?

GG: Yep. We did on air; 290 fsw. I personally felt that that was pretty close to stretching the envelope. Beyond that, if you really want to accomplish something, you need to switch to mix. And that's my concern: accomplishing something. Not just getting there and saying you did it. But doing something when you get there. That's what we're planning for the *Ostfriesland.*

AC: What do you hope to accomplish?

GG: For me, it's an historical event. I'm a researcher and I've written about the *Ostfriesland* in my upcoming book, *Shipwrecks of Virginia.* I get a great deal of satisfaction out of doing the research—concluding that, yes, a wreck is supposed to be in such-and-such a location, then going out there and verifying and identifying the wreck to prove that my research was valid. That's what'll give me the most satisfaction on the *Ostfriesland*—to actually relocate it from when it was lost in 1921.

There's also the minor satisfaction of conducting a deep dive like I've never done before. But if you were to ask Ken Clayton, who I'll be diving with, the same question, he would give you a different answer. I think Ken's answer would be that his satisfaction will be to dive deeper. Mine is not; I'm coming from the historical perspective of actually being on that wreck. And I don't mean driving an ROV on it. I'm a person who enjoys the experience of being there myself. I want to be on the *Ostfriesland* myself.

AC: What are some of the planning issues you've had to confront in putting together the dive?

GG: The most difficult part was planning the mix, staging, and decompression. The initial step was arranging for the gas mix; Dr. Bill Hamilton worked with us on that. I see Bill and others like him as being the guiding lights on the evolution of mixed-gas diving in the future because they're the ones that are providing us with the wherewithal to do it. I'm not the expert on it. I rely on his expertise, just as I rely on the captain's expertise to run the boat out there and locate the wreck.

It all has to be put together. But once you do, the dive itself becomes relatively simple because there's no narcotic effect. It's just like making any other dive, except it'll take you longer to get to the bottom. Once you get there, you'll feel just as comfortable as you do on a 100-ft dive.

AC: As I understand it, you'll be making a fairly short dive to that depth.

GG: Eleven minutes. But the complication comes in that you're no longer self-contained. On air, you go down, come up, and decompress on your own air. But once you get into mixed-gas diving, in order not to have to decompress for something like four hours or more, you've got to go into an accelerated decompression schedule that requires multiple gas switches during the ascent to several nitrox mixes, and finally O_2, based on custom tables.

It means you need surface support personnel: support divers who are going to go down to 100 fsw to clip off the nitrox bottles, and have the oxygen hoses ready for our 20 fsw stop. It means you're no longer just jumping off the side of the boat, going off on your own, and coming back with your dive done. There's a lot of set-up when you get there and you can't do the set-up yourself.

We're taking clip-on stage bottles, of course, as a back-up. But the biggest thing all of this means to us is that we have to come back to the anchor line.

AC: What will your total decompression time be?

GG: Two hours and fifteen minutes.

AC: That sounds pretty reasonable. It's probably not any longer than a lot of your deep air dives.

GG: We did a two hour and forty-five minute decompression on the *Monitor*. *(Ed: the USS Monitor dives were approximately 220 fsw.)* After a twenty-five minute down-time on air, we used computers and O_2 as a safety factor.

AC: There's some complicated logistics.

GG: Mixed gas diving is complicated, and complicated means expensive. Much more expensive. But, remember: what were talking about is not just your everyday adventure. It's not for people who just sit home and watch the boob tube. It's for the kind of people who want to go out and experience something that

Deep Wreck Diver

not everyone can have. We're willing to do what is necessary to have that experience.

AC: Are you going to take pictures on the *Ostfriesland*?

GG: Unfortunately, we don't have a camera that'll go that deep.

AC: What are your personal diving goals over the next 12 months, Gary?

GG: Aside from the *Ostfriesland* trip, I'm in the middle of writing two books: one a science fiction novel and the other is *Shipwrecks of North Carolina*. That keeps me busy when I'm not diving.

As for diving, I'm still adventuring—looking for dives that I haven't done before. Not necessarily wrecks that no one has seen, but photogenic wrecks that *I* haven't seen. My emphasis is photography. It's hard sometimes for me to say that. My interests are split between adventure and photography; I blend the two together. Sometimes I feel guilty having an adventure without taking pictures. It's like having a good time without anything to show for it, so I always temper myself. I want to share those adventures with other people.

AC: What's your advice for the people who are interested in expanding their wreck diving skills?

GG: Work hard. Work hard to gain the experience necessary to do what you want to do. Everyone can enjoy these experiences if they're willing to put in the time. Just gain the expertise to do them safely.

AC: From a practical point of view, how should people go about doing that?

GG: There are not a lot of courses, but there are some. I know several dive shops teaching wreck diving courses and actually showing people how to make a decompression dive. So you don't have to do it the way I did it the first time; suddenly finding myself in decompression, scared to death because I'd never done it before.

If I'd done it half a dozen times when it didn't count, when the real time came, it wouldn't have been so emotionally difficult to handle. That's why I think the first thing people can do is to take a course or read up on the literature that's available so they can practice on their own.

Of course. There's only a certain amount you can do in a course; most of what you learn has to be gained in the field. You've got to get out there and do it. That means getting in the water a lot, practicing techniques, doing the diving, gaining the experience—you can't get that from a book. You just have to go out there and do it.

The issue in which this interview appeared was titled "Deep" because that was the subject matter of the articles it contained. Also in the same issue, Menduno published a transcript of another interview with me in which I addressed the topic of nitrogen narcosis. This interview was titled "Gentile on Narcosis."

AquaCorps: Gary, are you one of those people who doesn't get narced?

Gary Gentile (GG): No; I think that everyone gets narced to a degree. It's just that I have a high individual tolerance to it compared to the average diver. Because of my experience, I have gotten used to working under slight narcotic levels.

AC: What do you see as the risk or danger of narcosis in regard to deep wreck diving?

GG: The main risk is the mind fudging to the point that it's not able to respond quickly to emergency situations. Other than that, if there are no emergency situations, narcosis has never hurt me in any way or caused me to change my dive profile.

There have been times when I felt it severely and it cut down on my productivity. It prevented me from taking in all the information that was coming to me through my eyes, and I wasn't able to comprehend everything, such as deciphering exactly what that coral-crusted object was. Under the narcotic effect, things look a little bit fuzzy; my eyes tend to be a little

On Narcosis

bit out of focus.

I've noticed in particular that narcosis can be brought on very sharply by hyperventilation. In a strong current, if I'm working pretty hard on the way down the line, then I experience severe narcosis. That doesn't mean cancel the dive, but it does curtail my observational skills.

AC: How do you deal with it?

GG: The important thing in deep diving is not to run out of breath: to take things slower so that you can fight off the narcosis. Otherwise, the CO_2 buildup induces more of a narcotic effect. As long as I stay calm and there's not a lot of current, and I kind of work with things—sort of cruise around—I don't experience more than a mild effect—at least down to depths of 250 fsw.

My main strategy is not to get out of breath. I've learned that the hard way. If I have to dive in a strong current and pull myself down the anchor line, then I do it very slowly. I let my breathing dictate the speed of my work to conserve energy and not to get out of breath. I try to stay calm, cool and not to get overexerted. That's the main thing: don't get overexerted.

AC: You feel you're able to deal effectively and work at depths of 250 fsw?

GG: Absolutely. As long as I'm not out of breath.

AC: How about progressive adaptation to narcosis? Is that a factor when you're diving a wreck for a number of days?

GG: Yes. When I was preparing for the *Monitor* trip, knowing that I would be working at depths of 230 fsw, I made sure I got a lot of deep dives in before the trip. I made about a dozen dives between 200 and 250 fsw in the month prior, and I was really fine-tuned. By the time I got there, I had no detectable narcotic level. Others have found the same thing. The more you dive deep, the more you get used to it.

AC: A strategy to prepare for the "Big" dive?

GG: That's right. It's not just psychological either. It's physiological. The body seems to acclimatize to the narcotic level of the depth.

AC: What about gear management? Is building up routines a useful way to cope?

GG: Yes. I've trained myself to look at my gauges every two or three minutes, especially in deep water. It may seem silly to look at them that often, but I think it's a good habit to get into because it's so easy to just forget about it and all of a sudden find yourself beyond your time on air. I'd almost say that I'm paranoid about watching my gauges.

AC: What about mix? I heard you quoted as saying that the first couple of dives you made on mix scared you because you weren't worried all the time.

GG: Its true. What normally keeps me out of trouble on deep air dives is fear. Let's call it apprehension; it's not necessarily fear. I admit that I am very apprehensive during deep dives. I *want* to be that way because that's what keeps me in tune with my gauges; it keeps me from being too bold, getting too far away from the anchor line, or getting out of control. As soon as I see anything occurring that is out of the ordinary, I'm ready to haul it in, head up. I'm used to that narcotically induced apprehension to keep me out of trouble.

When I first starting diving on gas, I didn't have that apprehension. I was absolutely calm—as if I were sitting in my living room—and that really scared me because I didn't have the natural inclination that was helping me to not be too bold.

It became an intellectual exercise. I had to consciously remind myself that my situation was just as challenging and potentially difficult as if I had been diving that same dive on air. I could be far away from the anchor line, making preparations to return, and I wasn't scared. The fear didn't keep me there. My intellect did.

AC: So, an important aspect of mixed-gas diving is staying aware, staying alert, and staying "apprehensive," as you would say?

GG: Yes. The gas keeps you alert, and your mind is clear, but I think it may also give a diver a false sense of security. That's exactly what I felt. Without that apprehension, I was perfectly secure. I had to remind myself that I was in deep water, to look at my gauges. Yes, it does say 250!

I think that's important for people to keep in mind when they're using gas: the gut feeling is gone.

AC: Do you think mix will eventually replace air diving at the 200-fsw-plus range?

GG: No. I don't think it'll replace it. Personally, I see no reason for me to use mixed gas on a 200-ft dive. Or even down to 250 fsw. I feel comfortable on air, and there's no reason for me to incur the complications and the expense of mixed gas.

But I do see it working for some people who, because of their individual tolerance, experience more of a narcotic effect at 200 fsw than I do. I think those people will be able to use mixed gas to overcome that. It's not like they are overcoming a deficiency, or a lack of expertise—it's overcoming an individual body tolerance, a physiological limitation. It has nothing to do with their experience level. It will help those people to be more productive at depths beyond which they normally can go.

And I think mixed gas will certainly become a standard for dives that are deeper than 250 fsw. Two-fifty is kind of a breakeven point. It's not that people can't dive deeper than that on air, but their productivity becomes limited.

AC: Interestingly enough, that's just what Lad Handelman, who was one of the people who helped pioneer the use of mixed gas in commercial diving back in the '60s, was saying. A 250-fsw air dive for 20-25 minutes became the limit that the industry was bumping up against, and that eventually opened the way for mix. Beyond that, productivity fell away, as you say.

GG: And, of course, on SCUBA, the effects are accelerated because you have the additional fear of knowing your air supply is limited. Gas goes quick at 250 fsw.

AC: The subject of a future article.

Travesty of Justice:
Wrongful Passage of the Abandoned Shipwreck Act

In the early 1980's, a minuscule minority of marine archaeologists and petty bureaucrats first attempted to force upon an unwilling public a bill that would take from American citizens every shipwreck within the territorial waters of the United States, and turn them over to the adjacent States. This was done in the wake of the fantastic trove of treasure found on the *Atocha* by Mel Fisher and his investors after sixteen years of dedicated and self-funded searching for the Spanish galleon's mother lode. Instead of locating shipwrecks on their own - and at their own expense - marine archaeologists, estimated at less than fifty in number, sought to usurp the tremendous efforts of treasure salvors by bureaucratic fiat. Their philosophy was: why earn something when we can take it by passing laws? That might make theft legal but it doesn't make it right.

The story is one of epic proportions, with enough conflict and background material for a full-length book. Perhaps someday I'll write it. The most appropriate title would be *The Treasure Wars*. Here is a condensed version of the plot.

Under the guise of "historic preservation," marine archaeologists lobbied for the nationalization of American shipwrecks as a way to ensure future employment among their ranks. Quick to jump on the bandwagon were opportunistic bureaucrats who came to perceive shipwrecks as a valuable political ploy. Historic preservation was enjoying enormous popularity, and popularity equates to votes. Thus there were economic incentives to such an endorsement, not only for the politicians' continued occupation of office, but for the States they represented - in the form of tax impositions, licensing fees, tourist attractions, and so on. The proposed legislation was unequivocally anti-democratic, at the expense of private enterprise, and against every principle on which the Constitution was founded. This didn't bother some lawmakers, however.

The bill that was framed was called the Abandoned Shipwreck Act, a semantically appropriate title. "Abandoned" was intended to refer to shipwrecks without traceable ownership and those that were derelict or had otherwise been deserted by their owners: in other words, every wreck on which there was no current claim of commercial salvage - and this included unknown and as yet undiscovered wrecks. The dictionary also defines "abandoned" as "shameful" and "immoral" and "corrupt," terms which come closer to the truth as descriptions of the Act and the purposes for which its passage was sought, especially considering the manner in which the Act was ultimately passed.

The underlying theme of the Abandoned Shipwreck Act was control and the lust for power. In their shotgun approach to shipwreck "preservation," archaeologists sought to possess totalitarian authority over all wreck sites in the country, aggregating to some tens of thousands of wrecks of which only a trivially small fraction were historically significant. The majority of wrecks had already been destroyed by time and the elements. Nearly all were the remains of commonplace vessels such as barges, ordinary sailing ships, and twentieth century steamships.

It is patently absurd to spend taxpayers' money to "preserve" a wreck when ships just like it still ply the seven seas. It's even more absurd to suffer unfounded beliefs that a wreck under water is preserved from the awful forces of nature. One might just as well "preserve" rare works of art by exposing them on windy, snow-covered mountaintops.

The archaeological community was a juggernaut gone wild on bad faith.

Founded to contest the ASA was the Atlantic Alliance for Maritime Heritage Conservation, a nonprofit organization that was headed by Charles McKinney, an archaeologist with the federal government and whose full-time job was to investigate proposals for historic landmarks and places; and Duncan Mathewson, the outspoken and volatile consulting archaeologist who worked with Mel Fisher on the *Atocha*. Seed money and primary financial support for the Atlantic Alliance was provided by Mel Fisher and other treasure salvors seeking to protect centuries-old Admiralty jurisdiction and to preserve private enterprise. Fisher had already made his millions so he had little to gain by getting into the brawl, yet not only did he travel to Washington, DC to protest the ASA, he brought with him his brilliant oratorical attorney, Dave Horan.

I began supporting the Atlantic Alliance as soon as I found out about it, in 1983. I attended meetings, and later joined some of its members in testifying before the House of Representatives in opposition to the ASA, citing my tribulations with NOAA over denial of access to the *Monitor* as an example of bad faith on the part of the government. By that time the fracas had reached a virulent level of hostility. I feared that my testimony would be purely incidental and largely ineffective, particularly in light of the opening statement made by Minnesota Representative Bruce Vento, who was the head of the subcommittee to which I presented my evidence. He announced haughtily that the hearing was a mere formality and would not affect the outcome of the bill. Bureaucratic minds were already made up.

I testified on May 3, 1985, along with other members of the Atlantic Alliance, including Mel Fisher and Dave Horan. We sat together at a long table, and took turns in presenting our views. We also submitted materials to support our convictions. I doubt that any Committee members bothered to read our supporting documentation. Listening to us - those members of the public who were the most adversely affected by the proposed legislation - was merely a formality which the

Committee was forced to endure.

Here is a transcript of my testimony:

> Dear Madams and Sirs:
>
> You will find enclosed a manuscript which is the bulk of this letter. It is copyrighted, but I encourage you to photocopy it and pass it around in order that its importance be understood by members of the Committee involved with H.R. 25.
>
> Although it is self explanatory, I will make further comment. As implied at the end of the article, divers are not merely concerned with recovering artifacts: they are proud to display them. Unfortunately, there are few opportunities presented to divers to display their finds. In the past ten years there have been only two such occasions in the Philadelphia area: 1976 at the Philadelphia Civic Center, and 1982 at the New Jersey State Museum in Trenton. While diver attendance at these displays was good, the plain fact that there has not been more need for shipwreck artifact displays leads to an obvious conclusion: lack of interest from the nondiving public.
>
> This lack of interest reached its epitome for me when I offered my entire collection of several thousand artifacts to the Philadelphia Maritime Museum - and they refused! Even a *maritime* museum was not interested enough in shipwreck history to make an effort to educate the public. So where do we go from here?
>
> It is apparent that only a select group of people really care about recovering artifacts: wreck divers. They are the ones who hold impromptu displays at club meetings and underwater seminars. The world in general does not care. If they did, there would be no problem in starting repositories where artifacts could be kept on display. Most divers would love to give

up their artifacts if they could be put somewhere and be seen and appreciated by more people.

I conclude, therefore, that instead of working *against* divers, the Committee should consider ways of working *with* them. After all, you'll never get a force as large, or as cheap, as wreck divers, to recover all those relics that the anti-shipwreck bill is supposed to preserve. I think that education is the way to go: by competent and interested archaeologists, and with a positive influence. People like being involved, they want to be included in projects, and will gladly volunteer their services - if only they were asked. I invite your comment.

Neither Vento nor any other Committee member deigned to comment.

Despite his stance of arrogance, Vento was mistaken. The bill did *not* pass, his presumptuous prediction to the contrary notwithstanding. Although we won the battle, we eventually lost the war. But at least we were able to stall a gross injustice for a few years.

By 1987, the Abandoned Shipwreck Act had been proposed for seven years straight, and had been defeated every time. It would seem that the people didn't want it. But what the majority wanted didn't matter to the infinitesimal minority whose personal agendas and ambitions denied accountability to the American public that they were supposed to represent.

Communism may have its politburos, but democracy has polit. burros and donkeys of a shadier kind. Chief ass in this case was Senator Bill Bradley of New Jersey. Since he couldn't get the ASA passed honestly, he resorted to chicanery and deceit in the bill's ultimate session. On the surface it appears that he presented a forceful oral argument to a full and attentive Senate, pleading that the august body should overlook seven years of undesirable legislative proposals and the strong opposition that they engendered, and should this time pass the bill. His speech was published in the Federal Register, which purportedly records all Senatorial dialogue as well as preliminary discussions on proposed bills and the votes themselves. The Federal Register duly noted that on December 18, 1987 a vote was taken and the Abandoned Shipwreck Act was passed by majority consent.

Like a merchant vessel, a proposed bill requires two passages in order to complete a voyage. The bill was required to pass in the House before it became law. Congress generally rubber-stamps bills that are already passed in the Senate, and vice versa, on the supposition that an unpopular or controversial bill wouldn't have gotten passed by the majority in the opposing house. Representatives don't like to appear antagonistic toward their counterparts in the legislative assembly unless there is a compelling reason to do so. Otherwise, one house might find itself opposed by the other when the situation was reversed and some other pet bill was proposed for vote.

Furthermore, representatives don't generally like to go against the tide. If they do, they get a reputation as obstructers, they lose the favor of their constituency, and they find themselves without backing in their own favorite causes. Since nearly half the States in the Union have no coastline, and therefore were not affected by the Act, those State representatives had no vested interest in the bill, and no self-serving reason to oppose it.

The Atlantic Alliance was quick to organize a protest before the bill came up for vote again in the House of Representatives. This afforded another opportunity for me to testify before the so-called august body.

A hearing was scheduled before the Subcommittee on National Parks and Public Lands, of the House Committee on Interior and Insular Affairs. I delivered the following testimony on February 4, 1988:

> In an already overlegislated country, where new laws continue to erode the premise of per-

sonal freedom and free enterprise on which this great nation is founded, the Abandoned Shipwreck Act serves as yet another harness strapped to the taxpayers. While the reins of injustice are boldly yanked by bureaucratic puppeteers, we cannot allow the blinders of political rhetoric to take the place of reason and foresight.

In a democracy, the purpose of the state is not to own or to rule, but to protect the rights and property values of its citizens. Abandoned shipwrecks, by the very nature of abandonment, are not the possessions of the government merely by the fact of their existence. If shipwrecks belong to anyone, it is to those individuals with the will and the incentive to dive on them at their own cost and expenditure of time. The confiscation of this property under the guise of "the public good," coupled with the subsequent denial of public access, runs against all the grains of the democratic principle.

As an example of the manner in which government has already dealt with these issues, consider my confrontation with the *Monitor* National Marine Sanctuary. Despite its location in international waters, the U.S. government has laid claim to, and placed off limits to all Americans, the site of this historic Civil War ironclad. Under present law, those charged with the responsibility of preserving that wreck for the American people, have been empowered to monitor access to the site. They have instituted a permit application system which, in the words of one Sanctuary spokesperson, "was specifically designed to keep divers off the wreck."

Furthermore, meeting the requirements of the permit application is costly and time consuming to the applicant. My own permit application, including detailed descriptions of objectives, equipment, diving methods, and resumé and complete medical examinations for all participants (all of which is required by the Sanctuary before it will consider a permit application) was over one hundred (100) pages long. My purpose was not to salvage, not to damage, but merely to behold this piece of history, to photograph the remains, and to share those images with the public. Yet, despite the sincerity of my purpose, my efforts were preordained to fail by the very nature of the permit system. My permit application was arbitrarily denied on the grounds of safety. Reviewing personnel wholly ignored my extensive diving experience, despite submitted proof that I had already made *hundreds* of dives identical to that proposed for the *Monitor*.

Legally, the *Monitor* has been set aside for public benefit. But, in actuality, it has been spirited away in the name of "preservation." Since its inception as a Marine Sanctuary, *no* private citizen has been allowed to visit the site. Photography has been permitted *only* by expeditions sponsored by the Sanctuary. Clearly, the Sanctuary has failed to serve the American public; it serves only those government employees whose livings are earned by their positions on the Sanctuary payroll.

The result in this case of government aggrandizement is a complete abrogation of popular sovereignty, against which this country once waged revolutionary war. This is what can happen when government takes control. This is what *has* happened in the case of the *Monitor*. This is what will *continue* to happen should a select few paid government employees be allowed to dictate the terms of freedom to the American public. I felt strongly enough about the *Monitor* debacle to take it to Federal District Court, where a decision is now pending (*Gentile v. NOAA et al.*, C.A. #87-2192 (E.D. Pa).

In order to advance the cause of freedom in this country, and to set an example for the world of democracy, it is important that we not give in to any form of wholesale takeover. The Abandoned Shipwreck Act seeks to appropriate vested interests that have been in the public domain for the entire history of the United States. In many cases, these shipwrecks are known only because of diligent research by private individuals. To take away from them the fruits of their labors is equivalent to nationalizing a business after it has been shown profitable, with the stockholders ousted of their ownership.

While the issues in this case have been clouded by proponents of the Abandoned Shipwreck Act, who have arbitrarily assigned *every* shipwreck as a national resource without adequately describing what makes that shipwreck a national resource, one truth is self evident: that individual property rights in a free democratic society must be preserved in order to uphold the integrity of that society. Legislative action should not take away those rights. The brash enactment of laws that prohibit free enterprise is not within the spirit of the Constitution, nor within the bounds of freedom for all.

The sea is ever changing, ever destroying. As a shipwreck disintegrates, it passes before our eyes like a movie in extreme slow motion. Each frame is ephemeral, existing only for a brief instant in time, and must be viewed quickly before it dissolves.

Only by permitting unrestricted access to these shipwrecks can public awareness be expedited. To place off limits the tens of thousands of shipwrecks (most of which have no historic or archaeological significance) that are sunk off the American coast, and to usurp from more than four million (4,000,000) wreck divers their rights, is grossly unfair to the majority of shipwreck enthusiasts. Admiralty Law, as codified by HR-2071, has worked for over two centuries. Let it continue to work.

My plea fell largely on deaf ears - or, more properly, on ears that had their own agenda. Nonetheless, I continued to write to my Congressional representative, Bob Borski, in order to voice my opposition to the bill. I also sent stern letters of protest to other representatives.

Congressional advocates of the bill proceeded to bring it up for vote, but not without strong opposition from fellow members of Congress.

On March 28, 1988, the ASA was raised for discussion before the House. Concerns of opponents of the bill were typified by Texas Representative Jack Fields, who not only stated his reasons for opposing the bill, but who added historical context for its origination. I quote his speech in full:

"I rise in strong opposition to S. 858 [the Congressional version of Senate bill H.R. 74], the so-called Abandoned Shipwreck Act of 1988.

"Frankly, this bill has no business being considered under suspension of the rules. It is flawed in a number of important ways and Members of this body should have an opportunity to offer amendments to improve it.

"I believe the amending process is particularly important in light of the fact that our colleague from California, Congressman Norm Shumway, has an amendment to protect the rights of sport divers, which I have yet to hear a single word of opposition. In fact, the House sponsor of this bill, Mr. Bennett, has not only indicated that he supports the Shumway amendment, but that he would introduce legislation to eliminate this major deficiency in S. 858.

"Mr. Speaker, this is the wrong way to legislate. Let's improve S. 858 here and now and let's stop worrying about what the other body will or will not do. In their unrelenting attempt to avoid real debate, the proponents of this legislation have asked us to accept a flawed bill by denying this body its legitimate right to work its will.

"During our committee's consideration of S. 858, there were several amendments offered which address the concerns of our Nation's 4 million sport divers, the Department of State, and several other groups which are deeply troubled about certain provisions in this bill.

"What is wrong, Mr. Speaker, with giving this body the chance to vote 'up or down' on each of these amendments? Isn't that how our legislative process in this, the people's body, is supposed to work?

"Mr. Speaker, in addition to the procedural problems I have in bringing up S. 858 today, I also have a number of serious reservations about this legislation which I would like to discuss.

"Before doing that, however, I would like to briefly touch upon the origins of this legislation. As many of my colleagues may know, this bill is a direct result of the failure of the State of Florida to win its battle against Mel Fisher in Federal district court.

"After more than 7 years of litigation and hundreds of court challenges, the State of Florida was unable to convince even one Federal judge that it had any legal basis or right to the *Atocha* treasure.

"While the State had no success in court, Federal District Judge James Lawrence King made admiralty law work in that case by establishing an "East Coast Shipwreck Project." As a result of this cooperative effort involving private salvors, archeologists, and sport divers, more archeological data was gained from the shipwrecks of the 1715 Spanish Plate Fleet in Florida water than had been collected during the entire 20-year program controlled by the State of Florida.

"Unfortunately, the State of Florida refused to accept the mandate of the courts and instead turned its attention to the U.S. Congress. As a result, the first Abandoned Shipwreck Act was born.

"While proponents will argue that their sole interest is the protection of the abandoned shipwrecks, the real goal of this legislation is to severely restrict, if not prohibit, access to these vessels.

"S. 858 is a blatant political attempt to throw out 200 years of admiralty law, and the precedents of hundreds of court cases, by granting to the States, with little or no guidelines or restrictions, ownership to these vessels.

"And, once States have these vessels, how will they manage these resources? Well, if past history is any indication, the answer is: Not very well. We have already seen a number of States, including my own, enact regulations which outlaw all private salvage operations and restrict sport diver access.

"Mr. Speaker, there are no reported cases where a shipwreck under the jurisdiction of Federal admiralty court has been destroyed. Yet, States have a number of blights on their record. For instance, no one talks about the H.M.S. *Debraak*, an 18th-century British warship which sank off the coast of Delaware. In this case, the State of Delaware attempted to salvage this important vessel and ended up destroying it. Instead of following prescribed archeological procedures, the State yanked the ship from its watery grave, deposited it in the open air for several weeks without proper preservation, and then dumped it into a big hole at one of its State parks.

"What you ended up with was a shattered piece of junk instead of a beautiful underwater monument which could have been enjoyed by thousands of recreational divers.

"And what about the 572 artifacts found by Mel Fisher that the State of Florida confiscated and then lost during the 7 years of court litigation. If a State can't even safeguard a few valuables, can we really expect that they are going to protect hundreds of shipwrecks. Sadly, the answer is no!

"Mr. Speaker, these examples clearly indicate that State ownership is not a guarantee of historical preservation or protection. The private sector can and has provided adequate protection for the public interest. And the *Atocha* is a good example of that - more than half of the *Atocha* treasure will end up in museums and galleries for the enjoyment of all Americans.

"Mr. Speaker, sadly, I must conclude that by enacting this legislation we will end up doing far more harm than good. Without the incentive to find these vessels, they will not be found, and they will continue to deteriorate off the coast of States throughout America. And, the real losers are the American people - as they will be denied the opportunity to enjoy and appreciate this important part of our history.

"Finally, while much has been said about the protection of the rights of the 4 million sport divers in this Nation, there is nothing in S. 858 which guarantees or mandates sport diver access to any shipwrecks in State waters.

"While it is true that the author of this bill has included a 'Sense of Congress' statement about reasonable access to the general public, this provision is unenforceable and nonbinding. Once enacted, the State can and will restrict access to these vessels.

"I was hoping that at a minimum we would include language in this bill which guarantees sport divers the opportunity to continue to enjoy their hobby. As one of my constituents so articulately stated, 'There is no desire on the part of sport divers to destroy items of historical significance. In fact, more items are on public display as a result of artifacts that they have donated to museums and galleries than from any other source, including archeologists.'

"To restrict sport diving access is also counterproductive because there is no question that it is the sport diver and not the professional archeologist who finds the vast majority of shipwrecks. According to the Atlantic Alliance for Maritime Heritage Conservation, in 1 year, sport divers discovered more than 2,500 wrecks while Federal and State archeologists together found less than 200. And of all these finds, there has never been anyone who has sighted [sic] examples of looting, scavenging, or destruction of these ships or their artifacts.

"Mr. Speaker, the authors of this bill don't like to

hear this but admiralty law worked well: shipwrecks and artifacts have not been destroyed. Moreover, admiralty law provides the necessary incentive for private individuals to go out and discover shipwrecks and it assures access to all interested groups.

"Mr. Speaker, we must not discriminate against these 4 million Americans and those latter-day Christopher Columbus' who are willing to find and salvage these shipwrecks in a proper, safe, and archeologically-sound way.

"I urge my colleagues to vote 'no' on this bill so that it can be considered, as it should, in the normal and proper legislative manner."

Fields was not the only one to recognize that wreck-divers were being struck by shrapnel that was intended for commercial salvors. Michigan Representative Robert Davis spoke next:

"Mr. Speaker, the recent discovery of a number of historic shipwrecks, whether they be in Federal or State waters, underscores the interest the American public has in these underwater treasures. My office has been flooded with mail concerning S. 858 that we are considering today.

"Recreational divers have urged me not to support these bills because of the danger that a State could shut the door on diving access to many of these wrecks, depriving them of an enjoyable and harmless hobby and driving those who operate diving operations out of business. Salvors also protest this legislation, citing the Admiralty law provisions in our Constitution and the specter of huge penalties.

"On the other hand, historic preservationists admonish me to vote for passage of the Senate bill with no changes, fearing that if the bill should be returned to the other Chamber, it would never see the light of day again."

If Davis only knew how close to the truth he hit. But more on that later.

California Representative Norman Shumway repeated the concerns of Fields and Davis, with special emphasis on collateral damage to recreational divers:

"Mr. Speaker, this bill should be voted down today on both substantive and procedural grounds.

"First, the substantive reasons. In my mind, there is a constitutional question as to whether this bill is a good idea, even in theory. At the very least, however, if the House is to pass S. 858 and send it to the President for his signature, the bill should be amended to correct the legal and policy problems it poses in its present form.

"First, by far the most glaring problem with the bill is that it fails to protect the interests of sport divers, and the private sector generally. Proponents of the bill point to section 4's so-called rights of access provision as protection for sport divers. That is simply not true. Section 4 contains only nonbinding recommendations regarding rights of access.

"Simply stated, there is no legal, binding, or enforceable way, under this bill as it is written, to ensure that sport divers' right to dive on these wrecks, even for purely recreational purposes, will be protected by States. Moreover, there will no longer be the same private sector incentive to go out and discover wrecks as there is now under the present system. I can't stress these points enough. These two factors - the failure to protect sport divers and the elimination of private sector incentive to discover shipwrecks - more than any, are, in my mind, why this bill should be voted down under suspension.

"Because of these gaps in S. 858, the 4 million sport divers throughout the United States are virtually unanimous in their opposition to the bill. And they are by far the largest constituency group affected by the bill."

Shumway went on to cite numerous instances in which States had acted irresponsibly with regard to shipwreck salvage, as opposed to the responsible conduct of recreational divers and commercial salvors.

He also repeated Davis' sentiment: one that demonstrated prescience: "I offered amendments to correct all of these problems with the bill last Wednesday. The only argument that was made by Members, including the author of the House bill, Mr. Bennett, was that if we change the bill and improve it, *there is no guarantee that the other body will pass it again.* No one raised a substantive or policy reason as to why my amendments shouldn't be adopted." (The italics are mine, and are intended to emphasize a point that I will make later.)

California Representative Walter Herger reiterated the key objections to the bill: "We have been told by the proponents of this legislation that S. 858 would help preserve and protect shipwrecks of historical significance. As some of my colleagues have pointed out, however, this particular bill does nothing of the sort. The bill creates no systematic means for preserving shipwrecks beyond ceding control over these vessels to the States. There are no guidelines for States to follow which would enhance preservation. In fact, taking the right of exploration away from individual divers might easily prove counterproductive from a preservation standpoint.

"As I mentioned earlier, the bill grants all control over certain shipwrecks to the States, and unfortunately, few of those States have the economic resources necessary to launch publicly financed exploration and recovery efforts for the numerous wrecks which might lie in their coastal waters. Under this bill, States may restrict access to ships and prevent private divers from working to assist in their preservation. The vast majority of these divers share both an appreciation of the importance of the wrecks, and the resources and the time to search for them and ensure that adequate steps are taken to preserve their remains.

"In fact, history has shown that those States which have title to vessels in their waters, have gone so far as to completely deny sport divers the right to even search for such wrecks. Texas for example has taken this very approach, and many interested parties are worried that as a result, important archeological treasures will never be discovered.

"The bill only serves to further expand Government's control over yet another area which has previously been left to private individuals. Individuals who have contributed substantially to our understanding of our Nation's history. Sport divers have been instrumental in the discovery of a number of shipwrecks which have proven to be extremely valuable to those interested in history.

"I do believe that the Government has a positive role to play in the discovery and recovery of such vessels. I do not, however, feel that it is wise for us to establish a system that will actually discourage sport divers, who historically have been far more successful than the States at locating ships lost for centuries on the ocean floor, from helping to preserve a piece of American history. For these reasons, I oppose S. 858 and would urge my colleagues to do likewise."

Adherents were silent against these reasoned diatribes against the bill's obvious and objectionable deficiencies. Other representatives also questioned the validity of the bill, as well as its constitutionality.

Only two representatives rose to speak in favor of the bill. (Neither of these was Walter Jones of North Carolina, the Chairman of the House Merchant Marine and Fisheries Committee. He was the most aggressive proponent of the bill when I testified in opposition.)

The most vocal proponent was Bruce Vento. He glibly attempted to gloss over the bill's inequities by disclaiming the objections of his fellow Members. His repudiation was weak: while pronouncing the bill's so-called intents, he admitted that those intents would not be binding upon the States.

In other words, although he stated that the bill was not *intended* to deny diver access, he *hoped* that the States would comply with the guidelines to that effect. He then admitted that those guidelines would not be written until *after* the bill was passed. This was equivalent to asking Congress to issue a signed blank check on which the recipient could write any amount.

Florida Representative Charles Bennett, the sponsor of the House bill, committed perjury by claiming that the Senate version of the bill had been passed "enthusiastically." Bennett was more honest when he stated, "The Senate sponsor, Bill Bradley, of New Jersey, said that probably won't happen again."

He was right about that. You will soon see why.

Despite the momentous objections, Vento moved "to suspend the rules and pass the Senate bill." Suspension means "that no amendments were allowed to be offered." In other words, Vento wanted the bill passed exactly as written, without modifications or alterations.

Shumway took exception. "Mr. Speaker, I object to the vote on the ground that a quorum is not present."

The Speaker agreed. He ordered the Sergeant at Arms to notify absent Members. A vote was taken the following day "by electronic device."

Of the 432 Members who were polled, thirty chose to abstain. After the votes were cast and counted, it was found that Congress "failed to gain the two-thirds vote required for passage in the House on March 29 [1988]."

One way to get an unfavorable bill passed is to keep reintroducing it, in the hope that the next time the defeated bill is put to a vote, a sufficient number of its opponents would not available to vote against it, so that the proponents could succeed in having it passed.

S. 858 was reintroduced two weeks later, on April 13, 1988. This time it squeaked through, helped no doubt by Bennett's lying proclamation that the Senate had already cast its vote of confidence in favor of the bill.

President Ronald Reagan signed the bill into law on April 28, 1988.

When the Abandoned Shipwreck Act became law, it became the greatest land grab since the Louisiana Purchase. The submerged territory added untold thousands of square miles to State ownership and control.

Yet, as I discovered, the ASA was based upon a fraudulent premise and passed by Machiavellian machinations that, although technically legal under the present system of government, are not condoned by the spirit of the law under true democratic principles.

The Atlantic Alliance has been unfairly criticized by some for failing to achieve its objective to overthrow the Abandoned Shipwreck Act, partly because of in-fighting among the competing salvage outfits that were its sponsors, and partly because it did not effectively coordinate the voices of recreational divers who were adversely affected by the shrapnel of archaeologists' shell fire aimed primarily at the treasure salvors. This isn't true. Salvors may have had their differences, but they offered a unified front, else the Atlantic Alliance wouldn't have existed.

Regional directors such as Joyce Hayward and Pam Warner expended considerable personal energy toward galvanizing sport divers for the cause - and were greeted largely with yawns and inertia. Recreational divers were content to let someone else fight the battle. They weren't willing to be inconvenienced. They languished with indifference and, through apathy, let their shipwrecks be legislated away from them.

The opposition camp, on the other hand, was not only strongly organized but it was infinitely well subsidized - by taxpayers' money. And whereas Atlantic Alliance members were volunteers, all the archaeologists and politicians who framed and supported the bill were paid full-time to do so. That was part of their job. Despite these obstacles to freedom, the Abandoned Shipwreck Act was overthrown seven times in seven consecutive years.

What ultimately enabled the bill to get passed was trickery and conspiracy: the hoodwinking of the American people through political opportunism. McKinney told me that, according to rumor on the Hill, only a handful of senators were in session when the bill was passed: perhaps as few as three. I didn't believe him - didn't *want* to believe him - and spent years tracking down the truth. When I blew the lid off the truth, it was more sordid than I could possibly have imagined.

I became suspicious right away when Bill Bradley refused to meet me in person, refused to talk with me on the phone, and refused to reply to my letters.

Travesty of Justice 39

After more than a year of persistence, one of his underlings condescended to speak with me on the phone. All he would tell me was that the bill was not passed with a roll call vote, and that therefore the names of the voters were not recorded.

I immediately protested, "But Bradley was *there.* It was *his* bill. He must remember how many senators were in attendance."

The aide would tell me nothing. A follow-up letter (written by a Bradley aide and stamped with Bradley's signature) reiterated Bradley's refusal to provide information. The following letter was dated June 8, 1989:

> Dear Mr. Gentile
>
> I recently received your letter of April 14, 1989, asking for additional information on the passage of the Abandoned Shipwreck Act. I understand that you have spoken to members of my staff regarding your request.
>
> I am enclosing a copy of the Congressional Record from December 19, 1987, showing the passage of the Act. In addition, I have included the Department of the Interior's report printed in the Federal Register on this subject.
>
> As you can see, the bill was passed under a "unanimous consent agreement." Under this agreement, a bill is passed by voice vote as long as no Senators in the chamber object to the bill. All members offices are alerted that the issue is coming to the floor for vote. If no Senator formally objects the bill is then passed. Therefore it follows that if no Senator objected during this procedure than [sic] all Senators present "unanimously" agreed to the measure. Because there was no roll call vote, it is impossible to determine which Senators were present at the time of passage.
>
> I hope that this answers your questions. Feel free to contact me on any other matters of mutual concern.

This letter certainly did *not* answer my questions. Nor was it "impossible" to determine which Senators were present at the time a bill was brought up for vote.

What Bradley meant was that instead of requesting written ballots, the chairman simply called for a show of hands and asked for "ayes" and "nays." In such a case, the Federal Register simply shows whether or not a bill was passed, not by what percentage. It was my contention that this situation was irrelevant. Since it was Bradley's prize bill and he was there to promote it, he would certainly remember the details. Undoubtedly he did, but he wouldn't talk to me because - as I finally discovered - in order to answer my questions he would have had to admit his culpability.

On June 14, 1989, I sent the following letter to Bradley:

> Thank you for finally responding to my plethora of letters (fifteen at last count), the first of which was submitted to you well over a year ago. While at first glance your June 8 letter appears to contain no information, a careful reading infers that, on the contrary, it conceals a great deal. Let me explain.
>
> When I first asked you to respond to questions pertaining to the passage of the Abandoned Shipwreck Act (see enclosures), my purpose was to quell the rumor circulating around the District that only three (3) Senators were present during the vote: you, and two others. I did not want to believe that a United States Senator would wait until late Saturday night just before Christmas, when most other Senators had already returned to their home states for the holidays, to put on the floor a bill so controversial that it had been vigorously fought down for eight consecutive years. I sought vindication of this accusation, and reaffirmation of the integrity of the senatorial office.

Now, my heart is saddened. Your continued and blatant refusal to reply to my queries, your squirming under direct questioning, and your misleading statements, seem to point to a cover up. Your statement "it is impossible to determine which Senators were present at the time of passage," is not true. Because the Congressional Record does not list the Senators present during passage does not make such a determination impossible, only more difficult. Please note that I did not ask the Congressional Record to answer my questions, I asked you. You, not the Congressional Record, have refused to answer.

I would like to see you cleared of these charges, but you will not let me. You promoted the bill, you were there during its passage, so your notes, personal memoranda, and recollections can answer my questions. Because of the importance of the bill to you personally, and because you finally saw it pass after so many years of rejection, I am sure you have indelibly imprinted memories of that moment of triumph.

At this time I form my question in such a way that your refusal to answer will be constituted as incrimination; that is, unless you refute in writing the accusation, it will go on record that you were unable to make such a refutation, and that therefore the rumors are to be believed. (Since you rely heavily on negative communication, this method precludes my having to write multiple letters.)

If more than three Senators were in attendance, were there less than ten? Less than twenty? Less than fifty? Even the admission of only a hazy recollection allows you to pick a category of approximation. If you prefer to use the convenience of "loss of memory," please state so.

I seek only the truth. Please help me find it.

That Bradley did not deign to reply speaks for itself about his guilt.

I am not one to give up easily. I took a different tack by submitting a FOIA request for all of Bradley's "documentation, personal memoranda, telephone transcriptions, and senatorial debate" relating to the ASA; before, during, and after passage of the bill. I did this concurrently with my repeated attempts to elicit an honest response from Bradley.

James M. Kovakas, Attorney in Charge of the FOI/PA Unit, Civil Division of the U.S. Department of Justice, sent me the following letter (dated June 15, 1989):

> Dear Mr. Gentile
>
> This letter is in reply to your letter dated June 1, 1989, seeking to appeal under the Freedom of Information Act, the refusal of Senator Bill Bradley to provide you with information relating to the Abandoned Shipwreck Act of 1987. As I advised you by telephone, the federal Freedom of Information Act does not apply to the Congress or the Judiciary but only to the Executive Agencies.
>
> Since the statute does not apply to requests made to U.S. Senators, there is no appeal procedure and this office can not assist you.

I eventually uncovered the squalid and unvarnished truth after years of persistent effort and research. All Senatorial and Congressional proceedings were videotaped by C-Span. These tapes could be viewed at and purchased from the Library of Congress. Yet when I submitted a request to view the tapes of the Senate hearings that were held on December 18, 1987, after an unduly long passage of time my request was denied.

No explanation was provided with the denial. Follow-up demands for an explanation went unanswered. Eventually I submitted a Freedom of Information Act request. After another unduly long passage of time, my FOIA request was denied. I appealed, and after yet another unduly long passage of time, my appeal was denied.

Finally, I wrote a letter to my Congressional representative, Bob Borski. I had voted for Borski because he was one of those rare politicians who kept the needs and wants of his constituents constantly in mind. Unlike politicians who made empty campaign promises in order to get elected, and who then did what they wanted when they took office, Borski was a true representative of the people.

I explained my position and described the opposition that I met in accessing public information. Borski wrote a stern letter to the Library of Congress, demanding that the videotapes be released to me. Reluctantly, and after untoward delay, the Library of Congress acquiesced to his demand.

By this time, *two years* had passed since I had made my initial request.

The Library of Congress notified me by mail that the appropriate tapes would be retrieved from the long-term storage facility, and made available to me (for reasons that I never understood) at the National Archives in Washington, DC. This is what I saw.

December 18, 1987 was the Saturday before Christmas. Nearly all the senators had already gone home to spend the holidays with their families. Only a handful remained in Washington, and of those even fewer stayed in session. Those who had bills to propose or statements to make did so in the morning, then departed. By late afternoon only two senators were present in the Senate chamber: Robert Byrd and Alan Simpson. Brock Adams stood at the podium and resided as Chairperson. Bill Bradley did *not* appear.

Byrd and Simpson extended their stay in Washington for one reason only: to pass unfavorable legislation that would otherwise have been vetoed by those senators who were not in attendance. Byrd and Simpson had their own precious bills to pass, and they were in cahoots with Bradley to pass his bill. Byrd submitted a copy of Bradley's speech and asked that it be appended to the record *as if it had been read*. Thus, one perusing the Federal Register would be deceived into believing that Bradley was present that day and delivered his pleading in person. The Federal Register doesn't distinguish between written and oral statements, and surrounding dialogue is deleted so that the truth cannot be determined.

After the false submission, Byrd asked that a vote on the bill be taken. Adams waived the reading of the bill and went through the pre-voting formality as if the Senate were in full session. "All in favor?" The camera focused on Byrd and Simpson, who stood side by side. Both stated "Aye."

Adams then asked "Opposed?" He could clearly see that behind Byrd and Simpson the vast chamber was totally empty. The camera clearly showed that every seat was vacant. Byrd and Simpson stood side by side in front of the chairperson's podium. Adams knew that they had already voted in favor. Who was he trying to kid with this sham? After a moment of silence, he said, "The ayes have it."

That was how the Abandoned Shipwreck Act was passed. And it was legal. But that's not the end of the story. Byrd went on to propose another half a dozen bills, and Simpson parroted his agreement. The pre-voting litany was repeated for each bill, the chairman called for a vote each time, and these additional bills were passed into law. Still, the worst was yet to come.

The session closed. The Senate chamber dissolved from view and was replaced by a title screen which stated simply that the Senate was not in session. I was not able to *see* that the chamber was empty; I was led to believe that it was. There was no reason for me to expect the session to resume, but because it is my custom to be thorough, I fast-forwarded through eight hours of blank videotape. Incredibly, just before the official midnight closing, two senators sneaked into the chamber and reopened the session.

Byrd stood alone on the floor. Assisting him in his nefarious deeds by acting as Chairperson was John

Travesty of Justice

Glenn, the space hero turned senator and now a conspiratorial turncoat. Like an automaton, Glenn pronounced the procedural litany as if the full assembly were gathered. Byrd proposed a bill by name and number only, Glenn accepted the proposal as if it had been read in its entirety, then called for a vote. Byrd alone voted aye, whereupon Glenn asked the empty chamber for all opposed, and, hearing no dissenting voices, said "Passed. Next bill." In this manner Byrd forced through another half a dozen unpopular bills, all by himself and with no one there to oppose him. When Byrd passed these bills, he did not represent the majority of the nation's voters, nor did he represent the majority of their representatives. Yet his whim, his personal ambition, and his single vote constituted law.

Thus were passed into law that day more than a dozen bills that were binding upon some 240 million American citizens, because one or two people wanted it so. Thus were the American people raped by Senatorial fiat.

I must have been asleep in class the day my history teacher covered the legislative process and a legislator's responsibilities to the people he was supposed to represent. I don't remember being taught that such shenanigans could be conducted in the highest office of the legislative process.

Legal it may be; ethical it is not. Laws that are passed without the majority consent of the public are wrongful laws, or unlawful laws.

In this sense wrongful means "contrary to conscience or morality; unfair; unjust." Unlawful means "contrary to accepted morality or convention."

In my opinion, one is not morally obligated to obey wrongful laws. My defense of this position is that the illicit nature of the passage of such laws is questionable, and can and should be strenuously contested.

Beware the system that allows circumvention of the people's will; beware of leaders whose only interest is their own. Otherwise, liberty may be short-lived and freedom a hollow word.

Murphy's Law: Destroyer Extraordinaire

The axiom known as Murphy's Law states that anything that *can* go wrong, *will* go wrong. The dire consequences of this recognized truism apply not only to a certain U.S. destroyer during her abbreviated career, but to the underwater adventurers who explored her rusting remains – and ultimately to the entire diving community.

In 2000, a group of wreck-divers aboard the dive boat *Seeker* checked out a "hang" some eighty miles off the New Jersey coast, in 260 feet of water. A "hang" is an underwater obstruction on which a dragger or trawler snagged its net. Most hangs are geological obstructions: rocks, reefs, or ledges. This hang turned out to be a shipwreck.

The steel hull measured approximately 150 feet in length. One end terminated in the knifelike edge of a stem, while the other end was truncated abruptly, as if a giant axe had cut transversely through the hull. The origination of the hang "numbers" was clearly in evidence: draped over the navigating bridge was a large fishing net – a common but expensive device for locating shipwrecks.

Boldly apparent in Christina Young's video footage was a gun turret, which she recognized. She showed her footage to me, and I confirmed that the object was indeed a turret.

The presence of a turret established proof that the wreck was a warship. Armed merchant vessels were equipped with gun tubs during both world wars, but never with turrets.

The mystery wreck was not *just* a warship – it was

half a warship. No other sections of wreckage were found in the vicinity.

Despite the presence of a turret, Dan Crowell – the new skipper of the *Seeker* after the death of Bill Nagle – insisted that the wreck was a Liberty ship from World War Two. My contrary arguments fell on deaf ears. I maintained that the wreck was clearly that of a warship. At the cost of being repetitive, I explained to him on more than one occasion that no merchant vessel in history had ever been equipped with a turret. Merchantmen, including Liberty ships, had gun tubs with shrapnel shields, but never a rotating turret.

Contributing to the problem of identifying the wreck was Crowell's attitude. He felt so possessive about the wreck – perhaps because it was the only one that he had ever discovered, or perhaps because he wanted a monopoly on the charter business to the site – that he refused to divulge its location.

Trips to the wreck aboard the *Seeker* were limited to one or two per year, and in some years none. Furthermore, Crowell permitted only certain individuals to attend these trips. Only his favorite cronies got to go. He turned away others who wanted to see the wreck for themselves.

There was little opportunity to study the site. All attempts to identify the wreck were defeated by lack of good evidence.

Gun shells were littered among the debris, indicating that the vessel had not been scuttled, but must have been on active service at the time of her demise. A few artifacts were recovered, but none that identified the wreck. Eventually, among other artifacts, Richie Kohler recovered a steam pressure gauge. A tag that was mounted on the face of the gauge read "LAUNDRY STEAM". Beneath the tag was an inspection stamp that was inscribed with a date ("6.17.42") and an alphanumeric designation ("JG 603").

Meanwhile, Christina did some detective work. She took a compass heading from the dock to the wreck, and estimated the mileage from the *Seeker's* speed and running time. When she plotted this information on a nautical chart, and followed the 260-foot contour of the ocean bottom, she found a wreck symbol very close to her approximated position. The presence of symbols on the chart were explained in NOAA's Automated Wreck and Obstruction Information System. The symbol corresponded to Record 1401.

The AWOIS record listed the vessel as "Unknown," and denoted the location in latitude and longitude: 39° 39' 30" North, and 72° 34' 30" West. The position accuracy was given as one mile.

The background information was furnished by two sources: the Wreck Information List of 1945, and the Navy Wreck List of 1957. The second source was an outgrowth of the first. Both sources concurred in citing the originating source: the cryptic acronym ESF. The Eastern Sea Frontier reported the sinking of a vessel on October 22, 1943, and established the position.

Christina now knew where to find additional information about the casualty: the Eastern Sea Frontier War Diary. During World War Two, the ESF kept a diary in which all reported incidents were logged on a daily basis. Christina knew that the ESF War Diary was archived at the National Archives. This was a problem for her because the Archives was open only during weekday business hours.

She called Kohler and told him about her discovery. Kohler was so excited that he wanted her to go with him to the Archives the following day. Christina had obligations to her employer and was unable to take off a day at a moment's notice. Kohler was self-employed, so he could play hooky without fear of angering the boss. He told her that he would go to the Archives alone, and let her know what he found.

Because of Christina's fundamental research, he knew exactly what file to ask for, and what date to look up. The ESF War Diary duly recorded the name of the vessel that was damaged by collision on the date in question: the U.S. destroyer *Murphy* (DD 603). The number "603" was the same number as the one on the steam gauge tag.

That night, Kohler called Crowell and told him the name of the wreck and its approximate location. Crowell confirmed that the location was extremely close to the site of the wreck. He ordered Kohler not to tell Christina what he had found, for fear that she would post the information on her website, for all to see. Kohler promised not to tell her.

When Christina called Kohler later that night, he told her in an evasive manner that he had not found anything of importance at the Archives. This seemed odd to her. She called him again the following Monday. Christina: "It was obvious that he felt guilty and started giving me hints – the hints led to me revisiting the prior (dead-end) research we had done about sinkings, and this time I looked for all 'damage' incidents as well."

Eventually, he broke down and confessed his lies and deceits, including the fact that Crowell had ordered him not to tell her anything.

According to the *Dictionary of American Naval Fighting Ships*, the USS *Murphy* was a *Benson*-class destroyer that was commissioned in 1942, served admirably throughout World War Two, and was decommissioned in 1946. She was mothballed in the reserve fleet for the next quarter of a century, until 1970, at which time she was determined to be unfit for Naval service. She was

USS *Murphy*. (Courtesy of the National Archives.)

sold for scrap in 1972, and subsequently was dismantled.

So how did the *Murphy's* identification tag get on a shipwreck off the coast of New Jersey? I already knew the answer – and had known the answer since the discovery of the wreck – but the information was buried in the back of my memory along with hundreds of other shipwreck sagas. The sordid truth of the matter unfolded suddenly when Kohler called me and asked if I had ever heard of the *Murphy*.

His question sparked a memory. I replied instantly, "You mean the one that was cut in two by the *Bulkoil*?"

There was a stunned silence on the other end of the line. Finally, he gasped, "How did you know that?"

I told him that I had an extensive file on the *Murphy*. I had researched it six years earlier, when I started revising and expanding my original *Shipwrecks of New Jersey* to three volumes that were to be subtitled *North*, *Central*, and *South*. I added quite a few wrecks to the New Jersey segment of my Popular Dive Guide Series. I finally elected not to include the *Murphy* because I had so many other wrecks to cover – wrecks that were closer to shore and of greater interest to divers and armchair historians. Even my threefold expansion in coverage had space limitations. There were thousands of shipwrecks off the New Jersey coast. I could not write about all of them. I had put the *Murphy* on the back burner.

I was chagrinned over the fact that I had not thought of the *Murphy* as soon as Christina showed me her video footage, without having Kohler remind me of the incident several years later. I could have kicked myself. Kohler was more forgiving than I was, and jumped to my defense. After all, he said, he had only one wreck to research, while I had hundreds. I agreed that it was easy to forget one among so many that were on my mind, and I was thankful for his commiseration, but that did not make me feel any better about not having solved the mystery sooner, and without prompting. I had clearly missed the boat on this one.

I had not finished berating myself when Christina called me several days later. She gave me the full story about the links that led to the ESF War Diary. Between Kohler's call and hers, I had reread my *Murphy* file so that the circumstances of the destroyer's loss were fresh in my mind. I congratulated her on her insightful research in identifying the wreck.

Several weeks later, the three of us met at Kohler's apartment, along with Dan Bartone, the skipper of the dive boat *Independence.* Kohler, Christina, and I brought our *Murphy* files in order to compare notes. Bartone had several sets of hang numbers in the area where he believed the wreck to be. Christina had hang numbers as well. Bartone felt confident that he could locate the wreck without Crowell's numbers. Increased exploration would help to tell more of the *Murphy's* story.

Afterward, I moved research on the *Murphy* from the back burner to the front. I tracked down the Court of Inquiry: more than 1,000 pages of investigative material and supporting documentation, including testimony of the survivors. From that I gleaned the tragic and dramatic events that were precipitated by the collision that occurred during the height of World War Two.

* * *

On the dark night of October 21, 1943, eastbound convoy UT-4 was on route to the United Kingdom. This convoy consisted of seventeen merchant vessels (some of which were troopships packed with American soldiers on their way to the European theater), and ten U.S. warships: the battleship *Texas*, the refueling vessel *Enoree*, and eight destroyers. In accordance with standard anti-submarine warfare protocol, none of these vessels was displaying any lights, navigational or otherwise. When the *Murphy's* radar unit detected the approach of an unidentified vessel, the Screen Commander on the USS *Nelson* was notified. The Screen Commander directed the *Murphy* to investigate the radar contact, and to force it away from the path of the convoy.

Meanwhile, southbound convoy CU-6 was proceeding to Curacao. The tanker *Bulkoil* became disabled, necessitating a reduction in speed and preventing her from keeping up with the convoy. The escort commander directed the *Bulkoil* to return to port unescorted at her best possible speed while complying with zigzag regulations. The tanker reversed direction. She was proceeding under blackout conditions when her torpedo detector sounded. The *Bulkoil* was not equipped with radar. Nor had the officers of the tanker been informed that the torpedo detector could not discriminate between a torpedo and a high-speed surface craft. The *Bulkoil* initiated a hard turn to starboard.

The men on the *Murphy* could not see the unlighted tanker because of the moonless sky. As the convoy was ordered onto the right leg of the zigzag – in order to avoid the oncoming vessel – the *Murphy* turned to starboard to herd the stranger away from the convoy. The tanker's radical course change caught the *Murphy* off guard. The *Murphy's* commander ordered "all engines ahead emergency flank," but before the order could be executed, the stem and starboard bow of the tanker struck the port side of the destroyer.

The *Bulkoil* cut the *Murphy* completely in two. Of the 255 men onboard the destroyer, six or seven were killed outright in the collision.

The stern section of the *Murphy* remained upright and afloat, and was in no immediate danger of sinking. But the forward section rolled onto its starboard side and commenced to flood; with the loss of electrical power, all interior lights were extinguished. Men who were topside either leaped overboard or slid down the slanted hull into the water. Gunners in the forward turrets escaped through the side hatches. Men in the fire director atop the navigating bridge crawled out of the overhead hatches. Officers in the wheelhouse climbed through the doorway onto the port side of the superstructure, thence to the hull. A number of men were trapped below deck in suddenly blackened compartments.

A group of enlisted men prepared two life rafts for launching – a difficult process considering the absolute darkness. Someone produced a flashlight. While some men abandoned ship on the rafts, others swam to the rafts as they were drifting away. One raft capsized – several times – resulting in the drowning of more than one man before the destroyer *Glennon* arrived to conduct rescue operations.

The most dramatic episode occurred in the communications office, located against the port hull. This compartment measured ten feet by twenty. As the starboard compartments flooded, the men inside the ship were forced to climb "upward" toward the port side. The decks were nearly vertical because of the crazy cant. The men scaled transverse bulkheads and trod on longitudinal bulkheads, crawling and clambering over furniture and other loose debris as seawater nipped at their heels. Emergency flashlights and battle lanterns faintly lighted the way.

Escape at first seemed impossible. One group of men working aft encountered another group of men working forward. Each group claimed that the way behind was blocked. Gunner's Mate Second Class Daniel Cafarelli climbed a ladder (staircase) into a "higher" compartment. From there he made his way along a narrow passageway that lay on its side, until he reached the communications office. This compartment had a porthole "overhead." The other men followed him into the room. Someone located a wrench and undogged the porthole.

This porthole measured twelve inches in diameter. Cafarelli stepped on a desk or table that was secured to the deck. He stuck his arms through the porthole and squeezed through the tiny opening into fresh air on the port hull. Two men were standing nearby: Lieutenant Commander Leonard Bailey (the *Murphy's* skipper), and Lieutenant William Klee (the executive officer). Cafarelli informed them that more men were trapped inside. Bailey was suffering from a broken sternum, and was painfully directing the launching of the life rafts. Klee helped Cafarelli to pull desperate men through the porthole.

As each man stuck his arms through the opening, Klee and Cafarelli grabbed his hands and yanked him out of the compartment and onto the hull. One man got stuck, and had to remove his trousers in order to fit through the porthole. Another was wearing a cork life belt; he had to drop down and remove it before he could squeeze through the hole. In this manner, Klee and Cafarelli managed to save five or six men in rapid order.

Then Seaman Frank Kupchak got wedged. Kupchak was described as "a heavy-set individual weighing approximately 200 pounds." The diameter of the porthole "was such as to make egress difficult for individuals other than those of a small stature." Kupchak could neither advance nor retreat.

Although the men inside worked frantically to release Kupchak, they did not panic. They did not know that time was growing short: water was lapping higher and higher as the *Murphy* gradually settled. By now the porthole was awash, and seawater spilled around Kupchak into the crowded compartment. Men inside started screaming.

The *Murphy* sank before Kupchak could be extricated. Bailey, Klee, Cafarelli, and the others were left adrift. At least twenty men were still trapped inside when the *Murphy* settled to the bottom.

Less than ten minutes had passed between collision and submergence.

The surface of the sea was covered with fuel oil. This oil impregnated clothing and coated skin: burning and making everything slippery.

Many survivors were separated in the darkness. Some fortunate survivors spotted a light in the near distance: it was attached to a life float. A few of the men managed to swim to the float, gather around its perimeter, and paddle toward the searchlights of the approaching *Glennon*. Half an hour later, they came upon a life raft that was crowded with other survivors. An injured man named Posey was transferred to the raft. Then the other men either climbed aboard or clung to the safety ropes. Soon they picked up the skipper. The *Glennon* rescued this group after an hour adrift.

The sea was littered with isolated sailors. Klee, a man named Pierson, and two other seamen supported themselves on a board until the *Glennon* picked them up. One pair of men "got on a piece of 4 x 4" until they were rescued. Lieutenant Young fought his way through the break – where the hull was cut in two – and found himself in the ocean. He drifted alone in darkness for an hour and a half before the *Glennon* found him.

The stern section continued to remain afloat with its crew on board. The *Glennon* rescued thirteen officers and ninety-five enlisted men. The USS *Knight* "picked up survivors and placed them aboard USS *Glennon*." The USS *Jeffers* pulled three firemen out of the dark and dismal sea.

When the final count was taken, thirty-five men were missing and presumed dead.

Men aboard the stern section shored the forward engine room bulkhead against leaks. The *Glennon* then took the stern section in tow. On the way to New York, the salvage tug *Rescue* took over the tow. Seven months and $2.5 million later, the *Murphy* returned to sea with a new forward section. She continued to serve admirably in the war against world domination.

The *Bulkoil* proceeded to New York under her own steam. Repairs to her bow cost $138,544.

Identification of the forward section of the

Collision damage to the *Bulkoil*. (Courtesy of the National Archives.)

Murphy initiated a bizarre series of events that is unprecedented in the history of wreck-diving. The prime motivator of subsequent machinations was Dan Crowell, the Judas of the diving community. Once the wreck was identified, he became more possessive than ever. He decided to make a videotape production about the wreck, and behaved as if he believed that he should be the sole custodian of the site.

As noted previously, in order to retain the *Murphy* as his own private domain, Crowell kept the location a closely guarded secret. But he failed to reckon with the

The *Bulkoil* in dry dock showing collision damage (Courtesy of the National Archives.)

initiative of Christina Young and Dan Bartone. Although Bartone did not have the GPS numbers of the *Murphy*, he had his hang numbers, Christina's hang numbers, and the AWOIS location in latitude and longitude. How far off could all these numbers be?

Bartone organized a search trip that included Christina but not Kohler. Bartone steered the *Independence* in a grid pattern whose focal point was the AWOIS location. It took him no more than three to four hours to locate the *Murphy*. Afterward, he continued to take divers to the site.

Crowell was infuriated when he heard through the grapevine that his exclusivity had been compromised. Christina: "And then to even infuriate him more, Mike Barnette posted the numbers on the Internet." The location of the wreck was no longer a secret.

Crowell ingratiated himself with the Naval Historical Center by notifying them that "unauthorized" divers were diving on the wreck of a Navy warship, and that he suspected that they were collecting souvenirs.

Before proceeding with the next sequence of events, it is important for the reader to understand the nature of the Naval Historic Center. Its initial purpose was to preserve Navy history, which it accomplished by archiving documents and photographs, and to disseminate that history to the public. Although the NHC is a division of the Navy, it is managed and operated by civilians. A handful of these civilians has taken it upon themselves to be the watchdogs of discarded Navy property. Over the years, these political control freaks have gradually (and insidiously) increased their power to a point that is totally beyond the pale. The NHC has become completely self-regulatory, without any system of checks and balances. Once their autonomy was assured, they commenced a witch-hunt against salvors, treasure hunters, and wreck-divers who sought to rescue Navy relics from oblivion.

Despite the fact that the documents archived by the NHC are public records, and are held in trust for the public, staff members have conspired to withhold certain documents from certain researchers. They do this by claiming that the requested documents either do not exist or cannot be located. I detailed these shenanigans at length in *The Shipwreck Research Handbook*. These archivists and research assistants decide among themselves which items of historical information they will release, and to whom they will release it. Thus a researcher who is "in" with the NHC can obtain documents that a researcher who is "out" cannot obtain.

This was brought home to me forcefully in 2000. On a routine research trip to the NHC, a newly hired research assistant was assigned to help me. He was a retired Naval officer who was working temporarily as a historian before deciding upon his next career. After discussing my current research topics, he went into the stacks to locate the information that I was seeking. Kathy Lloyd, Head of the Operational Archives, informed him in no uncertain terms that he was *not* to give me any information that contained shipwreck locations.

When the new research assistant (who requested anonymity) returned to the reading room, he asked me to accompany him to his office. In private, he told me about Lloyd's instructions. He had a personal problem with those instructions because he believed that public information should be made available to the public. But he could not bring out certain records because Lloyd was watching over him. Instead, a couple of weeks later, an inch-thick packet was delivered to my house. The packet contained the locations of hundreds of vessels that had fallen afoul of Nazi aggression. Many of these vessels had been attacked on the East Coast.

In the 1980's, when I was researching *Track of the Gray Wolf*, I spent a great deal of time going through Naval records at the NHC. Now I learned that important information, which I could have used in the book, had been maliciously withheld from me – and by consequence, from the tens of thousands of people who read my book about the World War Two German U-boat war off the American eastern seaboard.

By claiming discovery (if not identification) of the *Murphy*, Crowell forced himself "in" with the NHC. Certain others, myself included, were "out."

Bartone suddenly found himself about to be burned at the stake. Although he had not recovered anything from the *Murphy*, a photograph of him holding two relics from the *S-5*, a Navy submarine that sank off the coast of Delaware in 1920, was posted on Christina Young's website. Crowell made sure that the NHC was alerted about this photograph and the accompanying caption.

As a result, the NHC witch-hunters instituted a global Internet search for similar offenders – a search that became a regular activity in their quest to exert their authority (and incidentally, to justify their existence). The NHC now maintains files on people who are known or suspected to possess junk that they recovered from Navy shipwrecks. Some of these people have been prosecuted as criminal offenders for "theft of government property."

Crowell wanted the NHC to take action against Bartone, Kohler, and Christina. While the NHC dragged its collective feet, Crowell was insistent. He informed Navy affiliated groups about the trio's alleged activities, and he made accusatory postings on Internet forums, such as this vitriolic diatribe:

"It has been reported to me by an extremely reliable source that over Labor Day weekend divers, Richard Kohler and Christina Young, aboard the boat *Independence* owned by Dan Bartone, ventured out to the wreck sight [sic] of a US Naval war grave USS *Murphy* where on October 21, 1943, 35 sailors lost there [sic] lives after a collision with the US tanker *Bulkoil* sending the bow of the ship to the bottom. The trip was cloaked in secrecy as their intentions where [sic] to steal artifacts from the war grave. The report is that Richard Kohler removed the ship's binnacle as well as any artifacts that could be carried away while Christina Young photographed the event. The theft is being reported to several agencies in hopes of recovering the artifacts as well as the possibility of prosecution if applicable."

John Chatterton was the "extremely reliable source" to whom Crowell referred. Chatterton saw the artifact in the back of Kohler's truck, and reported the fact to Crowell.

Crowell also accused Kohler of stealing the GPS numbers from him.

Christina made a posting to set the record straight. She explained how she and Bartone had rediscovered the wreck using AWOIS and hang numbers, and affirmed that Kohler was not on the boat that day.

Kohler responded to Crowell's posting: "The fact that Dan Crowell no longer had a monopoly on the USS *Murphy* suddenly changed him into a hypocritical rat fink. After years of filling his pockets with the money from dive charters to other sailors and 'war graves' and not only encouraging the removal of artifacts, but grabbing some for himself, Danny Crowell now became the protector and guardian of the lost souls of the deep. He was compelled to write his acidic and false post to protect the USS *Murphy* from the same treatment he has meted out to every wreck he's ever hooked his dive boat into. Of course the fact that a History Channel documentary, possible book and further lucrative deals can be tied into the bleached bones of the USS *Murphy*'s dead sailors and put a little ching in his pockets doesn't hurt either."

Parenthetically, it is interesting to note that after this posting, Kohler adopted the very same attitude that he accused Crowell of adopting. With the notoriety that followed the publication of *Shadow Divers*, and after he spent years in recovering numerous artifacts from, among others, the USS *San Diego*, the *U-869*, and the USS *Murphy*, he became extremely vocal against divers (other than himself) who recovered junk from the U-boat which he then promoted as a military gravesite. As a true hypocrite, he didn't feel that way until after he got what he wanted, at which point he elected himself as the custodian of the wreck and the protector of the memory of the deceased German sailors.

Be that as it may, Crowell continued to call the NHC – again, and again, and again, and again. He kept calling the NHC until they promised to pursue the matter. Eventually, the NHC employed the Naval Criminal Investigative Service.

The NCIS ordered a Navy investigator to go to Bartone's house. After the investigator listened to Bartone's story, he did not think that the situation was Navy business. The recovery of discarded items from lost shipwrecks had nothing to do with national defense or homeland security: the Navy's congressionally mandated functions.

Crowell was not satisfied that the NHC did not enforce his exclusive rights to the *Murphy*. He continued to press his demand for action against competitors, using the NHC as a cat's paw to promote his personal vendetta. The NHC then ordered another investigator to retrieve Bartone's souvenirs from the *S-5*: items that the Navy abandoned after making 477 dives on the wreck in 1920 and 1921. This agent threatened to prosecute Bartone for criminal offenses unless he handed over the items. Because of the photograph and caption on the Internet, Bartone could not deny that he possessed these items.

The Navy investigator claimed that the NHC had valued the items – a cage lamp and a valve – at $5,000 each. When Bartone told me this, I told him that I suspected that the artificially inflated value was made so that the total reached $10,000, perhaps to meet a threshold that made the so-called theft meet the requirements for a grander "crime."

I appraised the items at no more than $500, and told Bartone that I would testify to that effect in his defense, should the need ever arise.

As a discretionary tactic, Bartone gave the items to the agent, and the matter was dropped (although the NCIS can reopen the case any time – a continuous threat that they can use to maintain their grip on putative offenders).

The NCIS also went after Christina. An investigator

parked in her driveway for two days while she was away at work. Apparently, NCIS investigators work banking hours, for each time the investigator departed before Christina returned home from her office. After the investigator left a message, Christina called and spoke with him. He wanted to know if she had removed any junk from the wreck. She told him that the only thing she took was video footage. He seemed to be satisfied with this, and let the matter drop.

Kohler was also the subject of investigation. After speaking with an NCIS investigator on the phone, Kohler suggested that they schedule a meeting at the investigator's office. This ploy kept the investigator out of Kohler's house. Kohler took with him to the investigator's office the artifacts that he had used to help in identifying the wreck – the very artifacts that were pictured in the report that he and Christina had submitted to the NHC: the steam gauge and tag. He gave a copy of the report to the investigator, and showed him copies of correspondence between him and the NHC. The report informed the NHC how the identification had been made.

The investigator claimed that the gauge was worth $5,000. He confiscated it. If the investigator believed that Kohler had recovered a binnacle, as Chatterton had told Crowell, he was either unwilling or unable to further prosecute a case that was based solely on hearsay, and on the unsubstantiated allegations of a disgruntled antagonist. It is likely that, under the circumstances, he could not have obtained a warrant to search Kohler's premises for the binnacle or any other artifacts that he may have recovered from the *Murphy*.

This put an end to the investigations that Crowell was responsible for initiating.

By this time, however, the snowball that Crowell had pushed down the hill was growing in size and momentum, and met with no other obstructions. Adding impetus to a situation that was already out of control, and using the *Murphy* situation as justification for its actions, the NHC decided that the best way to satisfy its thirst for power was to enact legislation which conferred absolute authority upon the NHC to reign supreme over all Navy wrecks – aircraft as well as vessels – everywhere in the world.

Legal process requires that proposed legislation undergo Congressional review, public hearings, political and public input, and debate. Anticipating that opposition to totalitarian control would be strong, the NHC relied instead upon stealth and subterfuge to achieve its nefarious goal. Just as the National Defense Authorization Act for Fiscal Year 2005 was about to be passed by both the House and the Senate, the NHC managed to insert a clause which asserted title of all "sunken military craft and associated contents" to the United States government, and, by extension, to the NHC as custodians.

The NDAA was an appropriations bill whose purpose was to assign funds for military spending. It was never intended to have anything to do with exercising control over lost, sunken, or abandoned military vessels by a handful of civilian powermongers. Nonetheless, the bill was passed along with its wrongful amendment (Title XIV of the Military Appropriations Bill).

According to the Prohibitions, "no person shall engage in or attempt to engage in any activity directed at a sunken military craft that disturbs, removes, or injures any sunken military craft" anywhere in the world unless authorized to do so, under threat of fine of $100,000."

A grapnel or other anchoring device can be construed as a means of causing injury.

There the matter rests.

Score another point for terrorism against democracy.

The reader should understand that the pogrom that I described above was instigated not by the United States Navy or its officers or personnel, but by a handful of civilian control freaks who dominate the Naval Historical Center. The leader responsible this evil initiative was the previous Director of the NHC, Bill Dudley.

*   *   *

Crowell showed raw footage of the *Murphy* to the Philadelphia chapter of the Explorer's Club. He introduced himself as the skipper of the *Seeker* and the discoverer of the *Murphy*. He then went on to say that the *Seeker* had also discovered the *U-869*. He neglected to mention that when the *Seeker* discovered the *U-869*, Bill Nagle was the skipper and Crowell was not even on the boat. By the use of careful wording, Crowell gave his audience the impression that *he* discovered the *U-869*. This kind of deceptive phrasing that misleads or manipulates the public is called newsmanship.

Crowell also neglected to mention that when his girlfriend, Jennifer Samulski, purchased the *Seeker* for Crowell to operate, Nagle's shipwreck location log came as part of the deal. Thus Crowell inherited the loran numbers that Nagle had accumulated throughout the years. In addition to known wreck sites were numbers that Nagle had obtained from the Bogans: a family of head boat operators who had been fishing on New Jersey shipwrecks and collecting hang numbers since the 1930's.

It was from the Bogans that Nagle had obtained the numbers of the *U-869* and the *Murphy*.

Crowell further neglected to tell his audience that, before the *Murphy* was identified, he vehemently repudiated the suggestion that it was a warship, and that instead he fervently believed that it was a Liberty ship. He also failed to give credit for identifying the wreck to Christina Young. By taking credit for "discovering" the *Murphy*, and by failing to give credit to those who provided the numbers and identified the wreck, he gave other false impressions that enhanced his spurious image.

Crowell continues to tell lies and practice deceit. On February 20, 2009 - one day before this book went to the printer - he gave a presentation on the *Murphy* to the Cape Dive Club. This time he went so far as to state unequivocally that *he* discovered the *U-869*. With regard to the *Murphy*, he said that, although he expected to see a Liberty ship on the bottom, he recognized the wreck as a warship. He danced around the issue of positive identification, but when pressed upon this point, he told his uninformed audience that he found the name on the AWOIS list.

He did not give credit to Christina Young; he never even mentioned her name. Nor did he inform club members that he sicced Navy investigators on her, Bartone, and Kohler. He took credit that was due to others, and refrained from taking credit for providing the impetus for the creation and insertion of Title XIV.

* * *

The *Murphy* was constructed to destroy the enemy during a time of war. In the process, she destroyed the lives of a number of her crew. Some sixty years later, during a time of peace, her wreckage helped to destroy some of the freedoms for which eighteenth-century American patriots waged revolution against tyranny. In that regard, the *Murphy* may be considered to be the greatest destroyer in the history of the world. She sank no enemy vessels, but she did much to facilitate the sinking of democratic principals and individual freedom.

As the saying goes, "Guns don't kill people. People kill people." The *Murphy* is an inanimate object. The true destroyers are the people who wielded the *Murphy* for their own nefarious purposes.

Once again, the kiss of death produced far-reaching consequences. It is too often quoted that the evil that men do lives after them. In the present case, in an insane bid for personal prerogative, a number of individuals conspired to appropriate for themselves some of the freedoms that once belonged to all the American people. That they did this by foul means will in no way alter the aftermath. Americans and their children will pay for these contemptible deeds forever.

When Brad Nolan solicited me to write a series of shipwreck articles for the inaugural and subsequent issues of Dive Chronicles, *I suggested a number of topics. The* Murphy *was one of them. He liked the idea of informing his readers about the circumstances that led to the passage of restrictive legislation with respect to Navy wrecks. However, he was concerned about creating turmoil within the diving community by mentioning the names of the culprits who were the most responsible for causing the controversy, and of the individual who suffered the most from their treachery.*

At his request, in the magazine version I used pseudonyms for these three people. Dan Crowell was called Judas, John Chatterton was called Judas 2, and Dan Bartone was called Victim.

Space limitations forced me to submit a somewhat abbreviated version of events. The present chapter is nearly double the length of the version that was published in the magazine. This book version gives greater coverage to Christina Young's significant and insightful research, which led to the identification of the wreck, and to the clandestine shenanigans of the Naval Historical Center.

As another example of Crowell's rabid craving for stardom and ill-gotten fame, on a television interview he asserted his overactive machismo by claiming to have made more dives on the Andrea Doria *"than anyone else on the planet."*

The next time we met, I immediately accosted him about this spurious proclamation. I asked, "Why did you say that? You know that I've made more dives on the Doria *than you have."*

Sheepishly, he acknowledged the truth of my statement, and admitted that he knew it for a fact at the time he made his unsupportable claim. Then he made excuses for his falsehood.

He estimated the number of trips that he had scheduled to the Doria *as "about fifty." He then assigned an arbitrary number of dives that he thought he could have made on each trip. By this guesswork reckoning, he arrived at an arbitrary figure that was nonetheless below my well-established number of dives.*

Except for two initial checkout dives, I have logged every dive that I have ever made. I also keep an addi-

tional and separate index sheet of *Doria* dives. In addition to maintaining a running tab, the *Doria* index annotates the date of every entry. This enables me to cross-reference my primary dive log and review the statistics of that particular dive (boat name, dive buddy, bottom time, artifact recoveries, and so on).

By comparison, Crowell had nothing. He did not keep a dive log and he did not keep a boat or trip log. Furthermore, I was onboard the *Seeker* on many of his *Doria* trips, so I knew that on some of these trips he did not dive at all. Sometimes he made only one token dive. He never made as many dives as his customers made.

Worse yet, not every scheduled trip made it to the wreck site. At least 25% of his *Doria* trips were "blown out" (canceled because of foul weather or an unfavorable forecast). Some trips were canceled because of mechanical problems with the boat, often due to the lack of preventive maintenance. In these cases the boat never left the dock. One year, more than half of the scheduled trips were canceled for one reason or another.

Of those trips that made it to the wreck, around 75% were cut short: some as a result of fatalities, some due to bad weather, and some simply because the forecast for the following day didn't look promising (or so Crowell claimed) and, since the participants had already paid him, there was no incentive for him to remain on site.

On more than one occasion the *Seeker* left the *Doria* in perfect sea conditions. Refunds were not made for curtailed trips.

Crowell's television statement was completely baseless - something that he made up for the camera in order to bolster his false image. His forced admission to me was gratuitous and useless. The damage was already done. Although he confessed the truth to me in private, the lie that he had told to the public would be remembered by the masses who had no access to the facts.

*   *   *

According to Christina Young, the GPS coordinates for the *Murphy* are 39-40.155 N / 72-33.854 W.

The Monitor:
America's Socialized Shipwreck

I have written a number of magazine pieces about my travails with the Monitor. *Two of these articles were reprinted in* Wreck Diving Adventures. *I have also written a book on the subject.*

I wrote the following piece during my six-year legal battle with NOAA, over access to the wreck site. It was published in the September 1988 issue of The Freeman: Ideas on Liberty. *It pretty much speaks for itself.*

For more than two centuries, Americans have defended the rights of sailors to move freely upon the open seas. But now, the international waters are again under attack. This time, however, we are fighting for freedom *under* the seas. And this time, the usurpers are minions within our own government.

At the center of the controversy lies the *Monitor,* one of the first ironclad warships, which was built for the Union navy by John Ericsson. Launched in January 1862, the *Monitor* measured 179 feet in length, grossed 1,200 tons, and featured a rotating turret that contained two 11-inch smoothbore guns. She was powered by steam, and had a screw propeller.

On March 8, 1862, the *Monitor* engaged the Confederate ironclad *Virginia* (formerly the *Merrimack)* near Hampton Roads, Virginia. In a historic struggle, the two ironclads fought a four-hour duel which ended in a draw. In May 1862, when the Confederates abandoned Norfolk, the *Virginia* was run ashore by her crew, and burned. In December 1862, the *Monitor* foundered in heavy seas off Cape Hatteras, North Carolina. This, it would seem, was the end of the *Monitor* and *Merrimack.*

However, the U.S. Navy knew the approximate location of the *Monitor*. But without adequate financing for an in-depth survey, the Navy was unable to find the wreck.

The Navy's primary concern was not who got credit for the find, but that the shipwreck be found. In 1953, to provide incentives for the private sector to conduct scanning operations, the Navy struck the vessel from the Naval Register and abandoned all salvage claims.

For two decades a veritable flotilla searched the shoals off Cape Hatteras, but it was not until 1973 that the Duke University research vessel *Eastward* located and tentatively identified the remains of the *Monitor* sixteen miles offshore. The following year the site was revisited, and positive identification was obtained when the research vessel *Alcoa Seaprobe* took several thousand underwater pictures which were assembled into a photomosaic by Navy specialists.

Almost immediately, several government agencies began vying for control of the *Monitor* wreck. The winner was the National Oceanic and Atmospheric Administration (NOAA), under the auspices of the Department of Commerce. Although the ironclad did not fit the criteria of any Act of Congress, the Marine Protection, Research, and Sanctuaries Act was the shielding mechanism deemed most appropriate. The *Monitor* became a sanctuary in the middle of a one-mile diameter tract of seabed and the accompanying column of water. It was designated the first marine sanctuary, and came to be

The sinking of the *Monitor*. (From the author's collection.)

known as the *Monitor* National Marine Sanctuary (MNMS). The *Monitor* had at last found a home—or was it a jail?

The *Monitor* as a marine sanctuary lies on shaky ground—and in legally turbulent water. By international agreement, territorial rights extend to twelve nautical miles from the mean high water mark. In this respect, the U.S. generously claims only three miles of territorial waters. In either case, the *Monitor* resides on land not owned by the U.S., and which is outside U.S. jurisdiction.

In addition, because the wreck was legally abandoned, its status falls under the common law principle of the maritime law of salvage, which, although expressed by various judges in different forms, generally provides that "the finder or salvor of abandoned property at sea who first reduces that property to his possession may keep that property." (*Treasure Salvors III* case).

In the 1981 *Cobb Coin* case, U.S. District Court Judge James Lawrence King further stipulated that "salvage law permits one whose salvage efforts are continuous and reasonably diligent to work a wreck site to the exclusion of others." In other words, the backers of the *Eastward* expedition could have kept a substantial claim over the wreck had they continued to work it. Since they did not, the wreck is unclaimed property. Anyone may salvage it.

Anyone, that is, except U.S. citizens. They are not even allowed to look at the wreck, much less recover anything from it.

While the stipulated goals of the National Marine Sanctuary Program are, in part, to "enhance public awareness, understanding, and wise use of the marine environment," and to "provide for maximum compatible public and private use," the case of the lost shipwreck has been wrapped in rolls of extremely sticky red tape.

Frustration and Delay

Four years ago, when I first applied to the MNMS for

a permit to dive on the *Monitor,* it was with full confidence of receiving prompt and professional aid. My simple letter of intent stated my purpose and objectives—to dive on the wreck of the *Monitor* in order to take pictures of the historic site. What I got was years of frustration and delay. At first, I received no response to my queries. Later, I obtained a grudging acknowledgment. Finally, intentionally rigid restrictions were imposed which would make compliance difficult and expensive. But, because I wanted to dive the wreck, I proceeded.

I wrote a six-page monograph, but MNMS found it inadequate. Eventually, this grew into a proposal of more than 100 pages in which I had to: itemize every piece of equipment I intended to take, and describe the function and use of each; submit a detailed cruise plan and time table of events; explain in intricate detail the techniques of scuba diving, even the most basic; furnish resumés and complete medical examinations for each participant; specify my goals, with no allowed deviation; and provide proof of funding. Doing this, I felt more like the board of directors of a university sponsoring an expedition than an individual desiring merely to see a sanctuary that supposedly had been created for my benefit as an American citizen.

During this time, not only did I receive no cooperation from MNMS, but the number of unanswered questions posed in my many letters was growing. And only one letter in four was answered. Worse, as I met the demands imposed upon me, the agency invoked discretionary procedures to conjure up more stumbling blocks.

In short, my permit application was denied. I was cited for safety violations due to depth (the *Monitor* lies in 220 feet of water) and for having photographic objectives which had already been met by previous NOAA expeditions. The *Monitor* National Marine Sanctuary took no cognizance of my experience and level of expertise: more than 700 open-ocean, decompression dives, of which nearly a hundred were made in depths equivalent to the *Monitor.*

In addition, MNMS officials asserted that my photographic efforts on the *Monitor* must produce viable results which in some way benefitted the Sanctuary. This obviates the ultimate aim of the sanctuary program: that sanctuaries, like parks, exist for the benefit of the people, not the reverse. Even if I chose not to make photographic documentation, this should not rule out my wanting to dive the *Monitor* because, like Mount Everest, "it is there."

Following administrative procedure, I appealed the denial. But my involvement with MNMS did not end there. Because of my tenacity, I became the focus of an investigation. Upon learning that I intended to dive in North Carolina close to the *Monitor* site, a MNMS spokesman alerted the Coast Guard and threatened me with arrest and a $50,000 fine should I be caught within Sanctuary boundaries. This brought up a curious situation: despite numerous requests for precise navigational coordinates, which I had needed for my proposal to calculate running times from shore to wreck, MNMS had steadfastly refused to give them to me. Now it enjoined me to stay away from a spot whose location I did not know. Nevertheless, officers of the Marine Fisheries Department were waiting for my chartered boat every day when it docked. They inspected our gear for artifacts which might have been old enough to have come from the Civil War ironclad. The surveillance continues.

Denying Access

I once cajoled an MNMS spokesman into admitting that Sanctuary regulations had been made purposely stringent so as to deny public access. The MNMS desires sole proprietorship over the site; it wants to have the only photographs of the wreck; and it wants complete control over publicity. It does not want to share the *Monitor* experience. Nor is it committed to having the wreck fully documented—it wants only that such documentation be generated within its own bureaucracy, free from outside competition.

The condition of the *Monitor* today is not the same as it was yesterday, last year, or at any other time in its history. The sea is ever changing, ever destroying. As a shipwreck disintegrates, it passes before our eyes like a movie in extreme slow motion. Each frame is ephemeral, existing only for a brief instant in time, and must be studied before it dissolves.

Even the most naive person must admit that the *Monitor* does not display the same graceful curves as it did when it slid down the ways in 1862. Its turret and Dahlgren guns are no longer thrust out defiantly against foes such as the *Virginia*. Its destruction is a continuous and ongoing process that is not stopped by the passing of laws, or by governmental intervention.

My case seemed totally lost until I met Peter Hess through the Atlantic Alliance for Maritime Heritage Conservation. This body of volunteers has lobbied for years against the many bills which seek to take, not just the *Monitor,* but all shipwrecks out of the public domain, and to place them under government control. Although the prime goal of the Atlantic Alliance is to teach underwater archaeology to interested divers around the nation, it has taken a staunch position in protecting people's rights to dive on shipwrecks.

Hess is a diver, shipwreck historian, amateur archaeologist, and an attorney with a background in maritime law. He has been intimately involved with diving legislation, has frequently advised on Atlantic Alliance policy, and has testified in Senate hearings against the Abandoned Shipwreck Act, which aims to place all shipwrecks under government control. He followed my *Monitor* pursuits with fervent concern. When my bid for justice died, he put life back into my sagging spirit.

After listening to my story and reading my correspondence, Hess was keen enough to note many improprieties in NOAA's handling of my permit application: improper delegation of authority, bias among MNMS staff members who had personal ambitions concerning the disposition of the *Monitor,* disinclination to consider proven scuba diving methods, and lack of impartial review. The denial of my permit was arbitrary and capricious.

Working together, we filed a complaint for declaratory judgment and injunctive relief in the United States District Court for the Eastern District of Pennsylvania. NOAA and MNMS were forced to commit to the administrative record such evidence as existed in their files. However, so vehemently did they resist interrogation that they filed a motion to have any further discoveries kept out of the Court's eyes.

Even so, several things became immediately clear: that, although mandated by Federal regulation, my permit application had not been circulated among members of either the Scientific Review Board or the Advisory Council on Historic Preservation—those very two committees for whom I had written my proposal in such painstaking detail; that, after stipulating that my photographic objectives had already been met by previous (government-sponsored) expeditions, NOAA spent $1.8 million of taxpayers' money on another photographic expedition; that, while not allowing my support vessel to place a 30-pound anchor near the wreck, in order to facilitate diver access and afford increased safety, NOAA permitted its own expedition to drop four *six-ton* anchors on the site, even though it used no divers and required no safety measures; that, after all the rhetoric aimed at protecting a valuable marine resource, NOAA let its own members fish on the wreck.

MNMS had pigeonholed my entire project right from the start, and never had any intention of letting it get a proper review.

I realized the full absurdity of this situation during a recent visit to Halifax. My Nova Scotian friends were dumbfounded to learn that they could take their boat down the coast and dive on the *Monitor* at any time. And no one, Coast Guard included, could stop them. Canadians, or the citizens of any other nation, are not bound by U.S. mandates when they are in international waters. The only people prevented from visiting the *Monitor* are U.S. citizens.

There is not much left of the *Monitor*. Its once sleek hull is pockmarked by the ravages of the sea: it is a mere skeleton of itself, unrecognizable to all but experts. The minimum estimate for raising the hulk is upwards of $40 million, not counting the cost of preservation, housing, and eternal maintenance—an unwarranted expense for archaeological provenience considering that, with all the photographs, plans, and written records of the *Monitor*, there is probably nothing additional to be learned.

The only thing ironclad about the *Monitor* today is MNMS's stand on no access. Instead of bouncing off cannon bails and solid shot, present arrangements deny access to the very people who are most willing to spend their own money and expend their own efforts to bring to the public the images of their adventures.

The time is long overdue to re-evaluate the entire status of the *Monitor*. Why should Americans be forbidden to dive on the wreck? Are there other ways to manage the *Monitor* which would involve less red tape? Why, in fact, should the Federal government maintain ownership and control? Wouldn't a private owner or salvager have strong incentives to put the remains of the *Monitor* to the best possible use?

In a truly free society, the purpose of the State is not to own or to rule, but to protect the rights and property of its citizens. Abandoned shipwrecks, by the very nature of abandonment, are not the possessions of the government merely by the fact of their existence. If shipwrecks belong to anyone, it is to those individuals with the will and the incentive to dive on them at their own cost and expenditure of time. The confiscation of this property under the guise of "the public good," coupled with the subsequent denial of public access, violates the most basic moral principles.

I won my lawsuit against NOAA in late 1989. As a result, I was awarded the first ever permit to dive on the Monitor. *I organized a two-week expedition for the summer of 1990. And the rest is history . . .*

The Monitor Goes Public

It is no secret that I have a long-standing feud with the National Oceanic and Atmospheric Administration, especially with regard to the Monitor National Marine Sanctuary. But my involvement goes much deeper than that (pardon the depth of the pun). I actually have a far longer-standing feud with a government that treats its citizens unfairly. You might say that I have a passion for justice, and I'm not afraid to fight for it.

I will make additional comments in this regard after you have had the benefit of reading this chapter and "The Stellwagen Bank Robbery."

The Civil War ironclad *Monitor* has had a long history of foundering, first in a storm off Cape Hatteras, North Carolina, then in bureaucratic red tape when it became this nation's first National Marine Sanctuary, in 1975. Until 1989, the National Oceanic and Atmospheric Administration (NOAA), which wrote the Sanctuary regulations, strictly forbade American citizens to have access to the site.

In November of that year, I took the National Oceanic and Atmospheric Administration to court in order to open public access to the *Monitor*. I won the case, but NOAA only begrudgingly permitted me and my fellow divers to photograph the wreck the following year, and that was contingent upon a policy of "no touching," even to the point of videotaping each diver's wetsuit before and after the dive in order to check for smudges proving that the diver had "brushed" against the coral-encrusted hull, which was considered a grave offense punishable by a $50,000 fine.

After finding an intact glass lantern globe in peril of being swept away by the currents, I suggested that the delicate item be rescued before it was lost forever. NOAA agreed, but refused to let me recover the relic. Instead, it chartered a submersible to do the job, at a cost of $15,000 a day. It took NOAA two days to accomplish what I could have accomplished in a few seconds.

The agency's continued adversarial posture resulted in two subsequent suits, affirmative action through Congressional intervention, substitutions in Sanctuary personnel, rewritten guidelines, and, at last, a somewhat enlightened attitude regarding the right of public access. Eventually, 1994 became a landmark year in the *Monitor's* ongoing saga, for it saw two monumental changes in the conduct of the Sanctuary.

Previously, access to the site could be obtained only by applying for a scientific research permit. Writing an acceptable proposal was burdensome and inappropriate when photography was the sole aim of the expedition. Now NOAA has instituted a system whereby access to the wreck can be gained via special use permits issued to approved concessionaires. That is a fancy way of saying that you can charter a boat to go to the wreck. The only two restrictions are reasonable: divers must be careful not to contact the wreck or damage it in any way, and a NOAA observer must be aboard the charter vessel in order to maintain an official presence. This is equivalent to the National Park Service policy of having a ranger lead guided tours through areas where hiking boots might trample delicate vegetation or destroy geological specimens. Wetsuits were not videotaped, and divers were allowed to dive unescorted on their own recognizance as responsible and law-abiding citizens.

NOAA also permitted recreational divers to recover artifacts under the aegis of the scientific research permit. Before an artifact could be brought to the surface its archaeological provenance had to be established. Provenanace means placement in relation to other components of the wreck. Each artifact was photographed, videotaped, and measured by tape with respect to nearby structures such as beams or bulkheads whose relative locations were already known or could be drawn on a slate and referenced to grids or positions within the hull. It is not as complicated as it sounds.

In this manner, nearly two dozen objects of the past were brought to the light of day. Chief among the items recovered were more than a dozen mustard bottles stamped "U.S. Navy," most with the contents corked tightly inside. (We were not permitted to spread the Civil War mustard on our sandwiches in order to ascertain its preservative qualities.) Also recovered were bottles of pepper and hair tonic, and a brass oarlock. Each bottle was slipped into a neoprene glove or mitt before being tucked into a mesh bag for its ride to the surface. The only casualty was a corked bottle which exploded during ascent due to trapped gas exerting outward stress against the glass as the ambient pressure decreased; the several parts were saved, and the contents sent to the FBI crime lab for analysis. All artifacts were shipped to The Mariners Museum in Newport News, Virginia, for preservation and eventual display.

John Broadwater, Sanctuary manager and observer on all expeditions, supports efforts to keep the diving community involved in the *Monitor's* future. In a new spirit of cooperative effort, both the *Monitor* and the American public will emerge as winners.

My most gratifying moment with respect to diving on the Monitor *was when I recovered a glass mustard bottle (a nest of which I had discovered the previous year). This simple act of artifact recovery - which I had done thousands of times on other shipwrecks - proved my point: that wreck-divers can perform valuable services in rescuing items that were at imminent risk of loss or destruction as shipwrecks collapse.*

I made certain that all the other divers on the trip shared the experience of recovery.

Unfortunately for the American people and the cause of freedom, NOAA's change in policy regarding shipwreck access was only a temporary expedient - as you will note in the following chapter.

The Stellwagen Bank Robbery

As I noted in the previous two chapters, I successfully sued NOAA for the right of public access to the Civil War ironclad Monitor. *Administrative heads have hated me ever since. I return the feeling. But more on that at the end of this chapter.*

The following polemic was published in Shipwrecks of Massachusetts: North. *The controversial issues are so important that I want them to reach a broader readership than is likely to be interested in wrecks off the State of Massachusetts - especially as NOAA's Ministry of Truth continues to rewrite history the way it wishes the public to perceive it.*

> "This is my last territorial demand."
> - Adolph Hitler

On October 11, 2006, I attended a meeting that was sponsored by the Metro West Dive Club, at which a representative of the Stellwagen Bank National Marine Sanctuary was scheduled to address the members and other interested attendees. The Sanctuary sent Matthew Lawrence as its spokesperson. To him fell the task of delivering carefully phrased claptrap that disguised the Sanctuary's true motives of territorial conquest and expansionism. He gave a spiel in which he touted the goals of the National Oceanic and Atmospheric Association to preserve the marine environment through its Marine Sanctuaries Program.

The insincerity that was obvious to me was not so obvious to those who did not have my long and dreadful experience with NOAA. I will digress for the moment in order to provide some background to NOAA's continuing saga of illegitimacy. The depth of NOAA's depravity is exemplified in this chapter. Read it and weep.

> "Government of the people, by the people, for the people."
>
> - Abraham Lincoln

In 1972, Congress passed the Marine Protection, Research, and Sanctuaries Act, the avowed purpose of which was to create marine sanctuaries in order to "preserve, restore, or enhance areas for their conservational, recreational, ecological, research or esthetic values in coastal waters." Areas deserving of such a designation were those that were "necessary to protect valuable, unique, or endangered marine life, geological features, and oceanographic features. Areas to complement and enhance public areas such as parks, national seashores and national or state monuments and other preserved areas. Areas important to the survival and preservation of the nation's fisheries and other ocean resources. Areas to advance and promote research which will lead to a more thorough understanding of the marine ecosystem and the impact of man's activities."

The MPRSA made no mention of shipwrecks.

The primary goals of the MPRSA were, among others, "to enhance public awareness, understanding, appreciation and wise use of the marine environment" and "to facilitate to the extent compatible with the primary objective of resource protection, all public and private uses of the resources of such areas."

On November 4, 1992, Congress designated the Stellwagen Bank as the twelfth National Marine Sanctuary since the inception of the program twenty years earlier. A National Marine Sanctuary is the underwater equivalent of a National Park. The focal point of this latest addition to the National Marine Sanctuary Program was the Stellwagen Bank: a shallow area that was a rich source of cold water marine life, and that was a major source of food for large marine mammals, particularly the humpback whale. The boundaries of the Sanctuary encompassed a number of shipwrecks.

The National Oceanic and Atmospheric Administration manages the National Marine Sanctuary Program. Historically, NOAA and NMSP have been antagonistic toward divers in the pursuit of their hobby. This antagonism was manifested largely in overly restrictive access to wreck sites, or in outright denial of access. Self-serving bureaucrats who were mandated by law to encourage research and to enhance public awareness have instead taken the opposite stance: they have tried to the best of their power and ability, and by exceeding their authority, to prohibit public access to wreck sites.

> "I will either find a way, or make one."
> - Hannibal

I learned this firsthand in 1984. A decade earlier, NOAA created the first National Marine Sanctuary for the explicit purpose of taking control of the Civil War ironclad *Monitor*, which sank in a gale in 1862 off the Diamond Shoals of North Carolina. It goes without saying that this shipwreck met none of the avowed sanctuary criteria for sanctuary status, as stated in the MPRSA.

When I requested permission to photograph the *Monitor*, NOAA denied my right of access to the site. This was tantamount to creating a National Park, but not permitting people to enter and see the sights that had been expressly set aside for them.

I objected to NOAA's self-serving attitude. I initiated a series of lawsuits whose cost to me personally was extravagant: it took eight years, five federal lawsuits, and thousands of dollars in legal expenses to force NOAA to grant permission for me to conduct a photoreconnaissance expedition to the wreck site. Finally I prevailed. I won the right for all Americans to visit the wreckage of the *Monitor*, and to see for themselves an historic piece of their national heritage. Previous to this, only NOAA personnel were granted the privilege of observing the *Monitor* firsthand, through the medium of videotape footage that was shot by means of remotely operated vehicles.

Even after my first successful *Monitor* expedition, NOAA continued to play hardball by denying my next diving application. NOAA's denial was overturned only by Congressional intervention. Thereafter, NOAA was forced to concede to Congressional mandates.

The landmark decision of the court was well worth the cost and effort, because it established two important precedents: it forever opened public access to the *Monitor*, and it forbade NOAA from using depth of water or safety considerations as excuses to prevent access. In the latter regard, although NOAA divers were prohibited by NOAA regulations from diving deeper than 130 feet on scuba, non-NOAA citizens did not have to abide by NOAA regulations. And many non-NOAA divers have far greater training and underwater competence than NOAA divers.

NOAA's attitude has not changed over the years. If anything, administrative conceit has worsened. In their bid for bureaucratic territoriality, NOAA's minions are serving themselves instead of serving the public. They continue to ignore the tide of public sentiment in order to expand their ill-gotten authority. Like Adolph Hitler, they keep saying that the next spree of territorial expansion will be the last. In fact, NOAA is administered by a host of control freaks who are insinuating themselves insidiously into the public domain much like a deadly cancer invading and destroying the human body. NOAA is a bureaucratic metastasis.

The minions in charge of the Stellwagen Bank National Marine Sanctuary have taken the same uncooperative tack as those who claimed access to the *Monitor* only for themselves. They have steadfastly refused to release public information that they hold in the public trust: among other data, the locations of the sites.

They have done this despite their avowed Action Plan whose language states specifically that the Stellwagen Sanctuary "is designed to protect these non-renewable resource sites and *promote responsible public access* for generations to come." (Italics added for emphasis.)

What NOAA wrote for public consumption was contradicted by NOAA's actions. According to law, NOAA does not have discretionary authority to either deny public access to wreck sites or to keep public information from the public.

"The great enemy of the truth is very often not the lie – deliberate, contrived, and dishonest – but the myth – persistent, persuasive, and unrealistic."
- John F. Kennedy

I discussed these issues at length with Dennis St. Germain. We decided to test NOAA's honesty and integrity by submitting a request pursuant to the Freedom of Information Act for the locations of the wrecks that lay within the borders of the Stellwagen sanctuary. Even after all these years, mention of my name still raises hackles among NOAA personnel because of NOAA's utter defeat in the case of the *Monitor*. So Dennis submitted the request under his name.

FOIA mandates the disclosure of information that is held by the government in trust for the people. "The basic purpose of FOIA is to ensure an informed citizenry, vital to the functioning of a democratic society, needed to check against corruption and to hold the governors accountable to the governed." FOIA provides that "every agency shall, upon request for identifiable records . . ., make such records promptly available to any person." Note that the law does not apply only to American voters and taxpayers, but to "any person," which by definition includes foreign nationals.

FOIA has been tested and upheld in federal court. For example, Judge David Alan Ezra ruled, "The Congressional message behind FOIA is unequivocal. The government must make available documents it possesses to anyone who requests disclosure. Congress explicitly listed the only possible exceptions in the Act. . . . The spirit and purpose of FOIA mandate a strong presumption in favor of disclosure."

NOAA responded predictably, as it did in my *Monitor* case. Assistant Administrator John Dunnigan's justification for denial was threefold: that the disclosure of such information might "cause a significant invasion of privacy," that it might cause "risk or harm to the historic resource," or that it might "impede the use of a traditional religious site by practitioners."

Dennis's appeal was a masterpiece of logic. "The public knowledge of the location of the shipwrecks within the confines of the Stellwagen Bank National Marine Sanctuary would not result in the occurrence of any of the three listed reasons for withholding the disclosure of said information. It is from this position that I base my argument that my FOIA request was wrongly denied.

"How can the knowledge of the location of shipwrecks which are tens, and in some cases, hundreds of years old cause a *significant* invasion of privacy? Can the known location of the wrecks impede the use of a traditional religious site by practitioners? Clearly reasons number one and three in no way apply. The only reason that the Department of the Interior could possibly remotely consider is number two: the risk of harm to the historic resource.

"I submit to you that it is an implausible idea to think that the public knowledge of shipwrecks submerged 200 to 400 feet deep, 20 to 60 miles or more from the nearest landfall would 'risk harm to the historic resource.' The location of the wreck of the *Monitor*, which lies at the shallow end of the depth range which we are discussing, was known to the public and no harm was done to that 'historic resource.' Quite the contrary, a case can be made that the expeditions embarked upon by Mr. Gentile and others to document the wreck fueled the public's curiosity and garnered support for the subsequent raising of sections of the ironclad vessel. The locations of the wrecks in the marine reserves of the Great Lakes are public knowledge, and they are situated in far shallower waters, and much nearer to land, yet no harm is coming to those historic resources. The invoking of 16 U.S.C. 470w-3(a) for not releasing the information is at best specious, and at worst absurd.

"It is with much surprise and great dismay that, as a tax paying American, my government is withholding information that I and others like me paid for."

The fallacy in St. Germain's argument was its discursive reasoning. Logic and reason work only with people who are logical and reasonable, or who do not have personal agendas; or, in NOAA's case, with people who are not self-indulgent controllers. One might just as well argue with a charging lion that it should give the matter a little thought before ripping off your head. Nonetheless, our purpose was to ascertain to what lengths NOAA would go to justify its unlawful position.

By no stretch of the imagination can any of the wrecks in Stellwagen be perceived as religious sites. By the exclusion relating to invasion of privacy, Congress meant invasion of a *person's* privacy, not a shipwreck's. Exclusions refer to a person's vital statistics, contact data, criminal convictions, and so on.

The three-page denial of St. Germain's appeal must have taken hundreds of hours to research and write by a Stellwagen bank of meticulous NOAA attorneys. In grandiose language, the denial simply reiterated NOAA's position that the "Disclosure of the Shipwreck Sites Creates a Risk of Harm." NOAA cited previous cases that were clearly irrelevant, but that proved two points: that NOAA attorneys had expended an inordinate amount of time in researching case law and prior suits, and that the denial was written as a pre-emptive rebuttal should the appeal ever go to trial.

Barbara Fredericks, Assistant General Counsel for Administration, ended her letter of appeal denial by stating, "This is the final decision of the Department of

Commerce. You have the right to obtain judicial review of this denial." In other words, her thinly veiled threat was: go ahead and sue. NOAA was fully prepared to spend its enormous resources to fund expensive and protracted litigation.

Few people have the means to litigate against the government, while the government has unlimited funds with which to mount a defense. In fact, the government's most effective defense – especially when it is in the wrong – is to prolong a suit with delaying tactics that continually increase the cost to the litigant. Instead of fighting a case on its merits, the government often tries to win a case by means of wealth and stealth: by making the case so costly that the litigant is brought to financial ruin. To add insult to injury, the government utilizes taxpayers' money to fund its wrongful defense against its citizens: a clear case of government gone awry like metastasizing cancer. Witness my *Monitor* case.

A rational person might wonder how a shipwreck could be harmed by divers looking at it, or by taking pictures of it. This pretext smacks of the primitive belief that a person's soul can be captured on film. Again, the application of intellectual thought has nothing to do with the true motives that underlie NOAA's illegitimate scam: bureaucratic territoriality. All too often, so-called "public servants" perceive themselves as owners instead of administrators. They view the public as trespassers upon the bureaucrats' private preserves. I call this misanthropic attitude the "junkyard dog complex."

A junkyard dog is an aggressive pet whose purpose is to protect a junkyard from thieves and trespassers when the premises are closed for business. At first, the dog barks at only those interlopers who attempt to enter the junkyard after hours or at places along the fence that are remote from the gate. After a while, the dog barks at all passers-by on the other side of the fence. Then the dog barks at bona fide customers who enter the gate in the normal manner. Finally, the dog barks at everyone but the junkyard owner. It may even attack people. The dog has lost sight of its original purpose. It now presumes that the junkyard belongs to *it* and not to the owner, and that every visitor is trespassing on its domain.

I wanted to determine how far NOAA would go to protect its junkyard of sunken shipwrecks from public access. I figured that at the very least NOAA would cooperate with local government. Vic Mastone, head of the Massachusetts Board of Underwater Archeological Resources, told me that NOAA had not even shared the locations with *him* – without even suggesting that it might share the information subject to a nondisclosure agreement. Even though the Sanctuary lay in federal waters and not in State waters, one would think that one government agency would cooperate with another government agency – especially with one whose primary responsibility was archaeological resources in adjacent State waters.

"There is a gap between one's real and one's declared aims."

- George Orwell

As a means to draw attention to the value of the Sanctuary, NOAA nominated the *Portland* for eligibility as a historic site with the National Register of Historical Places. This so-called American trust was designed primarily to protect old buildings from demolition, to prevent reconstruction that would change their original characteristics, and to enforce their maintenance in their present state. Since the NRHP was authorized by Congress in 1966, it has become a clearing house for "protecting" self-styled historic properties from destruction and modern alteration.

In the past four decades, the NRHP has granted historic status to more than 85,000 properties nationwide. In fact, NRHP personnel admitted that they never – *never* – turned down an application as long as the forms were filled out correctly.

The NRHP conducts no investigations to determine the historic quality of a site. It merely processes applications. There are no standards or guidelines for eligibility. The merits for eligibility are left entirely to the nominators to research and document. Once the NRHP determines that an application conforms to its guidelines for applicability – that is, that all the t's are crossed and the i's are dotted – it rubberstamps the nomination, and the rest is history (or historic preservation).

You could nominate your neighbor's eyesore garage as an historic building, and the NRHP would grant it protective status as long as you described the structure with sufficient academic pomposity and infused the text with enough bombastic phrases and buzz words – and they would never know the truth. This process begs the question: What is the value of acceptance as a historic site if no qualifications are required for granting such a status other than a nominator's knack for composing highfalutin language?

If the nomination process is merely a giveaway, then it follows that a site whose address is listed on the National Register of Historic Places is no more significant than that of a person whose address is published in the telephone directory, because no one ever gets turned down.

The listing of shipwrecks on the National Register of Historic Places seems to be one of NOAA's ways of bringing attention to itself, and to obtain funding and grant money in order to care for its so-called historic holdings. NOAA must believe that by calling a shipwreck a cultural resource – the political buzzwords that bureaucrats commonly overuse and abuse – the administration can maintain a firm grip on those wrecks for administration employees to explore and enjoy. Most people will swallow NOAA's song and dance routine because their only knowledge of the Sanctuary stems from Sanctuary propaganda.

Nomination applications that are submitted to the NRHP constitute public information. In order to test the honesty of the NRHP, Marcie Bilinski and I devised a two-stage probe to obtain a copy of the *Portland's* application form, which of necessity must provide its precise location. Buildings and other properties have street addresses; a shipwreck has GPS coordinates.

For the first stage, we drafted a letter in which we asked for a copy of the *Portland's* nomination. So as not to draw attention to the *Portland* per se, we also asked for the nomination of the USS *Arizona* (in Hawaii). Marcie then asked her nephew, Andrew Arnold, to submit the letter in his name. Because he was a high school student, which was mentioned in the letter, we hoped that the NRHP would look upon the letter as an innocent request for historical information.

In due course, Andrew received a package that included both nominations. Although the GPS coordinates were included in the *Portland's* original nomination, the numbers were redacted in the photocopy: that is, a NRHP employee used indelible ink to black out the numbers so that they were illegible. By this means we ascertained that the NRHP was in cahoots with NOAA to withhold public information from the public.

For the second stage, Marcie made an appointment to visit the headquarters of the NRHP in Washington, DC. In her introductory letter, she represented herself with her actual affiliations: she was a member of the Massachusetts Board of Underwater Archaeological Resources, and she was a member of Stellwagen's Maritime Heritage Resources Working Group. Thus she possessed an official status that should have provided her with VIP treatment.

Again, to draw attention away from the *Portland*, she asked to see several other nominations of Chesapeake Bay shipwrecks in which I was interested for a future book. The NRHP office and records were so disorganized that staff members were unable to locate any of the Chesapeake Bay shipwreck nominations. When they pulled the *Portland* file, there was a large red cardboard warning in the file that stated "address restricted." Marcie was not allowed to look at the original application. Instead, a staff member made a photocopy of the application, and redacted the GPS coordinates before giving the copy to her.

"Only two things are infinite, the universe and human stupidity, and I'm not so sure about the former."
- Albert Einstein

Despite these conspiratorial efforts to keep the GPS coordinates to themselves, NOAA was so unobservant as to air the location on public television and broadcast it to the world. In order to promote the Sanctuary, NOAA provided underwater footage that was shot from a remotely operated vehicle, or ROV. They also provided footage of the control room aboard the surface support vessel from which the ROV was deployed and operated. This topside footage focused on the ROV pilot who was watching the monitor that showed what the ROV camera was seeing on the wreck. Because a GPS unit was interfaced with the ROV, to enable the pilot to plot his course, the GPS coordinates were displayed on the screen and were duly recorded by the topside camera.

This informative scene was deleted from later broadcasts, but the damage was already done. NOAA's later attempts to cover up its stupidity, and its continued refusal to release the coordinates, came to naught. NOAA was pre-empted by its own inattention. NOAA's only saving grace was that most of those who noticed the errors of its televised ways did not write down the numbers, or think in advance to record the broadcast.

Others took a different tack. Bob Foster correlated published survey information with the historical record. This enabled him to pinpoint the locations of several wrecks that lay within Sanctuary boundaries. The GPS coordinates that have so far been ascertained – by Foster and others – are published in the present volume, both at the end of this chapter and in the GPS/Loran list at the back of the book. As other wreck sites are discovered (or uncovered), they will be published on my website and printed in future editions.

> "The smaller the mind, the greater the conceit."
> - Aesop

Now to return to the meeting that was noted at the beginning of this chapter.

After Lawrence's introductory poppycock, divers in the audience posed queries about access to shipwrecks within the Sanctuary. Lawrence danced around the issues with true political abandon by never directly answering the questions. Instead, he went off on tangents, during the course of which he expressed NOAA's avowed intent to consider the interests of the people by holding a public hearing.

I was well aware of how NOAA had conducted similar hearings with respect to other Sanctuaries. I was also well aware of their outcomes. Attendees were getting frustrated because they could not get a straight answer to a simple and straightforward question. Finally, I decided to provide what Lawrence refused to give them.

I announced, "NOAA is a totalitarian government agency that doesn't care what you want." I went on to explain that the only reason that NOAA promised to hold a public hearing was because it was forced to do so by Congressional mandate. But, although Congress demanded that NOAA had to *listen* to the concerns of the citizens, NOAA did not have to *act* upon those concerns – and never in its more than thirty-year history had it done so.

The public hearing was a smokescreen: a mere pretense so that NOAA could show Congress that the people had a say in the matter of Sanctuary regulations. NOAA was going to do whatever it damn well pleased.

Lawrence's appearance was a façade – nothing but window-dressing to convince the dive community that they were bound to be part of the decision-making process when in fact they were not. In effect, NOAA was trying to lull divers into a false sense of security, so that it could pass restrictions unopposed – restrictions that were not in the best interests of the public, and that were contrary to the wishes of the people who had the greatest stake in them. That was the way NOAA operated, and had always operated.

The proof of the pudding is NOAA's steadfast refusal to divulge the coordinates of shipwrecks that lay within Sanctuary boundaries. At a subsequent meeting (of the Bay State Council of Divers) on September 26, 2007, Lawrence reiterated NOAA's publicly avowed stance. It was no more believable to me then than it had been the year before.

When I told Lawrence that I had just surveyed the *Pentagoet* – a site whose location NOAA had refused to divulge – he asked me to submit a survey report. I told him that he could read it in the book (which you now hold in your hands). He added further insult by requesting reports of any other wrecks that I might survey in the Sanctuary. Marcie then asked him for GPS coordinates for sites that he wanted us to survey. With a smirk on his face, Lawrence refused to give them to us.

I turned to Marcie, and said, "NOAA doesn't believe in give and take. NOAA only takes."

Lawrence made no comment.

Even though Lawrence appears to enjoy his position of withholding information from the public, I do not mean to single him out from a large group of culprits. Despite the fact that NOAA has designated him as the spokesperson of its dictatorial doctrine, he is but a cog in an imperious wheel of chicanery that goes all the way to the head of NOAA, in the person of Dan Basta. On October 27, 2007, as part of NOAA's endless stream of self-promotion, Basta wrote that one of NOAA's accomplishments over the past thirty-five years was that it "involved people in its decision making, through the 14 advisory councils that provide a critical link to communities adjacent to national marine sanctuaries."

What Basta neglected to mention was that the advisory councils were stacked decks: their members were carefully chosen from among those who agreed with NOAA's policies. Most of the *real* people – those who actually lived near sanctuaries and who earned their livings in sanctuary waters – opposed further aggrandizement, but their voices were either stifled or ignored. Opponents had no say in the decision-making processes. NOAA listened only to proponents of its power-hungry policies.

Nor is there any end of NOAA's territorial expansion in sight. NOAA is now in the process of expanding the Thunder Bay National Marine Sanctuary *eightfold* in size. The absurdity of this situation is that Thunder Bay is not even a marine environment: it is a freshwater bay in Lake Huron. Like Hitler annexing neighboring countries, I doubt that NOAA will ever be satisfied until it controls the entire underwater world.

Fiefdom is alive and living in the NOAA hierarchy.

Millions of dollars have been spent on side-scan surveys and videotape reconnaissance from remotely operated vehicles. Yet when a member of the Massachusetts Board of Underwater Archaeological Resources asked for a side-scan image of the *Pentagoet*, Lawrence refused to provide it. NOAA has consistently declined to provide *all* other shipwreck information – photographs, footage, and side-scan sonar imagery – that is not published gratuitously on the Sanctuary website.

"Repetition does not transform a lie into truth."
- Franklin D. Roosevelt

Listed at the end of this chapter are the locations of those shipwrecks that I have been able to obtain from non-NOAA sources: wreck-divers who have spent their own time, effort, and resources to rediscover what NOAA maliciously withheld from them; and wreck-divers who are willing the share with the public the information that was so costly for them to procure.

Now that the publication of the present volume has let the cat out of the bag, NOAA will no longer have a reason to keep these locations secret. Yet full disclosure has never been part of NOAA's protocol. I doubt that publicizing NOAA's long history of dishonesty will force its administrators to change their tune. Based upon their past behavior, I suspect that they will continue to promote the Sanctuary program as if it is in the best interests of the public.

Consider this: NOAA's literature contains no mention of my victorious court battle against the Monitor National Marine Sanctuary. Both my name and my successful court battle have been expunged from NOAA's published history. NOAA has made no endeavors to inform the public that a legal confrontation occurred in which NOAA was found at fault. As far as NOAA's publications are concerned, the case never existed, and diving permits were always available to American citizens.

Despite my legal victory, the *Monitor* permitting process has again become a façade. Over the past three years, Todd Baldi has submitted five applications to dive on the *Monitor* – and has never been favored with an acknowledgment of receipt, much less the courtesy of a reply. His requests to see copies of existing applications, on which to model his own, have met with the identical treatment: no response. NOAA simply ignores him as if he does not exist, or like W.C. Fields saying, "Go away, kid. You bother me." Baldi wrote to keep me updated on his lack of progress: "I spoke to Jeff Johnson once over the phone. He guided me through the process and basically gave me the complete runaround."

It is the same story all over again. NOAA is doing to Baldi what it did to me, and what a bull does to a cow in heat.

I suspect that NOAA's cover-up will in large measure continue. NOAA may eventually publicize shipwreck locations after the fact of their publication in this volume – doing damage control for a fait accompli – but I doubt that NOAA will acknowledge the true reason for its grudging release of information. Instead, they will word the disclosure in such a way as to make it appear that they had *always* provided locations.

Nor will NOAA praise the achievements of those divers who were the first to dive on the *Frank A. Palmer* and *Louise B. Crary*: unless it is to belittle my predictions. I suspect that NOAA will write this book out of its history the way they wrote me out of the *Monitor's* history.

NOAA's blatant agency hype and self-delusion are ingrained in its policy and in the attitude of its administrators. I think that NOAA will continue to provide partial truths while refusing to admit to all the facts.

I also suspect that if NOAA ever releases the locations of Stellwagen shipwrecks, it will not mention that it did so because it was pre-empted by *Shipwrecks of Massachusetts: North*. Now that I have made the locations public knowledge, I suspect that NOAA might try to save face by making them available without acknowledging my priority: as if NOAA had never kept them secret. These suspicions are based upon NOAA's past actions. In actuality, these suspicions are more in the way of extrapolations rather than forecasts of future behavior.

Worst of all, I suspect that NOAA will endeavor to place at least some of the Sanctuary shipwrecks off limits. They are already laying the basis for this action by claiming that the *Frank A. Palmer*, *Louise B. Crary*, and *Portland* are "very fragile." These are the most intact historic shipwrecks so far discovered in the Sanctuary. Yet they do not describe other wrecks as fragile – those that are almost completely collapsed, such as the *Paul Palmer* and the false *Pentagoet*. It is oxymoronic – or perhaps just moronic – to claim that nearly intact wrecks are fragile, while nearly collapsed wrecks are not. But no one ever accused NOAA of sound reasoning.

> "Big Brother is watching you."
> - George Orwell

Other groundwork that NOAA is laying to preclude public access is water movement. NOAA claims that strong currents and tides pass through the Sanctuary. I would not dispute this claim, because strong currents and tides occur in every ocean, even in Boston Harbor. NOAA's current and tidal sophistry may sound plausible to a naïve citizen or his ingenuous representative, but it is no more meaningful than stating that the Moon revolves around the Earth. The truth that NOAA ignores is that divers do not dive during those times when the water is moving strongly.

NOAA also claims that dive boats utilize a seven to one scope for anchoring, implying that long mooring cables might sweep across and damage a wreck. While this ratio of anchor-chain length to water depth is true for large ocean-going vessels, it is not true for small boats. Small boats do not use a scope that approaches even two to one. By means of comparison, a large ocean-going vessel would use 700 feet of hard iron chain to anchor in 100 feet of water, whereas a dive boat would use no more than 150 feet of soft nylon line to anchor in the same depth. NOAA's imagery insinuates a false impression that is clearly deceptive.

Furthermore, many dives are conducted without anchoring at all. Live-boat diving is commonplace. In this technique, a weighted line is lowered next to a wreck, and is held aloft by means of a buoy, float, or tuna ball. Divers are dropped off and descend the line while the boat drifts or maneuvers in the vicinity.

NOAA commonly ignores well-established diving practices in order to justify its restrictions. If NOAA truly wanted to facilitate access, it would establish mooring buoys next to the wreck sites. I doubt that this will ever happen. NOAA's attitude is antagonistic and dishonest toward the public that provides its funding.

Sanctuary superintendent Craig MacDonald has laid the groundwork for a "switch and bait" scam. He professed to have the interests of divers at heart, but in aside admitted that the final decision for shipwreck management and control will be made at a higher level in NOAA. His disingenuous posture allows him to present himself as a supporter of the wants of the diving community, but lets him off the hook when high-level administrators overrule his putative recommendations in order to close the wrecks to the public. The situation is nothing more than a conspiracy that is designed to deceive gullible believers.

NOAA can prevent diver access by means other than direct prohibition. For example, one ploy is to claim that a wreck will be kept off-limits only until staff members complete a survey or examination of the site: a process which they can extend indefinitely while divers grow old and die. If site studies are never completed, the wreck is never opened to the public.

Another way is to claim that a wreck is too "fragile" for divers to explore. It goes without saying that a wreck cannot be damaged by ocular observation or by exposure to photographic processes. Yet the government has used this smelly red herring numerous times throughout its sordid history, and continues to get away with it.

Historically, NOAA's most effective means of denying public access has been abuse of the permit process. NOAA has already announced the likelihood of requiring divers to obtain a permit in order to dive on Sanctuary shipwrecks. This system sounds innocent at first blush. After all, the National Park Service requires backpackers to obtain a permit before entering the backcountry. But there is a substantial difference between the NPS permit process and the NOAA permit process.

When I backpack in a National Park, I either fill out a permit form at the self-service kiosk at the trailhead, or I stop at the visitor center and fill out the form under the guidance of a Park ranger, who advises me on conditions and the availability of water and camping facilities. On the one-page form I write my name, address, telephone number, make and model of my vehicle, my planned route, and the anticipated length of my stay. The permit enables Park personnel to determine trail usage. The permit benefits the backpacker by alerting Park personnel of his location and his anticipated date of return. If the vehicle is spotted at the trailhead after his anticipated return date, Park personnel possess information that is necessary to enable them to initiate search and rescue operations along the backpacker's projected route.

Now consider NOAA's history and proven track record: the process that I encountered when I submitted an application for a permit to dive on the USS *Monitor*. The first NOAA ploy was to ignore my written requests: about a dozen of them over the course of a year. After my persistence paid off by forcing a response to an avowedly hostile letter, Sanctuary manager Edward Miller sent me a multiple page outline of the information that I was required to furnish. He wanted lengthy essays on every aspect of the conduct of my proposed dive plan, backup procedures, and photographic objectives: the name and full background resume of every diver on the expedition; a complete Research Design to include the "scientific questions to be addressed;" a detailed budget "with sources of funding and amounts" and the "reliability and commitment of funding;" and a totally irrelevant Letter of Transmittal.

After I submitted a permit application that was eleven single-spaced typewritten pages in length, another year passed during which I received no answers to my written requests for a status report, and noncommittal answers to my telephone calls. When I finally received a response, it was only to notify me that my application failed to satisfy a new criterion. Long after I furnished the information to satisfy *that* demand, I received a notification that NOAA had found another part of my application that was unsatisfactory. Whenever I satisfied a new requirement, NOAA created another.

NOAA then pigeonholed my permit application for more than a year. This bureaucratic legerdemain continued through eleven applications over a period of several years, and would have gone on forever if I had not retained an attorney to take the case to federal court. NOAA knows that most people do not have the time, money, or energy to take it to court, while NOAA has unlimited funding (which is paid by the taxpayer) to prolong the case, to wear down the plaintiff, to drain his financial resources, and to prevail without ever adjudicating the case on its merits.

It took me six years and four federal court cases to obtain my permit. Then NOAA denied my next permit, and it took another two years and Congressional intervention to achieve a permanent permitting process that subsequent divers could utilize without having to take NOAA to court in order to dive on the *Monitor*. NOAA may very well employ these same tactics in the Stellwagen Sanctuary. The proof of the pudding is what NOAA is presently doing to Todd Baldi with respect to the *Monitor*. NOAA's shenanigans never cease.

There is no end to what a pack of creative autocrats can devise to hoodwink the public.

The NOAA thought police are keeping wreck locations and survey data to themselves. It is only through the efforts of private individuals that the locations of some of the wrecks in Stellwagen Bank have been made available to the public. Here are the locations that I have been able to obtain so far:

Fishing Vessel 1	100 feet deep	42-18.737
		70-17.824
Fishing Vessel 2	425 feet deep	42-31.679
		70-14.780
Frank A. Palmer (bow)	360 feet deep	42-29.030
		70-16.000
Frank A. Palmer (stern)	360 feet deep	42-29.942
		70-16.146
Granite Wreck	370 feet deep	42-29.140

		70-16.260
Josephine Marie	80 feet deep	42-10.925
		70-13.466
Louise B. Crary (bow)	360 feet deep	42-29.030
		70-16.000
Mystery Collier	405 feet deep	42-34.722
		70-15.672
Paul Palmer	80 feet deep	42-11.668
		70-16.311
Portland	450 feet deep	42-28.348
		70-17.238
Pentagoet (false)	165 feet deep	42-13.840
		70-09.067
Unidentified	110 feet deep	42-11.119
		70-12.062
Unidentified	100 feet deep	42-22.340
		70-22.220

There is a good reason for my predilection for quoting George Orwell's famous dystopian novel, 1984. It is the only book that I ever read that truly scared me. I read it as a teenager; I read it again as a young adult; and memories of the book still terrify me today.

I can conceive of nothing more horrible than a totalitarian government that rules its citizens as if they were slaves or, worse, livestock. The loss of freedom, the loss of identity, and the loss of reality are very real threats that I experienced firsthand when I was drafted into the U.S. Army and sent to Vietnam. It is the height of absurdity to take away one person's freedom in order to make that person fight for someone else's freedom.

As Thomas Jefferson wrote, "The cost of freedom is eternal vigilance." In relation to today's world, that means vigilance against aggression both foreign and domestic. The most insidious attacks are those that originate within the political system in which the citizens hold their trust.

When I wrote "The Monitor Goes Public," I harbored the mistaken belief that, once trounced and placed under Congressional scrutiny, the National Marine Sanctuary

Program would toe the line. How wrong I was. Congress has not been vigilant, so Program administrators have again gone astray. Like runners in a relay race, each power hungry Program bureaucrat has passed his obsessive abuse of authority to his successor.

The NMSP is so consumed by control and territorial expansion that I don't believe that it can ever be brought back into the fold - even by firing every administrator, staff member, and employee in any capacity, and restarting the Program from scratch. I am afraid that the infection is so entrenched in the system that it can never be eradicated.

There is only one solution to the problem. The National Marine Sanctuary Program must be abolished.

As an ironic side note, in the Introduction to The Technical Diving Handbook *I wrote about an incident that occurred on May 18, 1991. While diving on the freighter* John Morgan *off Virginia Beach, the anchor line broke free from the wreck. I did a drift decompression.*

On the boat were several NOAA employees who were making recreational dives. After twenty-six minutes of decompression, I surfaced in five-foot seas about a mile astern of the boat. I waved slowly to attract attention. One of the NOAA employees spotted me. He alerted the skipper, who raced the boat to my rescue.

Safely onboard, I jokingly suggested to the NOAA employee that he not inform his superiors that he was responsible for saving my life, or they would certainly fire him for stupidity. I was a thorn in the side of NOAA that its administrators wouldn't mind having plucked.

Apparently that NOAA employee did as I suggested, and kept his mouth shut. He rose through the ranks from a lowly underling to the highest position in the Administration. His name is Dan Basta. I wonder if he has any regrets about that day on the John Morgan.

Cast in Ink:
Hamilton and Scourge

Authors generally receive a fair amount of fan mail. I am no exception. With fifty-two books to my credit, I probably receive more fan mail than most authors receive. In addition, I meet a certain percentage of my readers on dive boats, at speaking engagements, and at underwater conferences.

Nearly all my feedback is positive. My readers like what I have to say, and they like the way I say it. Sometimes a reader was struck by a particular passage, and felt compelled to write how he or she was affected. Sometimes a reader had a particular interest in a topic, and wrote to comment about the reason for his or her interest. Sometimes a reader wrote simply to state: Keep up the good work. Such praise informs me that I am reaching my readers where it counts.

Every one in a while, however, I receive negative feedback. For example, one *Bible* belter was offended by a comment which categorized the *Bible* as a book of quaint parables that were not necessarily applicable in modern society. Times have changed in two thousand years, but not everyone has kept up with those changes. Nonetheless, I respected his opinion to differ. Religion can be a wonderful comfort to people who need beliefs, so I see nothing wrong with it. (Religious intolerance, however, I will not tolerate.)

More recently, after reading *The Lusitania Controversies*, Charles Steinman took exception to my slant on ethics in the legal profession. Steinman had a personal interest at stake: he was a lawyer, and had been one for more than thirty years. He ended his letter thus:

"It is with no little sense of trepidation that I violate Mark Twain's advice to 'never pick a fight with a man who buys his ink by the barrel.' Since you own your own publishing company, you may write as you please. But with that right comes the right of others to protest what you write, and I respectfully do so."

Steinman's objection was my castigation of attorneys who acted in blatantly unethical fashions. As my faithful readers know, I have fought for divers' right on more than one occasion. Those who have read the books in which I described the cases that I initiated, know that I take a dim view of the erosion of freedom in America, and of unscrupulous attorneys who will not let legalities get in the way of winning a case.

I call 'em as I see 'em.

My comments were based on personal experience. Yet, I cannot fault Steinman for maintaining an opposing view. He wrote, "It appears that you have been in court on a relatively small (albeit significant) number of occasions and have had been [sic] in contact with perhaps a few dozen lawyers. By contrast, I have handled thousands of cases over the course of my career and have litigated against almost as many attorneys from all over the country. Have I found some of them to be unethical and motivated by the basest of instincts? Unquestionably. Have I witnessed dishonest, and even criminal behavior by attorneys. Regrettably so. However, such behavior is by far and away the exception rather than the rule. . . . It is unfortunate that you have come in contact with lawyers whose ethics you found wanting."

Steinman's point is well taken. Even though I buy my ink by the barrel, I felt that it would be fair to give him the opportunity to use some of it to plead his case.

As for coming in contact with lawyers whose ethics I found wanting, his comment provides the perfect segue to remind my faithful readers of the legal tribulations that I recounted in *Stolen Heritage: the Grand Theft of the Hamilton and Scourge*. The book details my efforts to wrest control of two American warships from the greedy clutches of the Canadian government. As in the case of the *Monitor* (which I recounted in *Ironclad*

Legacy), all I wanted to do was to *look* at the wrecks. I filed my suit against the Canadian government because I am a staunch advocate of freedom and individual human rights, and the Canadian government was violating those rights and the cause of freedom.

Charlie, if you think the lawyers I met in my previous cases were unethical and unscrupulous, wait until you read about *this* case! Even my *own* attorneys did not have my best interests at heart. Order your copy now – before my inflammatory comments cause spontaneous combustion to reduce the books to ashes, or before the Canadian government files an injunction to prevent the sale of my remaining stock.

Above: *American Salvor*. Below: *Brother Jonathan*. (From the author's collection.)

Report on Salvage Operations on the Brother Jonathan Observed Between August 22-25, 1997

I have done all kinds of consulting work: for television; for museums; for publishers of books, magazines, and newspapers; for writers; for individuals with an interest in shipwrecks; for treasure salvors; and for lawyers - in the latter capacity mostly as an expert witness in civil suits.

My consulting work on the Brother Jonathan *case was a first for me. On the recommendation of attorney Dave Concannon, who had worked as a law clerk for Federal Court Judge Louis Bechtle, Bechtle hired me as Special Master to the Court.*

A Special Master is a person who is authorized to act in the absence of the judge. Bechtle needed someone with deep-diving qualifications because the wreck lay at a depth of 250 feet. Because the salvors had filed an Admiralty arrest on the wreck, the judge was responsible for ensuring that they acted in accordance with their salvage proposal.

In the event that it became necessary for the court-appointed representative to observe salvage operations firsthand - underwater - the judge wanted someone who could dive down to the wreck in his stead. In effect, my job was to be the eyes and ears of the court.

Bechtle resided and worked in the Philadelphia district. The wreck of the Brother Jonathan *lay off Crescent City, California. The West Coast federal courts were so overbooked that they farmed out some cases to courts that sat in other districts. Because Bechtle's case load was light, he accepted cases to be heard in San Francisco. He commuted regularly between the two cities.*

Bechtle gave me special instructions in his Philadelphia office. The salvors were planning a two-week expedition. He wanted me to arrive unannounced at some time during the operation, in order to catch the salvors off guard. That way they would not be able to put on a show to disguise any improper conduct.

The Brother Jonathan *was a sidewheel steamer that was transporting an Army payroll and privately owned gold coins from San Francisco to Portland, Oregon. On July 30, 1865 she struck a rock offshore, and sank with great loss of life.*

Treasure hunters searched for and discovered the site in the early 1990's. In 1996, the salvors in possession hired technical divers to recover the gold coins, which they did with incredible success. In 1997, the salvors hired a commercial outfit with saturation divers to recover more gold coins. I was involved in this second expedition.

I flew to San Francisco, rented a car, and drove 500 miles north to Crescent City. Here is the report that I wrote for the judge.

Prepared on August 30, 1997 by
Gary Gentile, Expert Witness for the Court

I spent three days and one night aboard the vessel *American Salvor* and one day ashore, observing various phases of the operation, interviewing participants, and visiting land-based sites. I obtained a broad perspective and overview of Deep Sea Research's activities with respect to the salvage of treasure, the treatment of non-treasure artifacts, the conduct of operations, and the philosophies of the principal personnel.

The *American Salvor* is more than 200 feet in length, with bunks and facilities aboard to feed and support twenty-five people (according to Coast Guard regulations). She served as the platform for all salvage operations. The primary function of the *American Salvor* is to salvage stranded vessels and to support diving operations when necessary. She is owned and operated by Crowley Marine Services. The vessel was held in place over the wreck by a four-point moor.

As soon as I came aboard, James Wadsley took me on a complete tour of the vessel. He introduced me to the people at their work stations, and explained every phase of the operation: ship handling, saturation set-up, bell and chamber mating system, umbilical hoses, recovery methods, artifact disposition, and so on. The vessel and the personnel were more than adequately suited for the job at hand.

Diving operations were conducted by Global Diving & Salvage. Two divers were saturated for the duration of the job; other divers acted as surface tenders and made surface jumps to assist the saturation divers on the bottom. The saturation divers lived in a deck decompression chamber which was secured on the stern of the *American Salvor*.

They were stored at a depth of 200 feet. They will not decompress until the operation is completed. Decompression will then take three days.

Each morning the saturation divers transferred from the chamber to a diving bell which transported them to the wreck. Their work day was about twelve hours long, not counting transfer time. Upon arrival on the bottom, one saturation diver exited the bell and made excursions on the wreck; the other diver remained inside the bell and tended the hoses. One hundred feet of umbilical hose give the diver sufficient range to explore different work areas. After about six hours the divers changed roles. The divers wore hot-water suits for warmth in the frigid sea. They breathed a mixture of helium and oxygen in which the percentage of oxygen was between 7% and 8%.

Each saturation diver carried a video camera mounted on his helmet. The video camera was hard-wired to two monitors on the *American Salvor*: one in the control van in view of Global's diving superintendent and DSR's supervisor of salvage, Harvey Harrington; the other monitor was located on deck for public viewing. Real-time 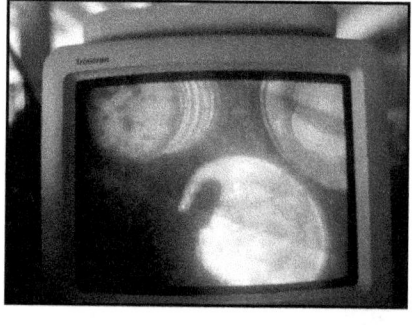 transmission permitted me to observe the diver's activities continuously, or whenever I chose to watch. Whatever the diver saw, I could see.

The divers established grid lines in the area in which they were working. This enabled them to orient themselves with respect to specific features of the wreck, and to keep a record of where recovered items were found. They worked primarily fore and aft of the port paddle wheel shaft, where treasure was found in 1996. They also worked abaft the starboard paddle wheel shaft to recover non-treasure artifacts.

Undersea Graphics supplied the one-person submarine *Snooper* for exploration farther afield. Don Siverts, owner and primary operator of the *Snooper*, made daily

reconnaissance flights in order to gather information for a drawing he was making of the wreck, and to identify other areas that might produce either treasure or non-treasure artifacts. The *Snooper* was deployed and recovered by a deck crane. The *Snooper* has a depth capability of 750 feet.

Transportation between shore and the *American Salvor* was provided by the twenty-five-foot shuttle boat *Negotiator*, owned and operated by John Nesset with assistance from Captain Pat Wilson. The *Negotiator* also transferred food and supplies.

The weather was ideal for the three days I spent aboard the *American Salvor*. It began to turn bad in the evening of August 24. Rough seas made the transfer from the salvage vessel to the shuttle boat a challenge. It was fortunate that I returned to shore that night, for small craft advisories were posted the next day and shuttle service was suspended. Had I remained on board I would have been trapped there for several days.

I spent only one night on ship. This was because the Coast Guard invoked a limit of twenty-five people. With the ship's crew, the divers, the *Snooper's* crew, and

DSR's supervisory personnel, the complement was full before my arrival. In fact, even investors were not permitted to stay on board. After my first day aboard I returned to shore. At the end of my second day aboard, James Wadsley went ashore in order to allow me to remain overnight. I slept in a sleeping bag which I brought from home for the occasion.

The time I spent onboard the vessel allowed me to observe nearly every facet of the operation. The only activities I did not see were the removal of entangled fishing nets, the rigging of the grid lines, and the recovery of treasure. Treasure had been recovered on the two days prior to my arrival, but coincident with my arrival the work shifted to the recovery of non-treasure artifacts.

Although I did not witness the recovery of treasure, I was present when James Wadsley and David Flohr made an inventory of previously recovered treasure. Treasure items were triply locked in a compartment constructed of steel partitions. The steel door was barred with a lock for which only DSR's principals knew the combination. All four principals were present when the door was unlocked (James Wadsley, David Flohr, Sherman Harris, and Harvey Harrington). The lock also had a Brink's seal. Harvey Harrington unlocked the door.

Inside the compartment was a spare decompression chamber in which the treasure was stowed. The door to the chamber was secured by two chain locks with different combinations. Two DSR principals were required to open the chamber because each knew only one combination. David Flohr and James Wadsley opened these two locks.

Each coin (or clump of coins) was itemized and sealed in a plastic bag in order to retain moisture. An inventory sheet was maintained, and this was cross-referenced

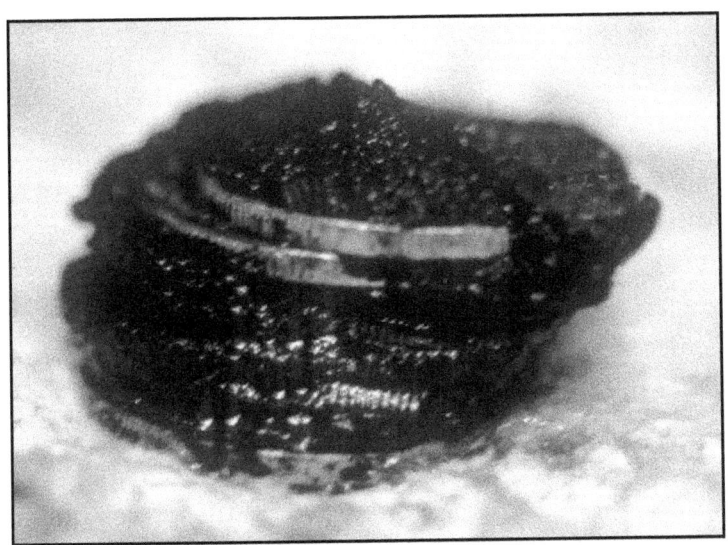

by Rob Reedy, the on-site archaeologist who was also present during the inventory process. The DSR inventory sheet was to be faxed to the court. An exact count of the number of coins recovered could not be made because some clumps were so heavily concreted.

One diver made a surface jump on umbilical hoses in order to move the downline. He did not have a video camera with him. He was on the bottom for forty minutes. He decompressed in the water (on the stage) for two hours, then spent another two hours in a deck decompression chamber (not the one the saturation divers were using, nor the one in which the treasure was stowed). He breathed a mixture of helium and oxygen in which the percentage of oxygen was between 11% and 12%.

I observed the recovery of many non-treasure artifacts. These were brought to the surface in a wire metal basket the size of a small animal cage. The saturation divers loaded artifacts into milk crates, and secured them with packing material so they would not get jostled or broken. The milk crates were then placed in the basket, which was then raised and brought aboard by the same crane that launched the submarine.

Rob Reedy was on hand to supervise the unloading of the artifacts, and to help transport them to the stern of the vessel which had been assigned as his work area. He uncrated the artifacts one at a time, conducted some initial cleaning, then bagged and inventoried each item. Recovered items consisted of dinner plates, cups, saucers, water pitchers, bottles of several types (wine, condiment, pharmaceutical, and so on), an ink well, a possible gravy boat, steam gauges, wooden handles (for chisels or screwdrivers), a glass lantern chimney, a clay pipe, and so on. One item that looked like a cannon ball and was about the size of a twelve pounder was probably a compensating ball from the binnacle; a knob that was recovered with it looked like the bolt that locked the ball to the binnacle arm.

Rob Reedy earmarked one recovered crate, plus some miscellaneous wood material, for return to the wreck. The crate was about 2' x 2' x 3', and contained lengths of wood that might have been chair back supports, although no final determination was made. He kept two lengths of wood, but decided that the entire crate would be difficult to conserve and not worth the effort. He also returned a box of iron nut blanks (that is, unthreaded nuts).

I watched on the video monitor as the diver plucked items out of the silt. The camera panned across fields of debris from which ceramic ware protruded. He picked up pieces that looked interesting, but did not pick up everything, and sometimes put back items that were broken or were duplicates of items already recovered. Thus he took only a sample of what was available. Except for the steam gauges, the recovered items appeared to be part of the *Brother Jonathan's* cargo.

Brother Jonathan

Don Siverts showed me his drawings of the wreck and the locations from which various items had been recovered. His drawings are based upon a compilation of video footage shot in 1993, 1996, and 1997. Harvey Harrington provided background information which explained where and why DSR's efforts were concentrated.

Willard Bascom, who prepared the report on the 1996 operation, was either in Crescent City or onboard the salvage vessel (in accordance with the personnel limitation restraints compelled by the Coast Guard). He has nearly completed writing a book on the *Brother Jonathan*, and is making observations for what he hopes to be the final chapter in the salvage of the wreck.

On shore, David Flohr and Sherman Harris guided me through the Del Norte Museum. This is a well established museum in a two-story building and has been a popular tourist attraction for many years. There are displays of Native American crafts and artifacts, textiles, antique implements, paintings, the Fresnel lens from a lighthouse, newspapers highlighting local events, and a small area devoted to the *Brother Jonathan*. Museum administrators are excited and enthusiastic over the prospect of increasing the size of the *Brother Jonathan* display with items recovered during the DSR venture.

David Flohr and Sherman Harris obtained the key to the conservation facility from the museum, then took me there (it is only a few blocks away) and showed me how DSR set it up. The storage and restoration facility is a two-car garage in a residential neighborhood and is adjacent to and on the same property as a two-story house.

The garage is wood construction on a concrete slab, the double door is locked, the side door is locked and equipped with a security alarm, and the back windows are barred inside and painted over so the interior is not visible from outside. The building appears to be an ordinary garage; it is unostentatious and not likely to attract undue attention or unwanted visitors.

The three interior walls have benches built against them in continuous sequence for a wraparound appearance and one-piece work station. On the bench sit plastic tubs filled with non-treasure artifacts that are individually packed in plastic bags and submerged in distilled water. There is plenty of room for the desalinization of more artifacts, and, in fact, those that I saw in temporary containment on the vessel were slated to be transferred to the

conservation facility as soon as weather permitted safe passage.

In one corner of the garage a battery charger and an electrolytic bath were set up for treating encrusted metal objects. At the time of my visit a porthole was undergoing such treatment. On the concrete floor sat a four-foot cubical heavy-duty plastic fish box in which the previously recovered safe resided in distilled water.

After interviewing the participants of DSR and the primary personnel involved in the salvage of the *Brother Jonathan* and the conservation and disposition of the recovered artifacts, I am convinced of their sincerity. They are experienced and highly trained professionals who are committed to salvaging both treasure and non-treasure artifacts in an archaeological manner that is consistent with their primary obligation toward their investors. That they spent $35,000 in operational expenses during the time of my visit, to recover non-treasure items for the Del Norte Museum, with no hope of returning a profit on that investment, speaks for itself.

Besides that, my many conversations with the participants divulged a broad knowledge of contemporary events surrounding the catastrophe, and a grand fascination of the historic significance of the *Brother Jonathan* with respect to Crescent City and to the West Coast in general, which I cannot believe was a well orchestrated fabrication put on for my benefit. These people are dedicated toward preserving history, while maintaining their integrity toward successfully salvaging that part of the wreck that will prove the most financially rewarding.

This concludes my observations at this time.

As you can see from my report, the salvors did an exemplary job. In addition to my firsthand observations, I testified twice in federal court in San Francisco. This was the easiest testimony that I ever had to give. In all my other court appearances I have had to deal with hostile prosecutors who tried their best to nail me to the cross. In this case, my testimony was merely informational: the judge wanted me to explain for the record how a salvage operation was conducted, how a saturation system worked, what kind of equipment was employed, and so on. If anyone should read the trial transcripts in the future, or if his decision was appealed, a complete explanation existed on record.

Ownership of the Brother Jonathan *was hotly contested by the State of California. As is typical of government, the State had never searched for the wreck, nor did it offer any financial support for its salvage. Instead, it manipulated the law as a way to wrest from the salvors the rewards of their multimillion dollar investment.*

The investors stole a march on the State by making a deal with the insurance company that underwrote the privately-owned gold. This meant that the provision of abandonment under the Abandoned Shipwreck Act did not apply. The insurance company never abandoned its claim.

Judge Bechtle sided with the salvors.

The State appealed the case all the way to the U.S. Supreme Court. The salvors liked my report so well that they submitted it to the Supreme Court along with their legal briefs. Judge Bechtle and I attended the hearing in Washington, DC. It was quite an experience to watch the Justices hammer the attorneys for both sides with hard-bitten questions. If you ever stood in front of a class while a teacher asked you questions about your homework, and didn't know the answer, you have a very small inkling of what it was like for those attorneys to be on the hot seat. They were in no position to not have an answer!

The salvors won the Supreme Court case.

It is interesting to note that technical divers recovered some 800 gold coins, while the saturation divers recovered only around 200 coins. This was not because the technical divers were more proficient; they discovered the stash and recovered most of the coins that were in it. The salvors hoped that the stash was larger than it was.

It is also interesting to note that the U.S. Army refused to make a deal with the salvors for a percentage of the payroll. If the salvors recovered any of the bullion, the greedy Army laid claim to all of it. (The insurance company bargained for 10%.) As a result, the salvors did not even look for the Army payroll, but left it on the bottom where it still resides.

The salvors wanted to sell the coins clandestinely, without informing potential buyers how many coins had been recovered. The judge disallowed this sales tactic as fraudulent. To numismatists, the value of the coins lay in their rarity. Some of the dates and mint marks were so scarce that only a handful were known to be in circulation. Dumping a large quantity on the market made them less rare, which consequently reduced their value. The judge made the salvors publish a complete inventory, so that potential buyers were aware of the new relative scarcity of each date and mint mark.

The collectors who lost fortunes were those who already owned coins that had once been considered rare, but were now made common. The recovery of gold coins from the Brother Jonathan upset the numismatic marketplace.

As Special Master to the Court, I had full authority to terminate salvage operations if I thought the salvors were neglectful in the performance of their duties. This authority was vested in me as the eyes and ears of the judge. In my opinion, this amount of power was too much to be entrusted in a person who, although this power was obtained through proper standing with the court, lacked a legitimate background in jurisprudence.

I realize that the judge wanted me to be able to act in his behalf, in consideration of his absence, but I think that such absolute authority might go to the head of a an individual who had self-serving motivations, and who was inclined toward exercising his temporary position of tyranny.

On one hand it demonstrated the faith that the judge held in me, but on the other hand such authority could all too easily be abused.

Ironically, when I filed my first federal lawsuit against NOAA for access to the Monitor, in 1987, the case fell into the court of Louis Bechtle. He threw out the case on a technicality. I then had to file suit in an Administrative Law Court. (The full story is told in Ironclad Legacy.) I don't know if Judge Bechtle remembered me or the Monitor case when I came to work for him ten years later. He never mentioned it, and I didn't bring it to his attention.

El Cazador:
For Lack of a Nail . . .

In 1783, the United States was a fledgling nation of pioneers who were fighting for independence and expanding westward across the broad North American continent, much of which was still unexplored by White Men. The war with England was winding down, and the erstwhile colonists found freedom ringing throughout the land; yet the country was unsettled both politically and geographically. While proclamations of law and order were being established in the new nation's capitol – Philadelphia – many people were restless and wanted to move to territory as yet unoccupied by non-native farmers and ranchers. These settlers headed toward the setting sun, beyond the jurisdiction of the original thirteen colonies – but were permitted to go only as far as the Mississippi River, for the vast tracts beyond, all the way to the west coast, were under Spanish dominion.

Spain as well as England was having difficulties with its American colonies – not so much with the people as with the economy. Much of the land that Spain controlled was inhabited by French Acadians who had been ousted by the English from Nova Scotia. Louisiana comprised about a million square miles of land between the Mississippi River and the Rocky Mountains, and had been ceded to Spain by France at the conclusion of the Seven Years War, in 1763. The "Cajuns," as the local French people came to be called, were forced to trade in their French money for Spanish paper currency, of dubious value long before Americans began counterfeiting it.

Although New Orleans was a thriving port city –

where thousands of tons of merchandise were landed every month by ships of many nations – the lack of a bullion standard to back up the currency created an unstable economy. Pieces of paper that were quite valuable one day were nearly worthless the next – a fluctuation that made the colony unprofitable for Spain, while causing chaos among merchants.

Enter *El Cazador*, and a bold plan to stabilize the failing Louisiana economy and perhaps prevent the irretrievable loss of the rich Spanish investment in North America. Charles III, King of Spain, determined to redeem the dispensable paper currency then in use by replacing it with a hard shiny metal whose value could not be contested: silver. Late in the year he ordered Captain Gabriel de Campos y Pineda to load the Spanish Brig of War *El Cazador* (*The Hunter*) with 450,000 pesos of newly minted coins from the Mexico Mint, with which to bolster the flagging paper economy.

The sterling ship left Vera Cruz on January 11, 1784 – and was never seen again. What misfortunes befell *El Cazador* and her valiant crew will forever go untold, for there were no survivors.

"For lack of a nail a kingdom was lost" may seem the stuff of fairy tales. Yet, as circumstances would have it, because *El Cazador* did not arrive in New Orleans with her precious cargo of silver, the Spanish colony in North America began to fall apart. Twelve months passed before another ship brought much-needed funds to Louisiana (some of which was needed to pay troops whose wages were then more than a year in arrears) but the delay proved disastrous, and economic distress continued to plague the colony. Later attempts to resolve the developing crisis failed. The Spanish colony languished for a decade and a half, losing money for everyone concerned.

In 1800, Charles IV, successor to Charles III, wiped his hands clean of the American debacle by trading Louisiana back to France for European considerations that were easier to control.

In 1803, France sold the ex-Spanish colony in its

entirety to the United States for $15 million – about three cents per acre. This was the historic Louisiana Purchase: a land deal that overnight doubled the size of the country. Pioneers by the thousands crossed the mighty Mississippi, bypassed the Indians or shoved them out of the way – with lead, if necessary – and filed claims on acreage in the greatest land-grab in history. The grand western expansion was underway.

While it therefore may be said that one kingdom was lost for the lack of a ship, another most certainly was born. Such are the vagaries of history.

In today's world, *El Cazador* threatens to topple another economic structure, not because of her loss but because of her discovery. As usual, when treasure comes to the surface, greed rears its ugly head.

Jump nearly 210 years, to August 2, 1993. Aboard the fishing trawler *Mistake*, Captain Jerry Murphy thought he was about to lose his expensive net on an uncharted "hang," usually a geologic outcrop whose exposed rocks snag trawler nets, sometimes forever. After much maneuvering, he was able to retrieve the net, although it was damaged by the underwater encounter. The crew hauled the net on board in order to make repairs – and were astonished by the sound of metal clanging to the deck: metal that was not part of a mineral vein or a stratigraphic formation, for it consisted solely of uncirculated coins bearing the portrait of Carolus III (the Latinized spelling of Charles III), most dated 1783. This was no rock pile that the *Mistake* had snagged, but a shipwreck that lay in 50 fathoms of water some 50 miles south of the Louisiana coast.

The *Mistake* returned to port, and Murphy immediately called the vessel's owner, Jim Reahard, and told him about the find. Reahard contacted attorney Dave Horan, who specialized in maritime salvage cases. By August 5, a partnership agreement was made, and on August 10 an action was filed in Louisiana federal court in the name of Grumpy, Incorporated. Wasting no time, the Grumpy partnership hired Marex International to conduct research and feasibility studies for salvage and recovery: Marex's full time occupation.

Very quickly, Robert Stenuit, among other areas of expertise a consultant in maritime archaeology, identified the wreck as *El Cazador*, and provided Grumpy with an outline of his historical findings and the ship's cargo manifest, which listed the rich trove of treasure that was aboard at the time she departed Vera Cruz.

A video camera lowered from a salvage vessel found very little signs of wreckage after two centuries spent lying on the bottom of the sea. Most of the wooden structure had long since vanished: food for hungry micro-organisms that inhabit the benthic regions. What the camera *did* see was far more dramatic: a mass of coins that was twelve to fifteen feet wide, thirty feet long, and that eventually proved to be several feet thick.

It was a king's ransom, almost literally.

The uncirculated coins may have saved the Spanish colonies from bankruptcy and a king from failure. Instead, they evoked an important footnote to the history of early American land development, offered numismatists the opportunity to obtain rare specimens for their collections, and provided a landfall profit for the Grumpy partnership in an otherwise ordinary fishing season. Everyone could be a winner. From yesteryear's tragedy would come today's triumph.

With a fortune in silver lying only a few hundred feet below the surface, Marex charged full steam into getting salvage operations underway before winter storms precluded any recovery until spring. Demonstrating the ingenuity and resourcefulness that has always typified the American spirit, Marex embraced the latest deep-diving technology available, mixed-gas scuba, and hired one of its chief proponents to conduct the underwater work: Billy Deans, owner of Key West Divers.

Commercial diving to depths beyond 130 feet is conducted with a surface supply rig: in the early days, a brass hard-hat and a heavy canvas suit, although now commercial diving dress consists of a plastic helmet or a full-face mask, and a conventional drysuit for thermal protection. The diver does not carry gas in tanks on his person; instead, umbilical hoses permanently connect the diver on the bottom to cylinders topside, ensuring an unending supply of breathing gas as well as wired communications and a guideline to the surface. A few years ago, diving self-contained and untethered to 300 feet would have been unthinkable. Now, among a select group of underwater explorers known as technical divers, it was commonplace.

The advantages of diving on scuba as opposed to diving tethered are several: increased mobility for the diver on the bottom, relief from the drag of a thick umbilical hose in heaving seas or swift current, and reduced logistical support, the latter translating into savings in equipment and personnel costs. In strong current, a tethered diver might be reduced to crawling across the bottom from handhold to handhold, or he might be swept completely off the work site and left dangling in mid-water like a piece of bait on the end of a deep-sea fishing line. The greater the depth the more pronounced the effect, as the water exerts its force against every foot of umbilical hose between the diver and the boat. The disadvantage is severe: limited bottom time.

Whereas a commercial diver can remain underwater for hours at a time, then decompress in a submerged bell or in the comfort of a topside decompression chamber (or stay saturated until the job is done), a technical diver relying on self-contained bottled gas can stay on the bottom only as long as the gas supply that he can feasibly carry with him, will last. No doubt, a tethered diver working several hours at a stretch can do more work on a given day than a self-contained diver can do in thirty minutes. But the cost differential is such that it is far less expensive to have a technical diver spend several days on site in order to perform the same amount of useful work that the tethered diver can accomplish in one day. Thus, Marex's decision to hire technical divers.

Diving operations began in November, supported by Marex's 150-foot salvage vessel, R/V *Beacon*. On deck were loaded 40 T-bottles (290 cubic feet each) of helium, 40 T-bottles of oxygen, and twelve sets of double tanks. By connecting a portable mix panel to a compressor, and using a set of doubles as a reservoir, trimix could be made to order. Hamilton Research provided decompression schedules. The final breathing mix consisted of 14% oxygen, 50% helium, the balance nitrogen: abbreviated trimix-14/50. This mix at 300 feet offered an adequate margin of safety from oxygen toxicity, and reduced nitrogen narcosis to a barely perceptible level.

Decompression gases consisted of nitrox-32 and nitrox-50, one tank of each clipped to each diver's side. During the final stages of decompression, divers breathed oxygen that was supplied from the surface; long low-pressure hoses were hung overboard and lowered to a depth of 20 feet. All decompression was done in the water. A double-lock recompression chamber was carried on deck for emergency purposes. It was never used.

It is important for a diving operation such as this to have a steady platform from which to work. For this reason the *Beacon* established a four-point moor – that is, four large anchors were taken out in four quadrants in order to stabilize the vessel while the divers were in the water. A boat on a single anchor line will swing with the wind or the changes of the tide, but with a four-point moor the boat is prevented from moving out of position. Furthermore, by alternately releasing and tightening the tension on the various anchors, the boat can be positioned anywhere over the wreck with a minimum of difficulty.

A five-ton crane on the *Beacon's* after deck lowered a weight to the bottom, from which an ROV (remotely operated vehicle) operated on an umbilical in order to scout the wreck – what little of it was exposed above the soft, unctuous mud of which the bottom sediment consisted. Little was seen other than a few worm-eaten timbers protruding no more than a foot above the muck. Once the ROV was deployed, its umbilical provided the divers with a guideline to the work site.

Down into muddy waters the divers descended. The surface water was lucid and blue, like the ocean lapping gently above a shallow tropical reef. Below 250 feet the water turned dark and forbidding, in hues ranging from chocolate brown to coal-tar black. Visibility dropped from crystal clarity to 3 to 5 feet. Once a diver settled into the muck, or scooped up a handful of coins to deposit in a bag, the wreck became a swirling cloud of fine silt whose enveloping blackness was claustrophobic. As Deans put it, "The bottom was like oil a half a million years before it became oil." A diver was lucky if he could see his gauges – and this at 300 feet.

The initial recovery operation lasted for a month, although not all that time was spent over the wreck. Bad weather frequently forced the *Beacon* to return to port, with the result that of the thirty-day duration of the expedition, only ten days were spent actually on the site, and of the time spent underwater, only half a dozen dives were made on the coin field. This was an exploratory expedition, the primary purpose of which was to ascertain the scope of the venture, so it was equally important to survey the site so that informed decisions could be made concerning future operations.

It was during one of these surveys that the ROV spotted a forty-pound bronze bell, which was then recovered. It might be the ship's bell, or it might be a small church bell. The bronze surface showed no markings that would aid in identification.

Diving in teams, six divers took turns in the water. Bottom times ranged between twenty and thirty minutes, decompression lasted from three to three and a half hours. Drysuits protected the divers from extreme exposure.

Most of the coins were brought up in clumps, or conglomerates: masses of coins that were melded together with solidified mud, in the manner in which stones are cemented in a matrix of paving concrete. The

El Cazador

outer surface of each conglomerate was encrusted with a combination of oxidized silver and marine fouling organisms. Thus the coins that were exposed to the sea were not in the best condition. But when a clump was broken open, the coins that were deeply embedded in the matrix, and which were therefore protected from electrolysis due to the current potential of the sea, were in an excellent state of preservation. Individual coins were tumbled, and their original shine was restored. They were truly uncirculated by all definitions of the word.

By early December, operations were running smoothly and progress was being made toward recovering the vast horde of silver coins. With much work still to be done, expedition members were hoping to capitalize on weather that was finally beginning to cooperate. Then, without warning, the U.S. Coast Guard arrived on the scene and terminated all diving operations. With hundreds of thousand of coins remaining to be recovered, the 1993 *El Cazador* expedition was over.

Because the treasure salvage job received so much media attention, the operation eventually gained the notice of the Association of Dive Contractors, an organization of commercial divers whose putative primary concern is safety in the underwater work environment. The ADC alerted the Coast Guard that an unsafe condition might exist, and asked the Coast Guard to investigate.

The Coast Guard has many duties and responsibilities, such as coastal defense, search and rescue, drug interdiction, vessel licensing and inspection, fishing quota adherence, and upholding American law in the seas over which it has jurisdiction. The Coast Guard has the authority to stop and board any vessel suspected of being in violation of federal law. It also investigates the conduct of commercial diving operations, and has strict regulations with regard to safety, in a manner similar to the way in which it regulates the construction and maintenance of commercial vessels that are licensed to carry passengers. The Coast Guard is authorized to enforce compliance to its diving regulations, at the point of a gun if necessary, but usually by imposing fines.

In the case of the *El Cazador* expedition, the Coast Guard found that the diving being conducted was commercial in nature – that is, the divers were being paid for their services – and that commercial diving safety standards were not being maintained. Therefore it had no choice but to shut down the operation, else it would be in violation of one of its own mandated duties.

If the diving had been recreational in nature – that is, without compensation to the divers – the Coast Guard would have had no authority to act as it did. In the spirit of freedom on which the United States was founded, recreational diving is unregulated.

As defined by the Coast Guard, OSHA (Occupational Safety and Health Act), and the ADC, commercial diving is permitted on scuba to a depth no greater than 130 feet, and in which no decompression is required. On any dive deeper than 130 feet, or on a dive in which decompression is required, the diver must have voice communication with the surface so that the dive can be controlled by topside personnel, and the diver must be tethered to the surface so he can be recovered by surface tenders without entering the water.

These commercial diving standards have evolved over many years, and have a proven record of safety. They are not arbitrarily restrictive. Nor is there any contention between the enforcing bodies (the Coast Guard and OSHA) and commercial diving companies. The ADC supports safety regulations because it helped to write them. It is a way of ensuring a high standard of safety in a working environment that by its very nature is potentially hazardous. Thus, when the ADC called the Coast Guard to investigate the complaint, the ADC was demonstrating concern for the safety of divers in what could not be construed as anything other than a commercial operation.

The initial reaction of the technical diving community was that the ADC was acting in its own self-interests and was protecting its turf; that it was less concerned about safety than it was about jobs being taken away from its member companies by "scabs." (A scab is a non-union worker who is viewed by union workers as a person who has no right to earn a living and no right to provide financial security for his family, notwithstanding the fact that the scab would gladly join the union if given the opportunity to do so.) That this may not have been the case was shown by the losses incurred by two of the ADC's member companies involved in the *El Cazador* expedition: those that furnished the chamber and the ROV. When the operation was shut down, those companies lost revenues that they otherwise might have earned.

As proof that commercial diving safety standards have made the underwater world a relatively safe place in which to work, Ross Saxon, executive director of the ADC, quoted this statistic: in 1993, commercial divers accumulated some 4.5 million hours of bottom time, during which only two fatalities occurred. To put this into perspective, when I was employed as a commercial and industrial electrician, I once worked on the construction of a thirty-eight-story office building, part of the time walking high steel. Less than 4.5 million man-hours were spent erecting the skyscraper, yet there were five fatalities, a number which the building trades accepted as ordinary. Nor did I feel unsafe on the job. Looked at another way, 4.5 million hours is almost eight times a person's allotted four score and ten.

Saxon also said that, of secondary importance, the ADC has legitimate concerns about the technical sport-diving community competing against commercial companies for jobs when those commercial companies must comply with regulations that technical divers may ignore, unfairly disadvantaging the commercial company that has its divers' safety uppermost in mind. The point being made here is that individuals may take risks on their own, but not when they are employed, because the conditions of employment are regulated by the government. Thus the ADC would have been derelict in its duties if it had not alerted the Coast Guard about unsafe commercial diving conditions.

Furthermore, Saxon believes that Marex did not save the Grumpy partnership any money by hiring technical divers who required less equipment and surface support than a commercial outfit, because a commercial company would have had divers in the water around the clock, operating out of a submerged bell, with a commensurate increase in bottom time that would have permitted the divers to complete the job in a few days. This is an opinion with which others might disagree.

As much as economics were a factor in utilizing technical divers to salvage *El Cazador*, in this particular instance the point might be moot. Government regulations apply to commercial diving. On the basis that the divers were paid for their services, there seems to be no choice about how such an operation can be conducted. Once the boundary is crossed from non-commercial diving to commercial diving, as commercial diving is legally defined, then the conduct of the operation becomes strictly regulated.

But, do technical divers qualify as commercial divers, when they are not union members and do not belong to the ADC? Should the ADC exercise control over non-members? Should OSHA and the Coast Guard group technical divers with commercial divers when their equipment and methods are so different? Should emerging technologies be formally recognized?

There appears to be a disparity between what technical divers can accomplish with the training and technology available to them (and which they have gone a long way toward developing), and the apparent limitations imposed by the long-time methodologies of commercial diving. Each group advocates that with which it is familiar. Progress cannot be stopped by governmental fiat, but the implementation of technical advances in the work environment will undoubtedly evolve slowly. There is a great deal to be said for the tried and true – because no responsibility for misjudgment devolves upon those who make expensive and grievous mistakes, as long as they were following the rules. That is the bureaucratic mindset, and the type of mentality that reduces progress to a crawl; and, on occasion, halts or reverses it.

According to Saxon, commercial diving uses methodologies with a proven record of safety, and until emerging technologies establish a similar record of safety, no changes will occur in the commercial diving industry. This is not necessarily a closed-minded approach, but perhaps a cautious approach. Commercial divers have a job to do underwater; they are not experimenters. So, while everyone acknowledges that new technologies must be embraced, it is the technical diver who must prove the validity of the technology.

It is also appropriate to acknowledge a more fundamental difference between commercial diving and technical diving, between diving for profit and diving for diversion. Whereas diving for dollars is a job, diving for Spanish coins is a grand adventure. To hear the exuberance in Deans' voice as he talks about *El Cazador* is to be infected with the adventure of diving into unknown depths, of exploring a sunken Spanish galleon, of touching a piece of history, of *being there* – not just watching actors on a movie screen.

Diving on an ancient shipwreck is much more exciting than inspecting a wellhead or welding a pipeline. It is an incomparable experience, and the prime motivation that pushes technical divers to the limits of technology – and beyond.

It is the modern manifestation of the pioneering spirit that drove mankind's ancestors in frail wooden craft across the unknown reaches of the Atlantic, and across the vast western plains toward the unsettled west. It is the same spirit that pushes mankind deeper into the ocean depths and higher into the vastness of outer space. It is a spirit that is unquenchable, and one that is unstoppable.

We can all still have our grand adventures. But if the ADC has its way, we cannot get paid for them, too.

The Lusitania in a Technical Way

I have been asked to write more articles about the Lusitania *than any other wreck (except perhaps for the* Andrea Doria). *The first technical diving expedition to the "Lucy" created quite a stir in the diving community. Each editor wanted a different slant on the subject. As I reread the following five articles, I saw very little overlap. So I am reprinting them pretty much as they appeared in their original magazine publication.*

I was wrong!

In the foreword to *Andrea Doria: Dive to an Era*, I wrote, "People asked to name some famous shipwrecks invariably rattle off the big three: the *Titanic*, the *Lusitania*, and the *Andrea Doria*. . . . The *Lusitania*, at a depth of 320 feet, has been dived by commercial divers wearing cumbersome and expensive oil rig apparatus, breathing a mixture of helium and oxygen, and tethered to a surface support vessel by means of umbilical hoses. Only a few divers in the world are qualified to operate at this depth."

When the book was published in 1989, that quote was an accurate assessment of the state of deep wreck-diving. I had no reason to believe that the *Lusitania* might be attainable by non-commercial methods. The farthest thought from my mind was that a short five years hence would find that most tragic of wartime shipwrecks within reach of free-swimming divers equipped only with scuba, and that I would be a participant in the exploration of her sunken remains.

This is not to say that individual divers had not previously attained and even exceeded the depth at which the *Lusitania* lay. Scuba divers breathing compressed air had dived deeper in the ocean, but they did not leave the vertical descent line, as their only purpose was to break existing depth records; they did not accomplish useful work or make any observations. On the other hand, mixed-gas scuba diving in deep phreatic systems was a long established fact. A select group of expert cave divers had made lengthy penetrations into Florida's seemingly bottomless sinkholes and extensive fresh water caves, greatly expanding our knowledge of ground water flow in the Earth's upper crust. Contrasted against this backdrop, it might in retrospect be acknowledged as inevitable that self-contained mixed-gas diving would expand its horizons into the highly variable, uncontrolled, and unforgiving environment of the open ocean.

Indeed, so rapid has been the progress of "high-tech" or "technical" scuba diving that it may justifiably be called an "advent" rather than an "advance," a "revolution" rather than an "evolution." The spurs that have pushed shipwreck exploration to deeper depths are the thrill of discovery, the spirit of adventure, and that most unquantifiable of human traits, personal challenge. In the overall scheme of this new era of deep wreck exploration, the 1994 *Lusitania* project was but a harbinger of greater things to come. I do not think I am going far out on a limb by predicting that the *Lusitania* is but a steppingstone to man's eventual conquest of the deep blue sea.

Complex and complicated though our expedition was, the "cumbersome and expensive oil rig apparatus" was reduced to nearly conventional scuba, with the addition of alternative tank configurations and innovative open water techniques coupled with proficiency in their use, particularly with respect to in-water decompression and computer-generated decompression schedules.

In order to give the reader a picture of how an expedition like this is conducted, I will present a simplified overview, then describe a representative diving day and insert explanations as I go along, including British vernacular equivalents.

No expedition can be expected to function smoothly unless adequate preparations have been made far in advance. Expedition leader Polly Tapson was primarily responsible for site analysis, boat charter arrangements, hotel accommodations, transportation logistics and ferry reservations from Wales to Ireland, and the delivery of gas cylinders, compressors, and boosters to our hotel, the Kinsale Folk House, which caters to dive tourism and maintains a tank filling station.

Kinsale is a sleepy tourist town on the south coast of Ireland, and a fairly remote location for the headquarters of an equipment intensive expedition. No close support was available, so everything we needed or anticipated needing had to be trucked in ahead of time or brought with us. This included all dive gear (or kit); nothing could be rented or purchased locally. For those flying from the States to the debarkation point in London, this meant air-freighting several weeks in advance all tanks, sling bottles, drysuits, and other paraphernalia, then having it shipped back after the expedition was over. Regulators, cameras, and other essentials were taken on the plane as baggage or carry-on luggage. The weight limit was severely stretched.

Each team member had an expressly assigned duty. When one's assignment was completed or if it was subservient to other tasks with higher priority toward the preparations for the next day's dive, one was expected to lend a hand wherever it was needed. There was no slack time for anyone.

Reveille was sounded at 6:30 a.m. by means of the telephone in each person's room. Of the twelve-member team, two were assigned each day, on a rotating basis, to act as dive masters (or marshals). The responsibilities of the dive marshals were manifold: from making wake-up calls to keeping everyone on the pre-established timetable to overseeing the dive to erecting the decompression station in the water. The dive marshals did not dive on the wreck on the day they were assigned to marshal.

Since the restaurant in our hotel did not open until 8 o'clock, we generally had a breakfast of buns and cold cereal washed down with juice, tea, or coffee, unless we could convince the owner to have the cook come in early to prepare eggs, sausage, and French toast. Christina Campbell was the hotel liaison, and because of her we each had a boxed lunch to look forward to, although, to be sure, it was not by any means the highlight of the day.

After breakfast we analyzed the gas in our scuba tanks. We began the expedition with thirty-two storage bottles of pre-blended trimix-13/52, but by the beginning of the second week, when our initial supply ran out and pure helium was delivered, we had to custom blend our own trimix, which required more time than simple cascading and topping off. Each person was responsible for analyzing his or her own gases, both bottom mix and nitrox. Some people chose to fill their tanks to 6/7 of their rated fill pressure, then top off with air, leaving a final blend of trimix-14/45. This cut about fifteen minutes off the decompression at the expense of a deeper equivalent narcotic depth.

Blending on site unavoidably led to slight variations in the final mix. It was not uncommon for nitrox blends to be off just enough to exceed the allowable tolerance for oxygen toxicity units according to the planned decompression schedule, or to affect the off-gassing curve adversely. When this situation occurred, Dave Wilkins quickly cut a new schedule on his laptop and printed it for the person in need. This procedure was quicker and easier than blending a new bottle of nitrox, especially as boat loading began promptly at 8 o'clock. By 7:30 the dive marshals were already swinging their paddles.

All gear that had not been left on the boat the previous day was loaded in the Peugeot van (or lorry) that was loaned to us by Peugeot for the expedition: ten sets of doubles, twenty sling bottles, ten oxygen bottles, all personal kit and drysuit underwear, and anything else we could think of. Paul Owen supervised the loading and drove the van to the dock. Most of us walked the pleasant half-mile along the narrow, empty streets through the picturesque town. There is no commuter rush traffic in Kinsale; there is no rush of any kind in Kinsale.

We used two boats. The 42-foot *Sundancer II* was our primary support vessel, owned and operated by Nic Gotto; it carried the divers and their equipment to the wreck site. The *Tornado* was a rigid inflatable boat (RIB) owned and operated by Howard Weston; it hauled the decompression station (dec station) and doubled as a chase boat. Each morning, all gear was laid out on the marina's sloping cobblestone ramp, the lower end of which was overgrown with slick seaweed that knocked more than one person on his bum.

Tanks and personal kit were loaded onto the *Sundancer II* in precise order, in such a way that the pair whose turn was to enter the water first was closest to the aft dressing station, and so on in sequence. We rigged our tanks before leaving the dock in case there were any problems with regulators, hoses, pressure gauges, buoyancy compensators, and so on, in order to effect repairs or obtain replacement parts. Sling bottles were set up and lashed to the rail next to our doubles. Backup gear was stowed below along with drysuit underwear, cameras, emergency oxygen bottles, and so on.

The dec station was partially pre-assembled and stowed in plastic buckets, then placed aboard the RIB by Richard Tulley in order for proper deployment. Each pair assembled their own portion of the dec station. This consisted of a large orange buoy to which was secured forty feet of rope weighted at the lower end with five pounds of lead. To the rope were affixed D-rings at 20 feet for clipping off two oxygen bottles complete with regulators and pressure gauges, and a six-foot length of PVC pipe for attachment to the adjacent segment. Final assembly was completed in the water by one of the dive marshals.

The Lusitania in a Technical Way

There was nothing to do for the hour and a half ride to the wreck site other than to ruminate in quiet anticipation (or perhaps trepidation) of events to come. A 300-foot dive is not to be undertaken lightly, regardless of experience level.

When Nic announced that we were twenty minutes from the wreck, the first pair began dressing (or kitting up) in the crowded cabin. There was the usual banter as they donned their diapers (or nappies). As soon as they had their drysuits on, they moved to the after deck, which was usually swept by spray, and the next pair began dressing. One dive marshal dressed in order to set up the dec station and to be prepared to render in-water assistance should that become necessary.

The waters around the Irish coast are tidal, with a flow generally too strong for diving at any time other than at slack (the turning of the tide). We timed our departure each day so we arrived on site just before slack. If we missed it, we would lose the day's diving, so timing was essential. It was also essential for the divers to be geared up and ready to hit the water as soon as the water movement stopped, for there was only a forty-five minute window before the tide began running again and soon reached the speed at which diving became impossible (especially when wearing doubles and two sling bottles).

Since the tide follows the phases of the moon, slack occurred fifty minutes later each day. By the end of the week we were diving in the afternoon, at which point we jumped back a tide and caught the new morning slack. This constant progression meant that when we got back to the dock late in the afternoon, tank filling and other jobs could not be completed before bedtime, and had to be finished in the morning. There was no respite from work.

The boat did not grapple the wreck. For ascent and descent we used a shot line with a buoy. When the first pair was ready, Nic maneuvered the boat into position near the buoy and the divers rolled overboard. The swim to the buoy was not difficult because the water was not moving. As soon as they were away, the next pair hustled their tanks into position. The dive marshals helped them with their sling bottles, lights, and so on. We all carried line reels and emergency liftbags in case we surfaced away from the buoy or for some other reason went adrift.

The shot line was nearly vertical when the tide was not running. I was able to slide down to the seabed in four minutes flat, and this included checking off my name on the slate at sixty feet. Bottom times were between fifteen and twenty-five minutes, depending upon the individual's preference and an assessment of the surface conditions. We sometimes dived in five- to six-foot seas with a short chop, a combination which made for an uncomfortable hang. Decompression times averaged ninety to one hundred minutes, putting the total run time in the two-hour range. That plus 47° water (52° on the surface) accounted for the diapers. Argon gas for suit inflation was a nice creature comfort, but not a necessity.

Ambient light on the wreck was zero. A thick layer of plankton absorbed all sunlight (if the sun was even shining). With a light (or torch), visibility ranged from eight feet to twenty-five. I speak only for myself when I say that swimming around at a depth of more than 300 feet, in body-length visibility, was frightening, perhaps even terrifying. Strobes were set flashing at the bottom of the shot line, and some people used line reels so they could find their way back in the dark. It was still scary.

The deepest depth we encountered was 310 feet. Although the commercial divers who salvaged the propellers in 1982 recorded a depth of 320 feet, it must be remembered that tidal variations can be extreme, and that a spring tide at certain times of the year can make quite a sizable difference. The average difference between consecutive high and low tides is ten feet, but throw in the alignment of the sun and the difference can be greater. And the commercial divers may have taken their deepest depth recording in a washout.

The deeper stages of decompression were conducted on the shot line, beginning at 150 feet. When the last diver to enter the water ascended to the depth of the slate, he would hopefully find a check mark next to the return side of everyone's name but his own. By that time the tide would be running, and those already on the dec station would be hanging on hard and waiting for release. The last diver would then unclip the carabiner that secured the breakaway line to the dec station, and everything and everybody went adrift.

At this point, the dec station consisted of a row of five segments connected by their PVC pipes. Once detached, the segments had a tendency to bunch up sinusoidally like the alternating sides of a rattlesnake, thrusting the divers against each other. Add the up-and-down motion of the waves, and you end up with a lot of tank banging and sore heads, both figuratively and literally. In order to alleviate this problem, the in-water dive marshal joined the ends of the station and added a length of PVC pipe as a spreader. The result was a geometrical figure that resembled the home plate of a baseball field, with a pair of divers at each angle. Crisscrossing ropes across the corners of the square prevented the sides from coming together.

By using long low-pressure hoses, we could spread out to either side of our oxygen bottles and have elbow room to spare. The in-water dive marshal flitted about like a mother hen (or father rooster), constantly querying divers to make sure that they were okay and had sufficient oxygen to complete the decompression.

When I think back on it, the drift decompression was the most relaxing and unstressful part of the day.

No sooner did the boat reach the dock than the real drudgery began. All tanks had to be offloaded and stowed in the van, along with personal kit that needed rinsing and undergarments that needed drying. Back at the folk house we unloaded the tanks and toted them to the various stations. Simon Tapson and Nick Hope were fettered to a ball and chain at the booster station (or Haskel land, as it was called) and rarely left the spot until they were called for dinner; they boosted the helium for bottom mix and oxygen for nitrox. John Chatterton and John Yurga were caged in the compressor room where each day they topped off more than forty cylinders with air, did preliminary oxygen analysis, and transfilled argon; they were often still pumping at eleven o'clock at night. Dave Wilkins stripped the used oxygen bottles of hose clamps and D-rings, and rigged ten unused bottles. Richard Tulley stretched out the ropes and PVC pipes that had been the dec station before it had been hauled out of the water and dumped in a heap on the RIB, and tried to untangle the mass of knots. Jamie Powell seemed to be everywhere, doing everything, and was especially good at doing repairs and making drawings of the wreckage and debris field. Barb Lander collected everyone's dive profile and decompression schedule for the expedition log, then pitched in wherever she saw a job that needed to be done.

Sad to say, I wound up being little more than chief gopher, grunt, and cylinder sherpa. My primary responsibility was working with the ship's plans: ascertaining where we were located on the wreck, keeping a written record of everything that we saw, and annotating interesting places to go – none of which helped the expedition's more immediate needs. I got most of my post-dive exercise by humping tanks back and forth between Haskel land and compressor country, a distance of a couple hundred feet through the hotel courtyard and along the sidewalk. Next time I'm opting for a more intellectual skill.

Dinner was between eight and ten o'clock, a dawdling, languorous affair that provided a welcome relief from the long day's laborious and never-ending workload. First came the debriefing session, during which we each had the opportunity to talk uninterrupted about the dive, to comment on performance, and to make suggestions for greater safety and efficiency. Then came excellent Irish cuisine, followed by a soft pillow to cuddle for a few short hours before that damned telephone rang and began the whole process over again.

Enough about logistics. What about the wreck? Well, folks, I must say that in twenty-five years of diving, the *Lusitania* was the most exciting wreck I have ever seen. Not because of the personal challenge, not because of its historic significance, but because of what was there to be seen and explored. There were portholes by the dozen and windows by the score, and more wheelhouse equipment that I have encountered on half a dozen virgin wrecks. The stern docking telegraph lay loose on the seabed amid a field of debris. The main navigating bridge has collapsed and rusted away, leaving behind such items of bronze as two telemotors, two telegraphs, and an annunciator. Only a true wreck-diver can appreciate what it means to behold such rarities in the untouched state. The *Lusitania* is not just a wreck; it is a solemn, seductive experience.

Inevitably I am asked by the meek why I and those who are like me choose to risk the unknown depths with seat-of-the-pants equipment instead of waiting for the technology to improve – such as the time when rebreathers become practical and are equipped with redundant systems.

In answer, I argue that Christopher Columbus did not sit idle at the dock waiting for transatlantic liners to be built, that the Wright brothers did not lie lazily on the dunes hoping for jet engines to be invented. We do today with what we have. And in the process, we pave the way for tomorrow's effortless ventures.

Lusitania
Historical Sidebar

When the *Lusitania* was constructed in 1907 she was the largest and fastest passenger liner ever launched. At 785 feet in length, she was 80 feet longer than her nearest competitor, the *Kaiser Wilhelm II*. Her beam of 88 feet ensured good lateral stability in addition to providing broad decks for spacious public rooms and passenger accommodations. Her draft of 33 feet required that docking facilities be dredged to clearance depths. Her gross tonnage was 32,500 (compared to 20,000 gross tons for the *Kaiser Wilhelm II*). She was powered by four steam turbines which generated a total of 68,000 horsepower, and which drove four manganese bronze propellers. Twenty-five coal-fired boilers provided steam for the turbines.

The *Lusitania* was appointed sumptuously and finished in rich woods and ornate decorations. The dining saloon was a two-deck affair topped by a domed ceiling of glass; 500 people could be seated in Edwardian era splendor. The smoking room, writing room, library, and lounge were commodious, each paneled with its own motif consisting of carved moldings and pilasters, embroidered valances, silk curtains, leather upholstered chairs, mahogany furniture, inlaid tables, and deep pile carpeting. The high ceilings and arched domes added an ambiance of open-air spaciousness.

The *Lusitania* wasted no time winning the coveted Blue Riband for the fastest transatlantic crossing. The speed record was broken by her sister ship, the *Mauretania*, after she entered service the following year, but the "Lucy," as the *Lusitania* was more affectionately known, quickly regained the trophy with a speed of 25 knots. During the next eight years, the "Lucy" made one hundred round-trip voyages between New York and her homeport, Liverpool. Despite the outbreak of war in Europe, in 1914, the "Lucy" maintained service between the continents.

On May 1, 1915, the day the *Lusitania* was scheduled to depart the U.S. for England, the Imperial German Embassy published this notice in New York newspapers: "Travellers intending to embark on the Atlantic voyage are reminded that a state of war exists between Germany and her allies and Great Britain and her allies; that the zone of war includes the water adjacent to the British Isles; that in accordance with formal notice given by the Imperial German Government, vessels flying the flag of Great Britain, or of any of her allies, are liable to destruction in those waters; and that travellers sailing in the war zone on ships of Great Britain or her allies do so at their own risk."

The notice was singularly prophetic. On May 7, 1915, as the *Lusitania* approached the Old Head of Kinsale on the south coast of Ireland, the German submarine *U-20* was steering a parallel but opposite course after a successful patrol in the Irish Channel, where it had torpedoed and sunk two Allied vessels the previous day. Although Captain William Turner had been warned by radio that U-boats were operating in the area, and was told to steer a zigzag course clear of headlands, he was forced to approach within sight of land in order to take ranges, so he knew when to turn northward into the Irish Channel.

Because the Germans had access to American newspapers, perhaps it was not just luck that the "Lucy" crossed the periscope sights of Kapitanleutnant Walther Schwieger.

Schwieger fired a single torpedo which struck the *Lusitania* on the starboard side abaft the forward funnel. A secondary explosion followed a moment later, causing Schwieger to write in his war diary "boiler or coal or powder?" The answer to that question is still hotly debated and still unknown: a controversy raging among historians to this very day.

Captain Turner turned his vessel toward shore, but the *Lusitania* sank in less than twenty minutes a little more than eleven miles from the rocky coast. Captain Turner never gave the order to abandon ship, because the "Lucy" was moving at considerable speed until the time she sank. Consequently, by the time his subordinate officers took it upon themselves to launch lifeboats, it was too late for most of the craft to get away. Of the 1,959 passengers and crew aboard, 1,198 lost their lives either by drowning or hypothermia. Among the dead were 128 Americans.

Many people today believe that the sinking of the *Lusitania* was the cause for the U.S. entry into the war. Not only is this belief untrue, the tragedy was not even the final outrage, as the U.S. did not declare war on Germany until nearly two years later, on April 6, 1917.

Of the controversies which surround the *Lusitania* disaster, people continue to argue over whether there was ammunition onboard. No argument is necessary since the British Admiralty freely acknowledged that a consignment of cannon shells was on the cargo manifest. The more important debate is whether gunpowder caused the second explosion. The Admiralty maintained that the shells were empty – nothing more than brass casings.

In any event, the magazine was located in a compartment that was situated forward of the wheelhouse. The second explosion occurred abaft the wheelhouse, about amidships. Thus it seems unlikely that gunpowder caused the second explosion. The compartments in the vicinity of the second explosion were coal bunkers.

More than likely, as Schwieger and others surmised at the time, the second explosion was actually a coal dust explosion. The jar of the torpedo blast would have tossed coal dust into the air in bunkers that were nearly empty at the end of the Atlantic crossing. This floating dust would then have been ignited by flames from the first detonation. The scenario is similar to grain dust explosions in silos.

Lusitania Bound

Conjure the ideal virgin shipwreck: portholes scattered about like leaves fallen from a tree in autumn, navigational equipment lying loose on the seabed, the hull contiguous but the superstructure sloughed off and rusted away so that only the brass fixtures remain. Add a forty-five degree list to starboard and three-quarters of a century of collapse, and you have a pretty good idea of what I saw on my first descent to what is the latest, perhaps the greatest adventure in deep-water, mixed-gas wreck diving.

My initial surge of excitement came when I spotted the first porthole. My excitement grew to ecstasy when I saw a whole field of portholes. And ecstasy became nirvana as I gazed upon the docking telegraph at the edge of the debris field. I had run out of superlatives by the time I beheld the wheelhouse annunciator and brass steering station. In twenty-five years of underwater exploration, this was without a doubt the most thrilling shipwreck I had ever seen.

There is more to the *Lusitania* than meets the eye. At least, more than the eye can see in a fortnight of daily twenty-minute dives. That's because the 780-foot-long wreck lies at a depth of 300 feet, in a zone of darkness where the sun rarely reaches, where visibility is limited by a soup of plankton swept back and forth by the never-ending tide, and where topside weather conditions are generally hostile, especially when diving off a 35-foot boat. If this imagery reminds you of your worst nightmare rather than a dream come true, then you must accept on faith that some people are driven by challenge rather than by convenience.

Just as climbing mountains would not be as meaningful if there were an elevator to the top, so diving

The *Lucy* in her heyday. (From the author's collection.)

shipwrecks would lose some of its glamour if there were no obstacles to overcome. Granted, diving on the *Lusitania* is no vacation trip or holiday spa, but what it lacks in creature comforts and Club Med amenities it makes up for with adventure and excitement. The far frontiers where people have seldom gone cater not to those to whom adversity is a hindrance. The *Lusitania* is not just another dive, it is a incomparable experience, made memorable by the difficulties in reaching the historic site.

I'm not talking about that uncomfortable flight over the Atlantic Ocean: six hours of boredom and jet lag on arrival. (It used to take two months on a rolling windjammer filled with rats, scurvy, and the stench of live food animals.) Or the rough boat ride through sickening seas. We've all borne those torments with varying degrees of discomfort. I'm talking about the additional difficulties of conducting a highly complex dive operation more than ten miles at sea off a remote corner of southern Ireland. *That* was a logistical nightmare.

To start with, the team of twelve divers required thirty-two K-bottles of premixed breathing gas, which had to be delivered by truck and unloaded by forklift in the parking lot of our inn. Then, a temporary wooden structure had to be built around the newly ordained storage facility. Also delivered was a low-pressure compressor that was needed to drive the two Haskel boosters which we brought with us from London; the compressor was gasoline driven, was the size of a small car, and came on its own trailer. And this was only sufficient gas for the first week of diving. After that, we had helium and oxygen delivered as needed and did our own blending.

We also needed half a dozen K-bottles of oxygen to make nitrox blends for decompression purposes. Then we needed V-bottles of oxygen for in-water decompression: one bottle per diver per day. Plus, there was argon for those unwilling to brave the 47º water (52º above the thermocline) without the additional heat-retaining qualities afforded by the denser gas. With run times in the two-hour range, warmth was a precious commodity.

Every day this mountain of equipment had to be loaded onto the boat, sometimes early in the morning after a cold breakfast of cereal or biscuits. This was because we could dive only during slack tide – a span of about 45 minutes. If the tide was early, we dived early; as the tide got progressively later (due to the phases of the moon) we could sleep later in the morning, have a hot breakfast, but then we did not return until late in the afternoon – with all those tanks to fill for the next day's diving. This meant a late dinner, then arising early to finish filling the tanks that we did not have time to fill the night before. There was no landside support – we had to do everything ourselves, except cook. The meals were superb and relaxing, and dinner provided the only relief in an otherwise long and wearisome daily routine.

The expedition was very much a group effort. As expedition leader, Polly Tapson constantly dealt with difficulties and reorganized our agenda. Her husband Simon and Nick Hope did all the gas boosting. John Chatterton and John Yurga ran the compressor, often filling tanks late into the night. Dave Wilkens oversaw our in-water oxygen needs, and rerigged the cylinders on a daily basis; he also ran new decompression schedules when the gas mixes did not come out exactly right. Every day Richard Tully assembled the drift decompression station for rapid deployment; he was ably assisted by Jamie Powell. Paul Owen was the driver and stowage master of the Peugeot van which transported all our tanks and personal equipment between the inn and the boat. Barb Lander constantly wagged her pencil at people in order to keep a strict record of everyone's dive profile. Christina Campbell was our liaison with the hotel and restaurants, and made sure that we had lunch every day on the boat. I was in charge of ship's plans and drawings, my primary responsibility being to record everyone's observations of the wreck; but there was usually so much more pressing work to do, in order to prepare for the next day's dive, that I filled in wherever help was needed, and usually ended up being chief grunt and gopher.

When all is said and done, the hardest work and the major difficulties of the expedition occurred topside. The twenty minutes spent on the bottom seemed effortless by comparison. True, the stress of just *being* 300 feet deep, totally self-contained, in utter blackness pierced only by a beam of artificial light, can be psychologically exhausting. On the other hand, the wreck has such a history, such meaning, such an aura for wreck-diving enthusiasts, that the exhilaration of being on THE *Lusitania* far exceeded the draining effect of what it took to get there.

In 1915, the *Lusitania* was eight years old, and was considered one of the crack ocean liners of the time. She plied the passenger route between New York and Liverpool with timetable regularity. On May 7, as she approached the Irish coast, she was spotted by Kapitanleutnant Walther Schwieger in the German submarine *U-20*. A single torpedo sent the massive vessel to the bottom in eighteen minutes. The loss of life was severe: 1,198 passengers and crew, of whom many were women and children. There had not been such a tragedy at sea since the sinking of the *Titanic* in 1912, and the *Empress of Ireland* in 1914.

Despite her notoriety and all that has been written about her, the wreck of the *Lusitania* has been fairly well ignored. Partly this is due to the depth. In the late '60's and early 70's, John Light and a small group of divers explored the wreck on scuba, breathing air. In 1982, Oceaneering's team of saturation divers cut into the specie room, which proved to be empty, and recovered three of the four propellers and some miscellaneous artifacts found in the stern where they were working. In 1993, the National Geographic Society sponsored a two-week expedition to film the wreck using remotely operated vehicles and a submersible; no divers were involved. Thus, from a wreck-diving perspective, the *Lusitania* can be considered a virgin wreck and a wreck diver's paradise where artifacts abound.

On one dive I swam along the high side of the bow, at 270 feet, and saw the entire name of the ship spelled out below me in large brass letters. On another dive I cruised past open hatches beckoning me to enter. On yet another dive I spotted exposed lavatories and ornate mosaic floor tiles. There were also some heart-throb-

The *Lucy* on her way to the bottom. (From the author's collection.)

bing moments, such as the time I missed the shot line in eight feet of visibility and had to circle for several minutes before I reoriented myself. And the time my fin got entangled in monofilament; I broke free in a few seconds, but those seconds seemed like millenia in the time-warped sense of subjective duration. Nevertheless, when the dive was going smoothly and visibility exceeded twenty-five feet, I felt a euphoria which was induced not by nitrogen narcosis but by my passion for new and exciting experiences. And I left the wreck each time with a feeling of incompleteness – there is so much more to discover. The *Lusitania* is a site to which I desperately want to return.

Yet, due to the wreck's uncertain legal position and nebulous claims of ownership, of which we were amply apprised by local police, customs and excise officials, the Receiver of Wreck, and American and Irish solicitors, the Starfish Enterprise team decided upon a policy of non-recovery. We did not want to "rock the boat" and jeopardize our unique opportunity to see and explore one of history's most famous shipwrecks, or, by irresponsible action, give cause to jeopardize the chances for others to share in the *Lusitania* experience. Even so, a commercial salvor has plans afoot to curtail future visits. The disposition of the wreck is uncertain. On the other hand, the world's oceans are full of wrecks of equal or greater appeal – not necessarily for personal gain, but for that rare occasion to see something firsthand that so few others have seen.

The application of advanced deep diving techniques and mixed gas technology – "high-tech" or "technical" diving – is opening new vistas in the field of shipwreck discovery and exploration, making accessible wrecks which a few years ago were considered beyond reach. This kind of diving is not cheap. It requires a great investment of time and money, training and experience, desire and initiative. But for those who are willing to pay the price, the inner rewards are profound.

Lusitania Turmoil

No worthwhile endeavor is undertaken without adversity, no campaign of exploration is executed successfully without overcoming obstacles. The *Lusitania* project was no different.

In addition to the logistical complexities of formulating and supporting an equipment intensive mixed-gas diving operation in the open ocean, with the difficulties of conducting in-water decompression for ten divers adrift, and the variables of an uncontrolled and sometimes chaotic environment, there occurred unpredictable events ashore which materially affected our group camaraderie and peace of mind and which conspired to hinder the achievement of our goals to explore and photograph one of history's most tragic shipwrecks.

Whereas one can accept with equanimity nature's insensitivity to man's trifling designs, the questing, rational mind has difficulty appreciating the evil perpetrated by those who would harm rather than help, who would destroy rather than create. Thus, when our expedition ran afoul of persons who, for reasons known only to themselves, chose to subvert our efforts by means either antagonistic or criminal, we were slow to recognize implacable meanness and an intentional scheme of obstructionism potentially more dangerous than the dive.

Initial interference came in the guise of F. Gregg Bemis, Jr., the millionaire who through sleight of hand swindled ownership of the wreck from its rightful owner, John Light. When Bemis learned that a group of technical divers planned to see for themselves the wreck of the *Lusitania*, he contacted expedition headquarters in London and tried to convince Polly Tapson to call off the dive. He gave as his reason a nebulous claim of ownership. Polly politely requested proof (copies of titles, deeds, bills of sale, and the like) which Bemis would not consent to provide. He simply insisted that she needed his permission to look at the *Lusitania*, and that for a fee and other outrageous considerations (such as copyright assignments for all photographs taken), he might tolerate our presence on the wreck. Polly was not intimidated by his threats, neither were the other team members, nor was the owner of the boat which we chartered, to whom Bemis wrote directly in an attempt to convince him to cancel our charter arrangement. Preparations for the expedition went on as scheduled.

But the Bemis issue was far from over. He made follow-up phone calls to me and to Polly. We were both away attending to other business, but his messages were duly recorded on our answering machines. Although I believe firmly in mature communication, under the circumstances and considering Bemis's hostility and intractable mindset, I opted for confrontational avoidance. I did not think that any compromise of positions could possibly result from further conversation. Bemis then got his attorney to call my attorney and through him tried to coerce me to back out of the expedition. I refused to respond to any kind of threat.

The final plea arrived on the eve of our departure for Ireland. A fax message from Bemis's attorney warned that if we proceeded with our plans against his wishes, he would file an injunction against us in Irish court. What otherwise may have been construed as a sincere petition for a bona fide legal sanction was made absurd by the accompanying accusation that our visit to the wreck might be considered an act of "international piracy." We laughed all the way to Kinsale, then discovered upon our arrival that Bemis had notified the provincial police of possible criminal activity, had alerted the Bureau of Customs and Excise about the possibility of illegal salvage operations, and had hired a local attorney to file for an injunction.

Not to belabor the point, during the course of the expedition we had to deal daily with the constabulary who had no idea what was going on; they were simply responding to a complaint which, we felt, was fanatical. At least one person, either a private detective or an official observer, surreptitiously appeared at the dock every day and watched us unload our equipment from the boat. Subsequently, reports were received at Customs and Excise claiming that we were smuggling contraband ashore.

Bemis never made good on his threat of injunction. The local attorney we hired to defend our position thought that there were insufficient grounds for the likelihood of success, and that Bemis backed down because a defeat would establish a disastrous and undignified precedent. But we never knew from day to day whether we would be officially enjoined from diving on the morrow, or whether we would be taken to an Irish jail in handcuffs. It was a stress we dealt with, but we would have been more at ease without it.

These legal manipulations pale to insignificance when weighed against a more dire menace with which we were constantly confronted. Nor is any collusion implied between the two. I refer to a continuing series of mechanical malfunctions which plagued both our surface support vessels. At first, the motor conking out on the inflatable chase boat was little more than an annoyance. We attached little significance to it other than to blame the operator for improper maintenance. After a couple of days of making motor adjustments at sea, he concluded that there was water in the gasoline, and solved the problem permanently by taking the gas tanks off the boat at night. No sooner was this problem fixed than the inflatable's steering linkage came apart, making us wonder if the sea gods were against us diving on the *Lusitania*.

Next, a float switch in the *Sundancer's* bilge failed to operate. We had just tied up at the wharf when the water level rose above the electrical contacts on the starter, causing a short circuit which not only burned out one starter but which ignited a fire. Smoke poured out from under the engine hatch, and when we lifted the hatch we found the engine engulfed in flames. The fire was quickly put out with an extinguisher. Had this occurred two hours earlier, before decompressing divers had been picked up, the results could have been catastrophic. In fact, the next day another fire burned out the starter on the other engine when no one was aboard but the captain and me. He replaced the bad starter with the one from the working engine while the engine was still running, and I swam a line to the floating decompression station and took it in tow – necessitated by the fact that the inflatable's outboard motor had conked out once again, leaving both boats dead in the water.

Despite this string of seemingly bad luck and coincidental breakdowns, we persevered.

Enlightenment came when the inflatable's motor suddenly ran rough. The motor was immediately shut down and, upon lifting the cowling, it was discovered that the oil had been dumped out of the reservoir, the oil feed line had been severed, and the electrical wires between the motor and the low-oil warning light on the console had been cut. A less astute operator would not have been aware of impending disaster until the motor seized up and was totally destroyed.

Now there was an explanation for our ongoing mechanical problems – sabotage! The police are still investigating.

We were also met with bad weather which complicated surface support procedures, made several people seasick, and was nearly responsible for a triple fatality. I was eagerly looking forward to my first dive on the wreck when we were forced to turn back due to high winds and an offending chop that shook the boat violently and sent spray across the deck. We canceled the dive for the day. On the way back to the harbor we picked up a mayday on the radio, and saw a fisherman gesticulating wildly for attention. We veered to intercept his boat without being able to decipher his Irish brogue. As we approached the vessel in distress we saw one man lying on the deck apparently unconscious, another shivering on a stool, and a third huddled in the cabin.

We were made to understand that a boat had swamped in the rough seas and three men had been dragged into the frigid water entangled in fishing nets. The lone fisherman who had called for help happened to see their boat go down, raced to their assistance, and dragged them out of the water one by one. Now the men were suffering from hypothermia, and one might be having a heart attack.

What better could providence provide for the occasion than a group of divers with a dozen sets of drysuit thermal undergarments and medical oxygen treatment cylinders complete with facemasks. We descended upon them like a swarm of flies. Thinsulate flew across from our boat to theirs like feathers in a teenage pillow fight. Soon they were all dressed in warm, dry clothing, and the one with heart problems was breathing oxygen. An ambulance was awaiting our arrival at the dock. We definitely helped to save one life that day, and possibly two or three. None of the men suffered aftereffects from the ordeal.

Even though I had not yet fulfilled my dream of seeing the *Lusitania*, I felt a warm inner content, a profound sense of humanity, and was satisfied that my purpose for being at that place, at that time, had found a grander meaning. The subsequent dives were icing on the cake.

A NEW ENDING

Cast in Bronze
Lusitania's Secrets Revealed

The sea was pale green like a crude chunk of jade. Plankton floated in the liquid realm much as intrusions marring a crystal lattice, causing the light to play tricks upon the eye. Distances were difficult to estimate because of the lack of perspective: the yellow polypropylene rope dropped away beneath me like a solitary strand from a giant spider's web, fading into the haze.

As I plunged through the stratum of floating microorganisms, the color of the ocean darkened. The water below was eclipsed by the living bulk that lay adrift in the broad Atlantic Ocean. Down I went into the biotic miasma, going deeper, growing darker. I had no sense of weight, or of cold, or of depth; only of the gathering gloom. Not until my eardrums grew taut did I have an indication of descent. I worked my jaw to relieve the unequal pressure.

I peered ahead eagerly. My controlled breathing pattern was timed to the cadence of my mitted hands pulling my body and five compressed gas cylinders down the limp shot line. Inhale, pull, pull; exhale, pull, pull; inhale, pull, pull . . .

The blackness became absolute. No ambient light reached these depths. Despite the sun shining brightly in the cool June sky, this was essentially a night dive. I could *feel* the "poly" rope but I could no longer see it. Masochistically, perhaps, I refrained from switching on my light in order to savor the unique experience of sensory deprivation. Then came a short burst of brilliance from far below, followed rhythmically by evenly spaced flashes. The team before me had secured a signal strobe to the chain at the base of the shot line.

I let go of the rope as I dropped past the strobe and

settled onto the rock-strewn seabed. *Then* I switched on my light and took a good hard look at my gauge panel. It had taken only four minutes to descend to a depth of 304 feet.

Because I was breathing a mixture of helium and air (called trimix), I did not feel the narcotic effect that was normally induced by a high partial pressure of nitrogen. I was as clear-headed as if I were diving in 100 feet of water. Yet my heartbeat quickened with trepidation for, although I could not sense the depth as I generally could when breathing air, I knew intellectually that I was far beyond the pale of traditional scuba.

I illuminated the area about me and had my first glimpse of the wreck of the *Lusitania*. Almost immediately I spotted a porthole lying loose in the debris field, then another, then one that was firmly secured to a steel plate. Because the wreck lay at a sharp starboard angle, the superstructure had weakened and sloughed off into a confused heap, much as a wooden house that had cascaded down the side of a hill in a California mud slide. Most of the rivets and thin metal had long since rusted away, leaving behind a jumbled pile of beams and broken bulkheads. In the near distance the hull rose upward. My partner had not yet arrived on the bottom, due, it turned out, to an ear-clearing problem. But I could clearly see two light beams thirty feet away, carving white swaths through the blackness like laser swords in a space epic. Since my projected bottom time was limited to twenty minutes, every moment was precious, and I did not want to waste even a second. I moved toward the other team.

I had traveled only a few feet from the shot when my attention was attracted to a curious brass cylinder the size of a partially smoked stogie; it was threaded at one end. I knew its import immediately, relegated the information to the back of my mind, then continued on my way to make the best of my remaining bottom time. The hull loomed above me beyond the slanted deck where once walked passengers through Edwardian era splendor . . .

When the *Lusitania* embarked upon her maiden voyage in 1907 she was the largest passenger vessel afloat. Her overall length was 780 feet, her beam was 88 feet, and she drew 33 feet of water when fully loaded; she grossed 38,000 tons. Propelled by four steam turbines which were fired by twenty-five Scotch boilers, the elegant behemoth could move at a speed of 25 knots, making her the fastest transatlantic liner in history and quickly earning her the coveted Blue Riband. For the next several years she traded speed records for Atlantic crossings with her sister ship, the *Mauretania*.

Affectionately known as the *Lucy*, the *Lusitania* maintained the epitome of decorum at a time when Victorian values were becoming part of the past. People of all classes thronged to sail on the *Lucy* because of the grace of her lines, the sheen of her brass, the dignity of her service, and the eloquence of her dining. Ornate domed ceilings arched high above her holystoned decks, while intricately carved woodwork adorned the walls of her public rooms. Her furnishings were of the latest style, with plush chairs and settees spaciously allocated so that one never felt crowded. Excellent cuisine was served on fine china embossed with the Cunard Line crest. Bulkheads were paneled in rich mahogany whose fluted surface was polished to a high gloss. Her lavatories were tiled with inlaid mosaic patterns. The *Lusitania* was a ship that was built for a country that still honored the lives of kings and queens.

... but I saw no majesty here. Instead, I was faced with a collapsing, shrunken ruin whose original beauty survived only in memory or imagination. The port rail that should have towered more than eighty feet above the seabed reached no higher than thirty feet. The interior decks that should have stood neatly atop each other like floors in an office building were squished together and buckled like a squeezed accordion. My impression was that a huge hydraulic foot had stood upon the wreck and tried to crush it flat – and very nearly succeeded.

Keeping an eye on the flashing strobe and the lights

of other divers, I followed the debris field along the starboard edge toward a point at which the wreckage of the wheelhouse had been previously located. Disarticulated hull plates offered no clue of order or logic in construction; the steel sheets lay scattered about like discarded chips of wood from an axman's handiwork. The farther I strayed from the shot the more apprehensive I became. It was paramount that I return to the surface up the "poly" rope in order to reach the decompression station and the oxygen cylinders which were suspended at twenty feet. When I got out of sight of the signal strobe, and when no other divers were in my field of view, I was ready to turn around. Just then I caught a glimpse of my objective: the carrot on the stick that kept me going farther despite the knot in my stomach and the chill in my spine.

No decks or bulkheads existed here, only the brass remains of the navigational equipment lying on the seabed like abandoned parts in a junk yard: windows, telegraphs, annunciators, and helm stands. Never in all my years of wreck-diving had I seen such an awesome sight as the concentration of relics that littered the rocky seabed adjacent to the wreck of the *Lusitania*. Furthermore, the story of the liner's last minutes afloat was spelled out before me – literally cast in bronze.

For a moment I was caught between increasing alarm and wild exhilaration. I was a long way from the surface both in distance and in time. Every minute down here added eight minutes to my decompression penalty, and time passed quickly at 300 feet. My gas supply was dwindling quickly. I checked my gauges to ensure that I could remain a few moments longer.

Hurriedly I brought my camera before my eyes and framed my shots. I detached the strobe in order to get a better angle on the subjects: a trick which not only reduced backscatter from the light that was reflected off floating particulate matter, but which added shadow to the picture and gave the resultant image a three-dimensional quality. I fired as quickly as the strobe would recycle. Finally, the anxiety became too much for me, and although I still had half a roll of film remaining, and much more of the area that I wanted to explore, I turned and swam back in the direction of the shot. I had lost sight of my fellow divers.

My heart was pounding hard despite the fact that all my equipment was functioning perfectly and I had sufficient gas to complete my allotted time on the bottom. I felt so far from help, so far from the surface and sunlight and open air. I was in a constant state of apprehension. At this depth, things can go wrong in a hurry. I needed to be on edge. Yet, although I recognized the necessity of threat-induced alertness, I did not enjoy the feeling. Even backtracking over familiar pieces of wreckage – symbolic breadcrumbs on the trail to the shot – did not dispel my inner doubts. This kind of diving is not to be taken lightly. Nor did I.

When I reached the point at which I should have seen the comforting flash of light from the signal strobe, and did not see it, I was gripped with the same measure of fear that must have gripped those who saw the wake of an oncoming torpedo that tragic afternoon of May 7, 1915 . . .

Off the Old Head of Kinsale, Kapitanleutnant Walther Schwieger lurked beneath the surface in a German submarine known only by its number: *U-20*. He had already had a successful patrol, having torpedoed and sunk three ships in the Irish Sea in the previous two days. With only two torpedoes remaining, and with the Irish Sea cloaked in fog, Schwieger turned away from his operational objective – Liverpool – and proceeded to sea.

About the same time, Captain William Turner received a wireless message from the Admiralty, warning him that a U-boat was active in the area that he was about to traverse, and cautioning him to avoid headlands and to steer a mid-channel course. Instead of passing the Old Head of Kinsale at a distance of two miles – his usual practice, in order to verify the vessel's position before entering St. George's Channel and proceeding into the Irish Sea – Turner maintained a distance of twelve miles from land. When the *Lusitania* encountered fog, he ordered a reduction in speed and, later, a turn to starboard (away from land). These maneuvers evolved into the fateful coincidence that brought the great liner to within a third of a mile of the watchful U-boat.

As the *Lusitania* passed the cross hairs of the *U-20*'s periscope, Schwieger fired a single torpedo. With unerring accuracy the deadly explosive device contacted the hull of the liner between the bridge and the forward stack. An explosion ensued, followed immediately by a second and larger explosion, causing Schwieger to note in his war diary, "boiler or coal or powder?" Thus was born the incident's greatest controversy: What was the origin of the second explosion? Did cold water rushing into the boiler rooms cause the hot boilers to explode? Was coal dust in the empty bunkers hurled into the air by the blast and ignited by flames from the torpedo's detonation? Or was the *Lusitania* carrying munitions? It has always been known that her cargo holds were filled with rifle cartridges and cannon shell casings – that is, empty shells without gunpowder. Conspiracy advocates conjecture that the cannon shells were not empty, but were fully loaded.

At the time, the cause for the vessel's accelerated

demise mattered little to the crew and passengers who were hastening to abandon ship. The rudder was thrown hard aport in order to steer toward land. Captain Turner gave no order to launch lifeboats because the *Lusitania* was traveling too fast: the boats would have capsized as soon as they touched the water. Nonetheless, the ship's officers took it upon themselves to lower away. Turner later testified that he was prudently waiting for the ship to stop before giving the order to launch.

The *Lusitania* listed drastically to starboard. Her throbbing engines and forward momentum propelled her downward beneath the waves. Overladen lifeboats capsized as soon as their keels touched the water, throwing their hapless occupants into the near-freezing ocean. Water poured into the *Lusitania's* gaping wounds. The excess weight dragged the hull down by the bow. Incredibly, the huge liner sank in only eighteen minutes, with the loss of 1,198 lives, many of them women and children whose last inhalations filled their lungs with water. Most of those who entered the water alive, soon drowned or succumbed to hypothermia.

. . . By now my gas supply was nearing the lower margin of safety. I was eighteen minutes into the dive, with only two minutes to spare if I were to maintain my twenty-minute schedule. An extra five minutes of bottom time incurred forty more minutes of decompression, and would seriously compromise my gas supply. I rose several feet above the seabed and worked my way forward. In total darkness, I played my light on the wreckage and looked for the yellow poly.

Then I saw the welcome flash of the strobe. Due to the angle of my return, a large section of hull had come between me and the shot, placing it temporarily out of my line of sight. Now, instead of being behind schedule, I had a minute to spare, so I hovered in the vicinity and looked for photo opportunities. If only I could relocate that cigar-shaped cylinder . . . Finally, it was time to ascend.

At 250 feet the water turned from stygian black to

somber green. At 200 feet I could read my gauges by ambient light. At 150 feet I paused for my first decompression stop; I was still breathing trimix from the tanks on my back. At 130 feet I switched to my first sling bottle, which contained nitrox-32 (that is, 32% oxygen, the balance nitrogen). At 60 feet I switched to my other sling bottle, which contained nitrox-50 (50% oxygen). Decreasing the partial pressure of helium and nitrogen in my breathing mix accelerated the decompression, which is inordinately long when breathing helium mixtures, because helium is absorbed by the tissues faster than nitrogen. Decompression on bottom mix would take twice as long.

After reading the names on the slate that was clipped to the downline, and ascertaining that I was the last diver to return, I unclipped the decompression station. By that time the tide was already picking up and putting a fair strain on my arms as I clung to the rope. Now all ten divers could drift effortlessly with the tide. After forty minutes of staged decompression, ascending slowly at ten-foot increments, I reached the "dec" station and found my oxygen cylinder. I pulled loose the extra-long hose, placed the regulator in my mouth, and for the next hour I floated next to the PVC pipe which separated my station from the two adjacent stations. Here, above the thermocline, the temperature was 52° (it was 47° on the bottom). As I was using argon for drysuit inflation, I was comfortably warm.

The surface support diver finned past and flashed a questioning okay sign. I returned the sign. There was always a support diver in the water in case anyone needed assistance or extra oxygen. Another support person remained on the boat, as dive marshall. We all took turns at the tasks, giving up a day's diving to do so.

I broke the surface after more than two hours of total elapsed time. The chase boat, a rigid inflatable, sped to my side and the coxswain asked if I was okay. I told him that I was. In the distance I could see the 35-foot fiberglass boat which was our primary surface support vessel. After recovering the diver who had surfaced previous to me, the boat turned in my direction and picked me up.

I was still on the ladder when Polly Tapson, expedition leader, asked, "How was your dive?" I gave her my typical enthusiastic response, "*Un*-believable," for truly it was. I had not only touched history, I had solved an historical mystery by bringing back some pieces of the *Lusitania* puzzle. On subsequent dives during the two-week expedition I made further observations. By exchanging observations with my fellow divers, we were able to construct in our minds an image of the wreck the way it exists today: from huge cracks in the hull to the interior decks crumpled together like the sections of a carpenter's folding rule.

At one time the *Lusitania* was a mariner's elegant mistress. Now it was a woeful wreck whose collapsed and rusted hull give mute testimony to the unstoppable dissolution induced by the sea.

I learned a great deal by diving on the *Lusitania*: about the wreck as well as about myself. The indicating arrow on the wheelhouse annunciator pointed to the side marked "ahead," implying that Captain Turner's order to reverse the engines was not acknowledged – probably because the engineers had been flushed out of the engine room by the incoming flood – thus hastening the influx of water and forcing the ship to settle more quickly, while obstructing the safe launching of lifeboats. The curious bronze "stogie" that I spotted in the debris was a primer, or detonator: the explosive device that screws into the base of a cannon shell. The implications are obvious, but I leave it to future historians to weigh the true meaning of the primer's presence on the wreck.

Now that I have dived on the *Lusitania*, it would be easy for me to say that I was fully prepared to undertake a venture of such depth, that I possessed the necessary skill, training, and experience. Yet I uphold the premise that overconfidence is an affectation to be avoided. I admit that I feel better about myself and my ability to perform in deep water under adverse conditions; but I will not let past positive feedback affect my judgment concerning upcoming endeavors. A cautious approach is always best. On the other hand, one never stretches oneself by always remaining within one's limits. The key to success is in understanding the difference between caution and progression. That difference is a fine line indeed, and one which each individual must assess for oneself – and for which one must therefore accept responsibility.

In the mean time, there are other wrecks to explore – both shallow and deep - and more history awaiting discovery. Adventure to the adventurous is never-ending.

The word "ASTERN" is clearly visible, while the needle points to "AHEAD" (not so visible). This annunciator can be seen in the lower right corner of the photo on page 157, beneath the telemotor. Compare with the photo on the front cover.

Forum: The 94 Lusitania Expedition - Seductive or Suicidal?

In The Lusitania Controversies - *in which I provided the history and evolution of wreck-diving - I noted that in my opinion, Michael Menduno was the person who did the most to introduce the concepts that were inherent in the activity that came to be known as technical diving. He started doing this in 1989 by publishing the first magazine that was dedicated solely to exploring the realms of deep diving with helium mixes, and using nitrox blends for decompression. The name of the magazine was* aquaCORPS Journal *(the typography of which varied). Indeed, it was the only magazine that would even* mention *these concepts in a positive light for the duration of its publication (until 1995).*

Decompression and nitrox were dirty words in other dive periodicals. It was forbidden to use the D word, the N word, heliox, and trimix in magazine articles, except to denounce their usage. Approbation came slowly. Years passed before other magazines jumped on an ever-accelerating bandwagon which, they finally admitted, was not going away, but was instead becoming the wave of the future.

Menduno diligently reported my mixed-gas initiatives, starting with the 380-foot dive on the Ostfriesland *in 1990, and continuing through the other scuttled German warships that I called the Billy Mitchell wrecks. I contributed to the magazine by writing and illustrating articles, including two on the Lusitania (see above).*

Slingshotting from the favorable reception of the aquaCORPS Journal, *Menduno later organized annual* symposiums that focused on evolving techniques and developing technologies in the newfound field of technical diving. He coordinated these "tek" conferences with the annual DEMA event. Members of the Dive Equipment Manufacturers Association could then present their products to a targeted audience of divers who came from around the world to see what technical diving was all about.

At Tek95, I gave a Lusitania slide presentation to a full house of divers that numbered in the hundreds. At the end of the presentation, I brought Polly Tapson onto the stage and introduced her as the leader of the expedition.

While the growing number of technical divers gloated over the acceptance of their rapidly advancing activity, not everyone was happy about it. One vociferous dissenter was commercial diver Lad Handelman. He perceived technical divers as encroachers in deep waters in which commercial divers had always reigned supreme. He countered this threat to his ego by disclaiming the success of the 1994 Lusitania expedition.

I first learned of his dissatisfaction after the audience dispersed. Only a few people remained in the auditorium as I gathered my materials from the projection stand. He rolled his wheelchair in front of me so as to block me in, then accosted me when no one else was standing within hearing range. He denounced me for presenting what he considered to be irresponsibility.

I didn't understand how anyone could repudiate a fait accompli. I listened to what he had to say, but poohpoohed his disapproving opinion as that of either a crank or a disgruntled antagonist. I had never met Handelman, and did not know who he was at the time of our only conversation.

As the saying goes, the proof of the pudding is in the eating. Handelman's objections to safety considerations were contradicted by the accomplishment.

He later voiced his opposition to Menduno. After the conference, Menduno decided to air both sides of the issue in the guise of a forum. He did this by interviewing the three of us (Handelman, Tapson, and me) separately via telephone, first by posing the axes that Handelman had to grind to Tapson and me, then by redirecting our responses to Handelman for his reaction. Menduno then combined the three viewpoints in a single narrative, and published the synthesis in the next issue of the magazine, number 10.

As you read the following interview, keep in mind that mistakes were made in the process of transcribing the voice recordings. Misspellings were the fault of the transcriber, not of the interviewee. I will not use the Latin word "sic" in brackets as a way to draw attention to typographical errors or usage mistakes. It is possible that the interviewee did not misspeak, but that the transcriber may not have heard the words correctly.

Parenthetical notes that are enclosed in brackets and printed in italics, are insertions that I have made for the purpose of clarification.

I have followed the original formatting with respect to paragraph indentation and boldfacing Menduno's questions. I have reprinted the synthesized interview in full, without redacting a single word that appeared in print.

Mike Menduno signed himself as M squared.

The 1994 Lusitania Expedition led by British wrecker Polly Tapson (aquaCORPS Journal N9) was the source of considerable controversy at the 95 tek.CONFERENCE, following an evening show presentation by author and expedition member Gary Gentile. Though the dive team, consisting of eight Brits and four Americans, conducted 120 dives on the wreck over a ten day period without incident, several tek participants, including Cal-Dive and Oceaneering founder, Lad Handelman, publically challenged the operation as being unsafe. This Forum presents some of the discussion that has ensued. The participants—Handelman, Gentile, and Tapson—were interviewed separately by phone and the results were combined into a single transcript. M2.

aquaCORPS: At the tek.CONFERENCE, you expressed some very strong opinions about the Lusitania presentation, and voiced them in the Safety Session and our closing wrap-up. Would you mind telling us how you felt about the expedition and what was presented at tek?

Handelman: First off, I knew nothing about this project until Gary Gentile's presentation at the tek.95. It was all I could do to contain myself during his presentation, and as each detail unfolded I became more and more disturbed. Out of respect for the people attending the conference who paid good money, I elected to withhold my questions until I could visit Mr. Gentile, one on one, directly after his presentation. I raised several, very direct safety issues with him and the response I received to the more difficult ones was, "that was Polly Tapson's responsibility. I suppose that was all she knew to do or had available." [*This quote is fictitious. I made no such statement nor anything similar which by allusion could be interpreted as such.*]

Who was the real leader of this project? As far as expedition credit and fame and glory would have it, Gary Gentile held himself out in that position. Furthermore, his lifetime of diving on wrecks in deep waters would appear to certainly make him the ex officio leader in my book.

Did you speak with Polly as well?

H: Later on. I decided then and there that this expedition needed to be really seen for what it was. That if it was left as the "leading example of technical diving," there would be all hell to pay in the form of future fatalities and injuries. I decided to seek out Polly and other involved expedition divers. The more I dug, the more clear it became to me that this expedition should never have taken place and further, should never have been publicized by aquaCORPS or given a platform at tek.95. The whole thing made me kind of sick.

Gentile: I think in one regard, Lad is seriously concerned, but the reason for his concern is his lack of understanding. He just doesn't know that this is the way things are done [in the technical diving field]. It's like saying, "We're going to take a chairlift up to the top of this mountain and ski down as fast as we can," and somebody says, "Well you don't have to ski down. You can take the chairlift down." We're saying, "But that's not the idea. We didn't come out here to take a chairlift; we want to ski." Handelman just doesn't have the background to understand any of this. That's not to put him down, it's just he's coming at it from a different point of view.

I would say it was the best run and safest operation I've ever been involved in, including those that I've run myself. The reason is that it was performed in what I would call a quasi-militaristic way. I don't mean you had sergeants screaming down your throat. What I mean is the organization was very well thought out. There was a protocol book that we went by, just like you do in the Army. Everyone was designated a job and that became that person's responsibility. That's what worked out so well. Everybody did his job. There was a great deal of cooperation between every member of the team, a real team glue, so to speak.

Polly, you were the expedition leader, how do you feel about this whole set of issues, and generally about your approach to planning the expedition?

Tapson: When I met with Lad, I could see his point of view entirely. He is looking back on a career in diving from a position where he is disabled and has a lot of time to think about his work in the diving industry. It's difficult for us—in what is to us a sport that we do during holidays and free time—to provide extremely expensive surface cover as in a major commercial diving operation. We are nonprofessional divers, but we organized our expedition amongst like-minded people who had mutual respect for each other, and had open

Lusitania - Seductive or Suicidal?

discussions on all aspects of the diving that we planned, as well as a great deal of training.

When aquaCORPS was in the UK last year you were holding meetings in your living room with the team, going through...

T: Yes. We had regular meetings, and discussed every single aspect of the dive over and over and over again. This is very different then deep mixed-gas diving as seen in the United States, where a diver with a trimix certification card can go to a shop, get her cylinders filled, and then just do a deep dive from a boat without necessarily knowing the level of experience of the other divers or the way the captain organizes the diving. As a group planning an expedition to the Lusitania, we all took responsibility. We were all involved in the safety discussions and planning.

Gary, how did you and Barb [*Lander*] and the other Americans stay in the loop? Did you meet when you got there, did you go through some of the planning?

G: Polly forwarded to us the minutes of the meetings so that we knew what was going on, could participate, offer advice or anything else, either by phone or by mail. I had a lot of conversations with Polly on the phone talking over the various aspects of the dive.

...BOAT SIZE...

Lad, I know that you have specific key safety issues with regard to this expedition. The first issue you raised was the choice and size of the boat, which was used for the 10 people on the diving team, plus a skipper and mate.

H: As I understood it from Gary's presentation, the Sundancer was a 35-foot vessel, and in the visual part of the presentation, one could see that it had a relatively small ante-deck, regardless of the length of the vessel. In my opinion, this size vessel might well have been adequate for taking four to six divers out to a mission in a hundred feet of water, but clearly was far too small for mounting this expedition. It was inadequate for a water depth that required additional gas supplies, decompression contraptions and a mountain of other equipment.

In sport diving, people rarely talk about boat size specifically, other than as a complaint. Explain to me why boat size is an important safety issue on an operation like this.

H: You can compare this to a refugee boat. It's one thing to have a boat size adequate for simply transporting people to and from a point. It's an entirely different matter to have the clear work space be sufficient to handle the very likely problems and emergencies which regularly arise on diving missions. Chaos and confusion are the climate. Too many bodies and too much gear in a situation where it's difficult to get on and off the vessel in expected rough sea conditions is a surefire recipe for inexcusable disaster. If you can't afford the right size and seaworthiness in the vessel, you shouldn't tackle the mission.

Gary, in looking at the video, it appears that you were really jammed in there, quite honestly. [An aquaCORPS volunteer videotaped my presentation.]

G: I'll admit that it was uncomfortable, but uncomfortable is a long way from saying that it wasn't big enough to support the operation. It was big enough to support the operation: the proof is in the pudding. We did it, so for anyone to claim now that it can't be done is like the engineer measuring the wingspan of a bumble bee and claiming that, according to their mathematics, bumble bees can't fly. Bumble bees are still flying. Now I would rather have had a larger vessel as far as comfort goes, but it would not have made things any safer. What really made things safe was the fact that we had two boats. That was the biggest plus.

The main boat and a chase boat, so if anyone cut loose and there were problems....

G: Exactly. That was a great thing to have and something I really promote a lot. Let's face it, if you're anchored in, the larger boat doesn't do you any good; you're still anchored in. You can have people decompressing on the anchor line, you can't cut free and go traipsing around after them.

T: In fact, although it seems crowded, it worked, and it was efficiency that made it work. It was the fastest boat on the South Coast of Ireland and we had the best electronic eco-sounding and sea-depth mapping technology. We also had the best skipper on the South Coast of Ireland, who had worked with [Robert] Ballard the year before. We went to use him and we knew that we had to limit expense on the boat, so we prepared accordingly. We had a great deal of space on shore, and each morning would assemble the equipment that we were to use in the dive on the slip. One person, Jamie Powell, was responsible for boat's steerage/storage and there were ten positions marked around the boat. Literally, pair one, pair two, pair three, pair four, pair five. Pair one would be closest to the exit point from the boat. Pair two would be second closest and so on, so there was never an obstruction between the point that you were hitching up and entering the water. Not only that, you only loaded on the boat the equipment that you were going to use for the dive. So all dive bags, unnecessary tools, and pieces of equipment were left back on shore. We had one spare box in the cabin which carried all the tools, all the spare chin straps, mouth straps that any one of the divers might need at the last minute, so there was one, plus the First Aid box.

...SHORT TIDAL WINDOW AND MOORING IN ROUGH SEAS...

My understanding is that the Celtic Sea is an intense environment. The sea is known for changing conditions, and has a short, very extreme tidal window. I think there was about a 45-minute window in between tides, with low visibility.

H: Exactly. In fact Mr. Gentile described it as a "frightening and perhaps even terrifying experience." Although he also explains this away by adding that the Lusitania "is not just a dive, it is a seductive experience." He chose the word "seductive;" I would have chosen "suicidal."

In the commercial world, a great emphasis is placed on having a stationary position, multiple mooring points and all that. The Lusey Expedition used a live boat and a downline. Can you talk about moorings, how that evolved in the commercial world and why that's important from a safety point of view?

H: To start with, my comments are as an experienced marine person who understands and has experienced all sorts of events as a sailor and fisherman. Nothing to do with commercial diving, except that's part of the great experience. Have you ever tried locating someone in a baseball hat who's fallen off the boat during a typical afternoon six-foot chop at a distance of more than 50 yards? I'm not much for relying on bells and whistles and maybe a flashing light if they are all working. I prefer the idea of a solid come-home base that's going to reliably be there when needed. And what happens when more than one diver is adrift in the extreme tides of the Celtic Sea. Yes. Management is a concern when any other to-be-expected complication arises like, God forbid, one of the divers does not reappear at the surface? Whose life does the captain choose to try to save?

Lusitania - Seductive or Suicidal?

There are perhaps some conditions where a solid mooring is not essential, but certainly not in 300 feet of water with only a 45-minute tidal window and eight divers hanging off on a makeshift decompression contraption.

In commercial diving, the boat needs to stay in one place because all your equipment is there. But you didn't do that, Gary. Why not?

G: In this case we didn't want to stay in one place. This boat is adrift and decompression is adrift. The worst thing is to be tied into the wreck because you're not only hanging in the water all that time, but hanging on in a tremendous current.

Commercial divers would follow one of two procedures. At those depths they would probably be in SAT and just pop into the bell and be hauled back up to the surface, or they'd do surD-02, where the divers would make it up to a 40-foot stop, then get out of the water and be popped into the chamber.

G: That's why I'm saying we have a different system, and that doesn't mean that it's better or worse than a commercial diving system. It means that it's different, and it addresses issues in a different way. Again, in the entire history of wreck diving, there has never been three- or four-point moorings. It's just not the way it's done. I think Handelman's problem is not so much that he doesn't understand about our backup systems as opposed to his, but that he refuses to accept our backup systems as opposed to his.

T: Given the fact we had free swimming divers, it was inappropriate to have a stationary mooring for various reasons. The boat drifts with the divers, and when the decompression station casts off, it drifted with them, so it's a totally different way of diving. We don't use commercial diving techniques and we've tailored our procedures to the environment. It is the best procedure for this environment tidal...

Drift decompression is a common practice in British sport diving.

T: I suppose our single biggest concern was if a diver needed to make an open water ascent, they'd be unable to find their way back to the down-line. We wanted them to have all the decompression gas that they needed for the dive. So we had a system whereby any diver who needed to would deploy a delayed surface marker buoy from a depth anywhere from 25 meters up before they needed their oxygen. It's a tube about one and a half meters long, about eight inches.

We call them sausages.

T: So they would deploy a sausage and the surface crew would put down a spare buoy with 30-meter down-lines attached to them, weighted at the bottom with oxygen cylinders, and whips attached at six meters, and then the support diver would go in to check that they were okay. There were always a minimum of two support divers. Plus the boat crew.

How did you handle the operation? You had a short tidal window, obviously very deep water, and changing conditions and a lot of divers. Your typical dive was about two hours, two-and-a-half hours, long. It seems like a lot to manage.

G: There was only a 45-minute slack in the tide, and that meant that everybody had to be up off the bottom before the tide got too strong. With 45 minutes, we had to be there right at slack, and as soon as the tide went slack, the first team went into the water. The rest went in at five-minute intervals. That meant that the last team was in the water 25 minutes afterwards, and they still had 20 minutes to do their dive, by which time the tide started to change and they'd be on their ascent. When it first starts to change, it's not really strong. But by the time they'd get up to the breakaway line at 60 feet, the tide would be picking up and fairly strong. It did require a fair degree of coordination. Then, of course, the last team out just broke the line off, a breakaway line with a carabineer on it, and the whole decompression station went adrift. Decompression was very simple. Everybody was drifting; we were all on the same escalator. That's essentially what it's like, being on an escalator.

What were the contingency plans if you missed the line or didn't make it back in your time frame?

G: Every diver carried a wreck reel and a safety sausage so if you didn't get back to the line...in fact it happened during the last dive, when the tide changed and three people happened to be down-current and had to swim up into it and couldn't make the anchor line. So they did a controlled ascent until they got to a hundred feet and then popped their safety sausage. Once they did that, we (I happened to be surface support that day) could see where they were. We just went over there and set a drop in the deco station where we were initially planning to drop it, and dropped it where they were.

There were only three divers in the water on that day.

G: Right. At any time, either one of the two boats could go chase somebody and drop an oxygen line. Each boat had its own buoy, which floated, kept the oxygen bottles at 20 feet, and had a weight on it, so technically everybody could decompress all by himself...

People were diving in teams?

G: That's right. Everybody went in as part of a team. The objective was to have five two-person teams, but it didn't always work. Sometimes we had people who bagged the dive. They said, "I don't feel good today," or, "The weather conditions are not to my liking," or whatever. In which case, that person's partner would triple-up with someone else, did not go in alone.

T: Most of the time it was really calm. On the days that it was rougher, we had much better support and fewer people diving.

What would happen if you got to the deco station and Team X didn't show up?

T: It's partly a judgment call, but I would first say that these are some of the best deep wreck divers there are, and with full redundancy to deal with any underwater emergency. All the divers had the training and the expertise to deal with any standard problems.

...NO CHAMBER ON BOARD...

Technical diving falls in between traditional no-stop recreational diving, where no one has an onsite chamber, and commercial and military diving that require recompression chambers. What are your thoughts on using recompression chambers for deep, technical dives, such as the one on the Lusitania?

H: There is no excuse for dives of this level of difficulty to occur without a chamber on board. That would apply to the Andrea Doria, Lusitania, or any similarly difficult wreck. Polly's explanation was that "they couldn't afford one." If you can't afford to do it right, you should simply not take on the mission until you can afford it. It doesn't matter how much value you place on life versus the thrill of showing you can do without the chamber.

Did you guys talk about having a chamber on board?

T: There was a chamber near the Lusitania, about 15 to 18 sea miles. There was also a helicopter base, and the support diver and boat skipper always had the helicopter number. The chamber always knew the dates and times that we were diving. It was an air/O2 chamber, rated to 50 meters. The potential incidents that we projected, which in fact we didn't have, were the kind of individual physiological hiccup. Maybe a skin bends, maybe a joint pain. We were not expecting embolisms. We were not expecting decompression sickness because the schedules that we were cutting were schedules that we had dived before. We weren't expecting someone to blow up or panic because we were confident enough in the divers. We weren't expecting equipment malfunction that someone couldn't handle.

G: I'm always concerned about DCI because it's so problematical. You can have it even if you do everything right. We had access to a Navy chamber within about 45 minutes. The main option was to have helicopter evac, and also to have one boat to transport someone if that proved necessary.
    What people need to understand is that there has never, ever, in the history of wreck diving, been an expedition that was run with a chamber onboard. That's like saying, we're going mountain climbing but we're only going to do it if there's a hospital at the summit. There are no hospitals at the summit, and there are no chambers in wreck diving.

One of the arguments the tech community raises against having a chamber is the expense and the space required. How much does it cost to get a chamber in the U.S.?

H: If one were to go out and order a brand new chamber designed for a smaller-sized sport boat, and probably limited to a pressure depth of, say, three atmospheres, then my guess is that built and fully outfitted, it could be had for $25,000 or less. On the other hand, the commercial industry was many, many ASAME-approved recompression chambers which they'd probably be more than happy to sell or lease, and my guess is one could be had for probably on the order of $10,000. I have one, a small one-man chamber on my 28-foot commercial abalone boat, which would be loaded on, hooked up with a hoist in the pier within 10 minutes, and I see no excuse for any deep diving effort not to have one.

T: It's a judgment call. Sometimes it's just not practical. We're not forcing anyone to come. We're not paying anyone to come. They're paying for themselves. They're signing a four-page contract saying they understand exactly what they're doing.

I would assume that, all other things being equal, you'd take a boat with a chamber?

G: That's true, but other things cannot be equal, particularly the cost. I once estimated—when I was running an expedition relating to the Monitor, because that was a prerequisite initially being used as an excuse to keep divers off the wreck—that a boat with a portable chamber was going to increase the cost of the expedition about three-fold to five-fold.

On a per-person basis?

G: Yes. Not just because of the chamber rental, but because the weight of the chamber requires a boat that is at least two to three times larger than what we normally use. Not only that, you also have the weight of all the compressed air bottles, the weight of all of the compressors, plus you need to have an operator. Then, of course, you need a crane to load it on a boat, and you need a boat with extra space and the buoyant capacity to carry all of this weight. When I totaled it all up, it was conservatively going to be between three and five times as much. That's a lot.

It's generally agreed that every minute of delay in getting a bent diver into a chamber greatly increases the chance for permanent injury or impairment.

H: I recall having my partner, Danny Wilson, blow up from 240 feet to the surface and we managed to pop him in the chamber within a few minutes, and he was never paralyzed. On an everyday basis, all deep commercial diving from the surface relies on the four–minute air gap where a diver exits at his 40–foot stop and returns to 40 foot in the chamber and wherein what would have been a severe bends case is a nonoccurrence. If one is decompressed in a matter of minutes, not hours, the explosive bends and embolisms have an excellent chance of either not occurring or being reversed. I cannot fathom why the leaders in the technical diving industry don't all have chambers on board.

T: I think Lad Handelman is being ridiculous, because anyone who wants to do this is going into it with their eyes open in most cases, and I'd certainly say we were. I'm not going to have someone like Lad Handelman policing what I do in my free time. I really, really don't mind if you print this: He can fuck off. Because what I do in my free time is my business; it's not his business. It seems to me that the people who are criticizing it...they're not the people who are involved in the sport.

Given the facilities we had available, the safety couldn't have been improved upon in my opinion. Now, if somebody had wanted to give us a chamber on board, I'm not even convinced of the merits of a chamber in that situation for a serious, serious mixed gas bend, unless it's a mixed gas chamber facility. Now you're talking about many thousands of dollars which, for a kind of recreational sport, is not really practical and quite unlikely to start appearing on the scene.

H: Eight weeks after this expedition, a diver blew up from the Lusitania on another expedition and was flown to a shore-side chamber. By that time, what probably was a mini-case of explosive bends could not be reversed and that diver is now a quadriplegic. A chamber on the spot, in my opinion, would have been an immediate fix. Sorry to bring this up, but in Polly's own interview [aquaCORPS N9, Interview with a Wrecker], she said, "what I don't want to do is to be an example of someone who acted irresponsibly and got away with it. And then have someone else do the same thing and subsequently ends up in a wheelchair for life."

Do you think that's what happened.

H: I think so.

T: I don't want somebody to follow in my foot-steps and get hurt, and I'd like to say that that person did not follow in my footsteps. If they had, they wouldn't have gotten hurt because they would have done a great deal more preparation. The team that came after us wasn't well enough trained. They just got their trimix tickets two months before. They hadn't done enough build-up dives, and dives with each other very often. The two that were diving hadn't really dived with each other more than a couple of times.

My understanding was that the Irish chamber was inadequate for treatment, and the injured diver had to be flown to the DDRC (Diving Disease Research Centre) at Ft. Bovisand.

T: Yeah, it was an air-O2 chamber, depth–rated to 50 meters. The medic was knocked off his face trying to deal with something he'd never seen anything like before. Lad Handelman claims that it's imperative that we start thinking about having chambers on board.

Now, to me, if we really talk about safety, we need to have a DDRC person on board. We need to have serious depth-rated chambers with seriously trained hyperbaric operators.

Gary, do you see a day when tech divers will have a chamber on-boat for an expedition like this?

G: By and large, no. For reasons I outlined above. I don't see most expeditions being able to afford them because most expeditions are not sponsored by groups or organizations or agencies. The individuals pay their own way. It's not something I'm going to go out and buy and have hanging around just in case I want to do an expedition. I see the logistics of ownership, and right now, chambers aren't for rent, so that means there's no option of "Let's just rent a chamber for this one expedition." If that occurred, it may be a possibility. Then we're talking lightweight, portable chambers, inflatable ones that a person can actually pick up and carry around.

...OPERATIONS...

The Lusey Team conducted about 120 dives in a 10-day window, with no injuries to speak of. In your mind what does that say about the safety of the expedition?

H: That God was watching out over them. He didn't hear the call on the next expedition, however. When Mr. Gentile said, "Why did we choose to risk the unknown depth with seat-of-the-pants equipment?"...that doesn't say much about the operation in my book. Also, in my personal interviews with some of the other team members, I learned that many incidences occurred during the expedition which were viewed by certain members as being unsafe, too risky, a few of which were called off and some carried out in spite of these fears. The predominant attitude was a certain peer pressure to go for it and not to be seen as the cry-baby. I think it's very unfortunate that that should even be a question.

The plan called for eight divers on the bottom and the two remaining divers to manage the decompression stage and other eventualities, and no remaining set of divers strictly limited for bottom rescues. For me that would be minimal, and I'd also limit the number of people on the bottom to one team at a time at these depths, and I'd better have a pretty extensive plan for how I'd get them out in the event of a break in the mooring or entrapment or blow-up. A plain old loss of body temperature will nail you if nothing else does. This is a very, very difficult expedition to take on.

G: This was a group effort. It is critical for you to understand that. It wasn't ten people who happened to be on the same boat together. This was a single unit, which worked toward a common goal of getting as many individuals on the wreck as possible. No one was ever on his own or out for himself. Certainly everyone wanted to make his own personal time, but there were times when that had to be sacrificed for the group. One time a couple of other people and I gave up a dive because another team missed the wreck and we had to go help them. Everybody said, "OK, right now we're talking about survival of the team." It wasn't according to plan, so we had to back up a step and the rest of the people did not get to dive that day.

T: We did 120 dives, 93 meters and not one single incident or call for any alarm. The point is that I do believe we did the right amount of preparation and training, and had the right equipment so that we didn't run a risk of serious DCI.

AQUACORPS' RESPONSIBILITY

Lad, you made some very pointed comments to me

about featuring the Lusitania as part of the tek.CONFERENCE. Would you mind sharing your thoughts about aquaCORPS' responsibility in all this?

H: At the risk of not being invited for any further issue commentaries, I hold aquaCORPS as accountable as I do the leaders of such expeditions for failing in their responsibility to only give platform and visibility to missions that are conducted according to some minimum level of safety and which will invariably be used as examples for new arrivals.

Debra Hill made a good point in our closing forum that there should be some kind of panel or group discussion after things like this are presented, so that different viewpoints could be aired. Her point was that if aquaCORPS holds someone up as a "leader," then we're responsible for promoting whatever that person's position is. If it's not safe, then we may be inadvertently responsible for hurting people.

H: I think that idea was shared by a number of people. In Mr. Gentile's last interview in aquaCORPS, following his statement about choosing to go with seat-of-the-pants equipment, he justifies this with the statement, "Why not wait for the technology such as rebreathers or hardsuits to become practical? Christopher Columbus did not sit at the dock waiting for transatlantic liners to be built." I would hardly compare the two gentlemen. Columbus spent years raising sufficient funds to build the most seaworthy ships available in the world at that time, and stocked the ship with only the select crews and ample provisions and backups to mount the mission he did. Hardly seat-of-the-pants. I compare Mr. Gentile more to a leader of a fleet of Cuban refugee boats than to Columbus, and one who happens to profit through lectures and books. I'm not very happy with all this, as should be evident by now.

G: I'd like to point out that my presentation was geared toward a high-tech audience which already understands all the principles. Lad's the one guy in there who doesn't understand these principles because he's not a high-tech diver. Everybody else can take it for granted.

I'm sure he's not the only one there, but the point's taken. The people in this area should understand this stuff..

G: We don't have to walk them through this; that'd be a waste of their time and talking down to people. "Here's how we did this and how we did that..." I do that in seminars, but I didn't need to in front of this audience because I assumed that most of the people there understand it, and if they don't, they accept it. See, this is Handelman's problem: he doesn't accept it. He may not accept it because it's different, not only from the way he's always done it in commercial diving, but he sees it as a threat to the way he's done commercial diving. They want to do it differently, fine; if it works, do it. That's why I said, what works works, and that's why you can't say anything against this particular dive operation: it worked.

A question came up at tek about how safe these dives are. Someone said, "Well, these are exploration dives," implying that they should come under some different risk assessment criteria. What's your take on that?

H: That's a tough one. These are individual choices and I support that notion. All I'm saying is that the leaders of such expeditions and movements need to act with added responsibility knowing the consequences that are likely to befall others who may try to follow in their footsteps. Sheck Exley exercised his own personal choice...I doubt he had planned for what happened, but nevertheless, he acted as an individual and exercised extreme caution in preparation and planning. Somehow I see a difference between his choices and lifestyle and what I see in what might be called glory expeditions, or where side profits can result from books and lectures about expeditions.

It seems to me that it's not necessarily the people doing the expeditions that we should be concerned about, but those who might be influenced by the "leaders," the "heroes," the Gary Gentiles... and go out and try to follow in their footsteps and get themselves killed.

G: I agree with you in that respect. Unfortunately, there's always the person out there who only sees the end result and does not see the training that goes into it. But I'm not my brother's keeper, so I can do what I want to do, and if other people choose, through their own ignorance, to follow in my footsteps without the training, then that is not my problem; it's their problem.

Do you think you glamorize your efforts in your books, your novels, and your presentations?

G: Not at all. In fact, I go overboard in the other direction to describe my own fears in doing these deep dives. I always say, any time it's deep, it's serious. Granted, I have more experience than most people, but that doesn't mean that it's less serious or that I take it with a grain of salt.

I think what you're asking is if my example of doing a dive like this is going to lead someone else to thinking he can do it, too. It's a very stupid person who would say, "Gary Gentile, with thousands of deep dives under his belt, can do this; therefore I can do it." That's like me saying, "Well, gee, Edmund Hillary climbed Mount Everest; that means I can."

I have no control over other people, nor do I want control. I would like to just set a good example of what can be done. It's up to people to be intelligent enough to say, "Yes, it can be done, but only with the proper training and experience." My books do not promote risk-taking.

CONCLUSION

There have been a number of publicized technical diving fatalities. In the commercial world that would simply not be acceptable. People aren't supposed to get waxed at their place of employment.

H: Absolutely not. The whole tech diving world, it seems, has yet to take on the responsibility and approach that, for example, the cave diving community has. I'm not that knowledgeable about cave diving, but from what I can gather, they realize that they're in a high-risk world and have done a lot to set their own standards and practices to avoid obvious killers and to have contingency plans to react to situations. Another good example is PADI with its extreme focus on quality assurance throughout all its teaching of their dive instructors.

I think in the technical diving world, without those types of realities having set in through experience, and with more and more would-be tech divers deciding to "go for it," it's inevitable that the pattern of fatalities will continue unless some leadership comes to the front. It should come from the ranks of this group themselves, and it should be heavily embraced and joined in by aquaCORPS as the current forum and voice for this community.

Gary, what do you think Lad, Jim Corey (FBI) and the others that spoke up at tek are reacting to so strongly with regard to this expedition?

G: I think they're reacting to their own experience, which has nothing to do with wreck diving. I think he's coming from the point of view of the commercial diver

Lusitania – Seductive or Suicidal?

who has more systems, who's in this for a job, and who has millions of dollars to spend on backup systems. I don't mean to sound aggressive or pejorative, but a diver who has more backups requires less skill. What we've done is we've made up for the lack of backups such as a chamber onboard by training and experience. You could put a monkey in a hardhat rig and put him down at the bottom of the ocean, and all he has to know how to do is breathe and he's going to come up fine. If he gets into trouble, you plug him into the chamber. We go a step beyond that: we have training which makes up for what Handelman considers to be the deficiencies in our system. Our perspective is, instead of dealing with backups and having inexperienced people who may need to be saved, in our case each person is competent to save himself or to effect his own rescue.

What would you do differently if you were going to do the expedition again?

G: I'd say the only thing that really bothered me was exhaustion. If I wanted to make it easier on myself in another expedition, I would have some landside people to handle all the tacticals in order to make it less strenuous for those of us doing the dives.

Lad, have you any closing comments?

H: I have another quote from Gentile's interview. He said, "In 1994, the Lusitania expedition paved the way for tomorrow's ventures." My comment: I hope not.

Polly, would you do anything different if you do it again?

T: No, I wouldn't do anything different if I was to do it again. In fact, I did do it again and we didn't do anything different.

History has proven Handelman wrong in his pre-

sumptions. Technical dive trips operate essentially the same today as they did in 1994. Dive boats are not equipped with recompression chambers or chase boats.

The only major equipment development is the wrist-mounted decompression computer that can be programmed for helium mixes and multiple gas switches. This has almost universally replaced reliance upon decompression software, in which schedules were written on a plastic slate, or were printed on paper and laminated for use in the water.

The only major modification in technique is that divers no longer rely upon surface-supplied oxygen for completing decompression. Nowadays divers go totally self-contained by carrying small cylinders that hold all the nitrox blends and/or oxygen that will be needed to complete decompression without any kind of surface support (although generally there is oxygen available for emergencies: either a hang bottle that is suspended on a line, or a long hose that is connected to an oxygen cylinder on the boat).

One thing that has not changed is that, for the most part, commercial divers still hate technical divers for their expertise and achievements.

Shadow Divers Exposed in Retrospect

The Truth Hits the Fan
The publication of *Shadow Divers Exposed* created a furor.

The book was both vilified and praised, in that order. Camps were pitched at opposite ends of the spectrum, with almost no one occupying the middle ground.

A curious pathology developed among those who disparaged the book, many of whom did so with the fervor of religious fanaticism. For the most part, these verbal terrorists hid their identities behind fictitious monikers or Internet handles. While their malign strictures generated feverish debate among fellow detractors, they ultimately had no effect upon the eventual acceptance of truth. Nonetheless, it is interesting to examine their malicious critiques if only to demonstrate how irrational people can be whenever their cherished beliefs are challenged.

There are two sides to every story: the truth and the lie. *Shadow Divers Exposed* told the unvarnished truth that contradicted the bold lies that were told in *Shadow Divers*.

Before I launch a compendium of ill-disposed criticism, I would like to annotate certain consequences that occurred in the wake of *SDX* – as I refer to the book in abbreviation.

Immediate Aftershocks
When Joe Porter inaugurated *Wreck Diving Magazine*, he wanted well-known bylines to attract subscribers. He contracted me to write a series of ship-

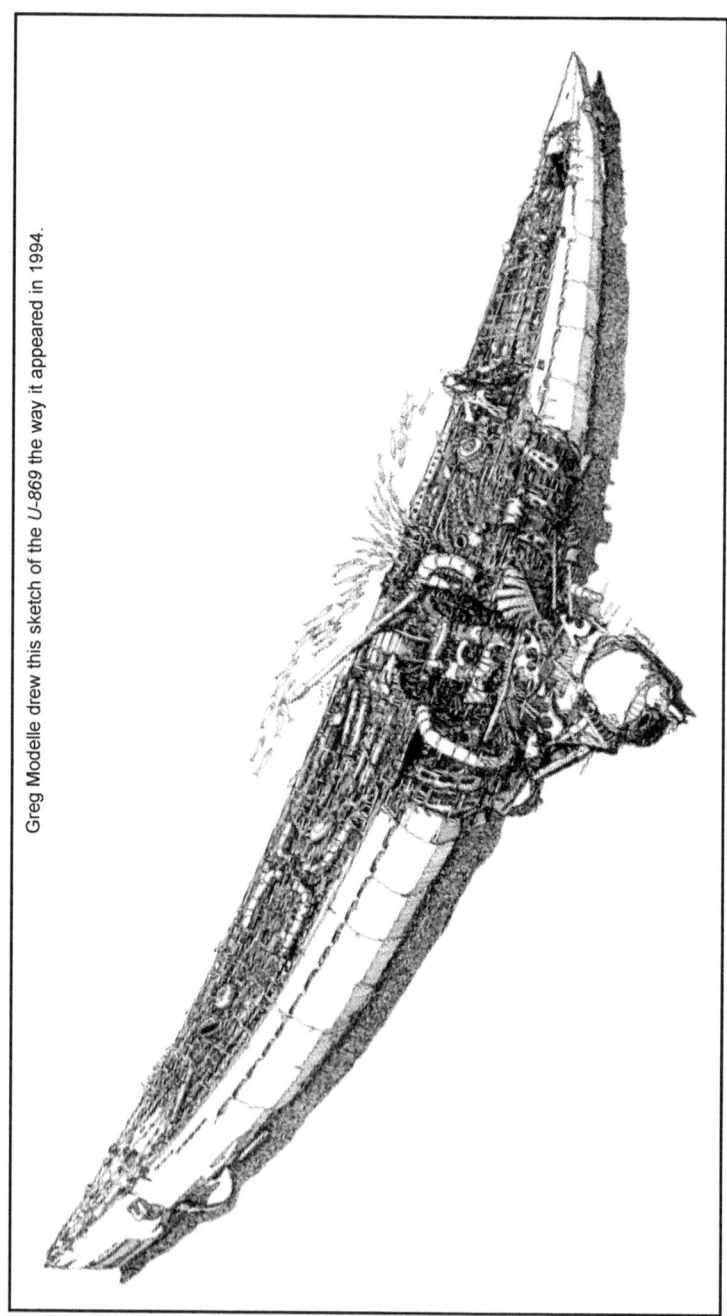

Greg Modelle drew this sketch of the U-869 the way it appeared in 1994.

wreck articles for his quarterly periodical. Each one was to be illustrated with my underwater photographs. As a photojournalist, I had performed in this capacity for more than twenty years. I could produce a wealth of material that was based upon my own adventures and experiences.

Things went smoothly for a year. My fourth article was about my discovery and recovery of the *Sebastian's* bell, which identified the wreck. (See *Shipwreck Sagas* for a reprint of the article.) I suppose it could be construed that John Chatterton was portrayed in a less-than-flattering light, as he was first in the water and swam past the bell without noticing it.

Porter then asked me to write a piece on "The Evolution of Technical Diving." I wrote the article and submitted photographs to accompany it. Porter paid me.

About this time, Chatterton and Richie Kohler invested heavily in the still-fledgling magazine, and bought large-size self-promoting advertisements. Their financial support was more than welcome to Porter. He took additional advantage of their ballyhoo by associating the magazine with their newfound (if misplaced) notoriety. When he showcased the magazine at conference booths, he displayed racks of business cards which spotlighted Chatterton and Kohler. He wanted the public to identify them with the magazine.

Wreck Diving Magazine then became a full-time promotional vehicle for Chatterton and Kohler, with Porter sucking up to them at every opportunity.

Porter shelved "The Evolution of Technical Diving." The article was an historical piece about how mixed-gas diving came into being. It said nothing about Chatterton and Kohler because they were never in the forefront of technical diving. They were third generation technical divers, and not the pioneers that they claimed to be in *Shadow Divers*. Porter canceled my contract to produce quarterly shipwreck articles for his magazine. This was the first and only instance in my writing career in which a publisher paid for a requested piece that he didn't use.

Although Porter never published "The Evolution of Technical Diving," I incorporated the article in my Introduction to *The Advanced Wreck Diving Handbook*.

When negative comments about *SDX* began to appear on Internet forums and chat groups, like-minded individuals jumped onto the bandwagon of castigation. Some people came to my defense, and championed the cause of truth that *SDX* represented, but they had a tough row to hoe. They were flamed in capitals for contradicting the urban legend that *Shadow Divers* had become.

(Note: because many people utilize fictitious names or monikers in correspondence and on the Internet, I will place such names within quotation marks unless I know the commenter personally. I will use the pronoun "he" when the gender of a stranger is in question. I will also use "he" for anonymous commenters. I would like to thank Dennis St. Germain for sending these negative interchanges to me, as I was not able to see them for myself because I don't subscribe to any forums or chat groups.)

Some of this contention aired on ScubaBoard. Two people who came to my defense were Dennis St. Germain and one whose handle was "shakehead." St. Germain noted some of the obvious departures from truth that appeared in *Shadow Divers* – gross exaggerations and grand embellishments that could easily be recognized for what they were without any knowledge of the events in question. "Shakehead" went so far as to itemize in exacting detail a large number of factual errors in *Shadow Divers* that I spotlighted in *SDX*. He appended corroboration for those opponents who were open-minded enough to regard.

It is well known that a devout disputant cannot be converted by means of reason and logic. My champions' protests fell on deaf ears.

Chatterton and Kohler then paid a hefty fee for a self-promotional banner on ScubaBoard. Immediately thereafter, all commentary that supported *SDX* was deleted, but all the censure that was made against it was left undisturbed.

As "shakehead" noted, "All of my posts demolishing shadow divers were removed. Reference page numbers, direct quotes, direct contradictions." "Shakehead" continued, "I spent hours posting Gary Gentile's informative quotes and facts, with the result that the usual 'keyboard bullies' had a field day with adolescent flames. The moderator joined the chortling and DELETED the quoted references, page numbers, and corrections."

It may seem to some that Chatterton bribed or "bought off" *Wreck Diving Magazine* and ScubaBoard, but I make no such allegations. Although these instances smack of censorship, I am merely reporting the facts – as I did in *SDX*. It is the responsibility of my faithful readers to interpret the meaning behind those facts.

The Motionless Picture

Coincidental with these shenanigans came the dissolution of the *Shadow Divers* movie deal. The motion picture was supposed to be directed by Ridley Scott. He quit the project a couple of months after the publication of *SDX*. Later, Peter Weir was assigned to take over the directorship. But the project was canned before it could get underway. Now, two years later, the film appears to be lost in limbo.

The Bliss of Ignorance

The *SDX* smear campaign commenced with people who had read *Shadow Divers*, but had only *heard* about *SDX*. I don't understand how a person could have anything intelligent to say about a book that he hasn't read. Be that as it may, in the final analysis, their denigrating remarks say more about themselves and their preconceived notions than they say about *SDX*.

I took a back seat in *SDX*, absenting myself as much as possible from events that I related, unless I was directly involved. I did this intentionally so as to not have the book perceived as a personal vendetta against Chatterton and Kohler. I divulged the facts from the point of view of an omniscient bystander. In this chapter, however, I must intrude myself as a matter of defense, as I was the person who took the heat over *SDX*.

One who signed himself as "John Blausey" sent me a scathing and castigating email in which he wrote, "I don't know why you haven't been sued." This sentence displays "John Blausey's" ignorance of the law of libel. In jurisprudence, libel is a false written statement that maliciously damages a person's reputation. By this definition, any statement that is true, no matter how heinous that statement may be, is not libelous.

There is nothing illegal about telling the truth.

For example, *Shadow Divers* claimed that both Chatterton and Kohler got divorced as a result of their single-minded preoccupation with identifying the *U-869*, and that they spent more time in their newborn passion than they spent at home with their wives. Were I to write that Chatterton got divorced because he learned that his wife was banging her boss, and that Kohler sued for divorce because his wife was having sexual relations with a number of lesbian women, these statements could not be considered libelous as long as they were true (or as long as that is what Chatterton and Kohler told me when these sordid events were unfolding).

I can understand why Chatterton and Kohler would not want to acknowledge publicly these salacious circumstances, especially in a book whose intention was to glorify them by means of fictitious achievements, because the truth might tarnish the false image that the book was trying to create. But the fact that *Shadow Divers* invented vainglorious myths about fictional characters does not make my unveiling of the truth in any way libelous.

Because *SDX* presented documented facts, a lawsuit would have died aborning as soon as witnesses corroborated those facts under oath. In any case, "John Blausey's" argument is now academic, as the time to file a lawsuit has expired.

Among other things in his page-and-a-half diatribe, "John Blausey" also vilified me for publishing *SDX* through my wholly owned small press instead of farming it out to a large publishing concern.

In *The Lusitania Controversies*, I explained at length how and why I started my own publishing business. I capitalized the venture with my savings, with royalties from my science fiction novels, and by taking out a large loan with an affordable interest rate.

The publishing industry was taking a nosedive at the time (1989), with the result that the sale of manuscripts dropped significantly. The manuscripts that I sold to other publishing houses were printed on poor quality paper, my color photographs were reproduced in black and white, and the artistic layouts were amateurish and substandard.

I thought that I could do a better job. By not having to cater to the whims of unversed editors, and to the low production values of cost-cutting publishers, I produced high-quality books that were printed in vivid color on slick paper. Not only did I have total artistic control over the product, but I didn't have to contend with editors who wanted to bowdlerize my work.

Entrepreneurial spirit is universally praised in American society. Yet "John Blausey" disparaged me for gambling everything I owned – and then some – in a risky investment that eventually paid off in spades.

Furthermore, I *did* submit the manuscript of *SDX* to a large publisher: Random House, the publisher of *Shadow Divers*. I provided a synopsis in which I revealed the inadequacies of *Shadow Divers* as a work of nonfiction. I explained that most of *Shadow Divers* was either fictitious or grossly exaggerated, that the so-called heroes took credit for the achievements of other divers (whose roles were either downplayed or expunged), that the book paid scant attention to the truth and instead invented improbable scenarios that never occurred, and that I had interviewed other participants whose testimony established without a shadow of a doubt that *Shadow Divers* was riddled with prevarications, distortions, deceptions, inaccuracies, and self-serving matters of omission.

I suggested that *SDX* would give Random House the opportunity to redeem itself for taking part in a literary hoax, and for foisting upon the public a work of obvious fiction that Random House promoted as a factual account.

No professional editor worth his or her salt could possibly have read the manuscript of *Shadow Divers* without recognizing the blatant embellishments that permeated the narrative. They had to have known that the story was sensationalized beyond the pale of belief. Conning an ignorant nondiving public was one thing; I cannot believe that Random House's editors could have been so easily deceived. Had they been honest and sincere, they would have exercised due diligence in ascertaining the truth by seeking the opinions of professional diving consultants.

If the editors did not make a conscious decision to ignore the conspicuous invention in order to earn ill-gotten profits for the company, then Random House is guilty of employing the most stupid editors in the business.

Even after I informed Random House of the actual state of affairs, the company did nothing about it. Random House continued to market *Shadow Divers*, and to advertise it as a "true adventure." Once informed of the facts, a reputable company should have replaced the spurious statement from the front cover of the book with "This is a work of fiction." Then, on the copyright page, it should have printed the warning that is the standard caveat for novels: "All incidents and characters in this book are fictional, and any resemblance to real incidences and to persons living or dead is purely coincidental."

The company declined to publish *SDX* as counterpoint. To do so would have been against the company's financial interests. After all, Random House had invested millions of dollars in the production and promotion of *Shadow Divers*. As long as the book was still earning money, profit motive was paramount and more important than truth.

I was not about to let that truth be buried by a publishing house conspiracy. I published *SDX* through one of my subsidiary imprints.

More Bliss, More Ignorance

One who signed himself as "rawls" wrote, "But exactly what part did Gary Gentile play in the discovery and subsequent ID of U-869?" Had "rawls" bothered to read *SDX* before posing a question in ignorance of the facts, he would have learned that I made no claim to having discovered or identified the wreck. "Rawls" implies that therefore I had no right to write a book about the *U-869*.

In fact, I played a greater part in the wrecked U-boat than Kurson played, yet "rawls" did not admonish him for writing a book about a subject in which he played no role at all. Unlike Kurson, at least I was a diver, and had penetrated the hull of the U-Who? before it was identified.

One anonymous poster claimed that he hadn't read *SDX*, but nonetheless the book "seems short on evidence and long on supposition." How could he have come to such a conclusion without reading the book that he had the temerity to critique? This poster is every prosecutor's ideal juror: one who passes judgment based upon the prosecutor's allegations, without listening to the evidence of the defense.

Another anonymous poster wrote, "If you title a book to discredit another book on the same subject, you expect it to be filled with facts and positively show how the previous book was inaccurate. That is not the case, it seems. By just giving a possible alternative to the original story amounts to just that, A POSSIBLE ALTERNATIVE. If you claim to EXPOSE then you must fullfil [sic] that goal and Gentile seems to be short, way short, of that goal." Keep in mind that this poster made his unsupported allegation without having read *SDX*.

Yet another anonymous poster claimed that I had no right to use *Shadow Divers Exposed* as a title. I disagree. As the book is an exposé of *Shadow Divers*, I cannot think of a more accurate and appropriate title.

"Caroln" shared the anonymous poster's opinion: "If he wanted to write another book about the sub, no problem, and I'd have been happy to read it, but just the title alone comes off as bitter and nasty, so I won't bother reading further."

Affirmative Indifference

An anonymous poster on the Deco Stop defended *Shadow Divers* against *SDX* by writing, "I don't give a rats ass if the hand of God reached down from the heavens and sunk [sic] the sub. The book was an interesting read."

I suppose that his attitude of indifference to the truth explains why he chose not to read *SDX*.

"Gibby" mirrored the sentiment: "Shaddow [sic] Divers was a great book. I could care less if it ever hapened [sic] or not."

On March 10, 2007, during a lecture engagement at ScubaFest in Ohio, I actually met a man who told me that he didn't want to know the truth about the *U-869*. He was so enamored with the story that he read in *Shadow Divers* that he didn't want his notions disabused.

There is no accounting for tastes. I suppose these people would be just as happy to accept a history of World War Two in which the Nazis won the war and took over the world – and never wonder why they were speaking English instead of German.

Character Assassination

Ad hominem is a Latin phrase that translates literally as "to the man." By definition it means "appealing to personal considerations rather than to logic or reason." The phrase is commonly used to describe instances in which a biased detractor is unable to find anything derogatory in a person's accomplishments, so he assaults his person instead.

One person who went out of his way to ridicule me the most with attacks against my character was Bret Gilliam. His vested interest in the *Shadow Divers* controversy appears to be in using it as an excuse to pour scorn on my reputation.

Gilliam's latest soapbox was an article in a magazine called *Diving Adventure.* In the first issue he used Chatterton as a vehicle to write about himself and to disparage me. In his so-called interview with Chatterton, Gilliam devoted more space to his "questions" (as a result of his parenthetical pontifications) than to the interviewee. In this case Chatterton was little more than Gilliam's sounding board.

Gilliam kept dragging my name into his lead-ins when I had nothing to do with the question or with the subject at hand. For example, he invented a fictional conversation that he and I supposedly had "in the early 90s."

He romanticized it this way: "I'll never forget one day he called me and asked me a question about managing oxygen exposure. I presumed that I was talking to someone who was fairly switched on to the subject, so I launched off on a 20 minute dissertation on oxygen exposure. At the end of what I thought to be a very basic explanation of the topic, there was silence for about ten seconds, then he replied, 'I have to tell you something, Bret, I don't have a clue what you're talking about.' I said, 'Where did I lose you?' He said, 'About a minute and a half into it.' . . . he didn't have a clue about what was going on with oxygen management. He was unable to even work the essential physics equations."

I reiterate: I have no recollection of any such conversation, I vehemently deny that it ever occurred, and I am willing to take a polygraph test to prove it - and to prove the rest of the following account. As far as I am concerned, the conversation is an invention of Gilliam's wishful imagination. But the conversation itself is irrelevant to the issue at hand. The real issue is: What was his objective in making a public denouncement more than a decade after the so-called event?

Gilliam has no idea about what I know. I took trigonometry and physics in high school, and calculus in college. In 1989, I had long talks about oxygen exposure with decompression guru Bill Hamilton, when I was planning a 380-foot dive on the German battleship *Ostfriesland* for the following year. Hamilton generated the decompression schedules for the dive. I wrote about oxygen exposure in the *Ultimate Wreck Diving Guide* (1992). If I did have a question about oxygen exposure, I would have called Hamilton, as we were in constant contact about the upcoming project.

Elsewhere in the interview, Gilliam deprecated the *Ultimate Wreck Diving Guide*: "Gentile published one book shortly after people started being introduced to mixed gas, where his knowledge was so fundamentally flawed that he thought all gasses had a "2" subscript. Since oxygen is O2 and nitrogen is N2, he published a book and listed helium as HE2."

Again, Gilliam cannot know or speculate about my knowledge base. Because I had taken chemistry courses in both high school and college, I was well aware that oxygen and nitrogen were diatomic, while helium – a noble gas – was monatomic. With limited exceptions, the noble gases are chemically inert, and do not combine with themselves or with other elements.

The chemical symbol for hydrogen is H_2 (2 being a subscript, not merely a small number as it appears in this text; in desktop publishing programs subscripts deform the leading, or space between lines). The chemical symbol for helium is He. A chemical symbol that was printed as H_2 was undoubtedly a printing error that was supposed to be He.

I was not willing to spend the time and effort to confirm his allegation by proofreading the book word for word, especially as it had been out of print for over a decade (replaced by *The Technical Diving Handbook*.) Gilliam later annotated two instances of misprinted chemical symbols in the *Ultimate Wreck Diving Guide*.

In Gilliam's article, the symbol for helium was incorrectly printed as HE2. In the symbols for elements that are expressed by two letters, the second letter is never capitalized. A chemical symbol in which two adjacent letters are capitalized refers to a molecule, not an atom. A prime example is CO_2, which is the chemical symbol for carbon dioxide, in which C stands for one atom of carbon and O_2 stands for two atoms of oxygen. Because no element is represented by the letter E, there is no such compound as HE2.

It appears that Gilliam is not as familiar with the Periodic Table of the Elements as he would like his readers to believe. The example in the previous paragraph certainly turns the Table on him. People who live in glass houses . . . Or was it perhaps a typo?

In a sense, I feel gratified that Gilliam found only two printing errors that slipped past the proofreader's eyes in a complex and highly technical book that was the first of its kind. But his arrogant satisfaction in finding those errors – and remembering them after nearly fifteen years – begs the question that I posed on the previous page: Why did he feel compelled to make such a harangue about a single-character typographical error among some half a million characters?

Let me take a detour that will provide the background to Gilliam's tirade and misplaced wrath. The story is worth the digression.

Copyright Infringement

In the 1980's, I wrote a piece about the various salvage attempts on the *Andrea Doria*. I sold the article to *Sea Classics*, a monthly periodical that focused on naval and maritime history. The article was duly published in the May 1984 issue. One of my underwater photographs graced the cover, and another sixteen of my photos were used to illustrate the text.

Yet payment was not forthcoming. I waited a reasonable amount of time, then called the publisher/editor in Canoga Park, California; his name was Edwin Schnepf. His secretary informed me that he was presently unavailable. I left my name and phone number and the reason for my call. After a week or so, I called a second time. Again his secretary informed me that Schnepf was unavailable. I called three or four days later. Unavailable.

This time I engaged the secretary in conversation. I asked her if she had given my messages to Schnepf. She assured me that she had. She had no explanation for his refusal to return my calls. I asked if this was the way Schnepf treated all writers to whom he owed money. She didn't know. I asked if she was being paid her salary. She was. I asked her if she didn't think that I should get paid too? She agreed that I should.

I called a few more times during the course of a month, but Schnepf was never available. Nor did he return my calls.

Then I hit upon a better plan. Instead of spending my money on long distance phone calls, I called collect. The secretary would not accept the charges, but she knew who was calling and why. Every time I called collect, I left a message for Schnepf to return my call. He never did. Sometimes the operator even let me have a short chat with the secretary about the reason for my call. She was totally embarrassed at having to field Schnepf's dunning messages.

I called every weekday, two or three times a day, morning and afternoon. This went on for about two months. In all, I made more than one hundred collect phone calls. It was obvious to me that Schnepf *never* accepted phone calls, and that the secretary was instructed to *always* say that he wasn't available. It didn't seem like a good way to run a business, but then Schnepf wasn't really running a business – he was running a scam.

The secretary was apologetic at first. Then she was embarrassed. Eventually she got so frustrated with my incessant calls that she put me through to Schnepf. That caught him off guard.

I gave Schnepf no opportunity to put up a defense. For about twenty minutes I lambasted him about the money he owed me. He was so cowed by my outburst that he didn't think to hang up on me. He backpedaled like a scared child and promised to send me a check in payment for the article – and to include the manuscript and photos that he had neglected to return. I put him in his place in no uncertain terms. I eventually received a check in the amount of $250.

That was only the beginning of the story. A few months later, a friend congratulated me on the fine job I did on the *Doria* article in a magazine that he had recently purchased. I was confused. The issue in which my article appeared had been out of print for a year. He showed me a magazine that was dated Winter 1984. It was a special issue that was entitled *21 Strange Tales of Shipwrecks, Survival & Salvage*. I had never heard the name before. Yet the magazine contained my article in its entirety, including all sixteen photos that had illustrated the original piece.

The magazine stole my article from *Sea Classics*!

Then I made a startling discovery on the copyright page: the publisher was the same one that published *Sea Classics*: Challenge Publications, alias Edwin Schnepf. I realized with some irony that as he was writing my check with his right hand, he was reprinting my article in a sister magazine with his left. Schnepf had simply lifted the plates from *Sea Classics*, and reused them on the new magazine.

This was no longer a simple case of nonpayment. This was outright copyright infringement. I had not authorized Schnepf to reprint my article and photos.

I retained copyright attorney Dwight Peterson to handle the matter. Peterson threatened to file a lawsuit for copyright infringement unless Schnepf made an out-of-court settlement that was large enough to exact retribution for Schnepf's deliberate breach of faith.

The legal process moves at glacial speed. Negotiations consumed the better part of a year. Peterson had the advantage over me in that Schnepf accepted his phone calls, and returned those calls that he missed. Peterson was not content to merely negotiate a monetary settlement. He wanted Schnepf to sign a written declaration that he would never use my materials again.

Peterson drew up the document. Schnepf eventually signed it. Schnepf also made restitution in the amount of $1,500. I would have been happy if he had paid me $500 up front, but honesty was not his policy. His attempt at grand theft was a costly mistake on his part. Or so it seemed to me at the time.

But the story is not ended. Not by a long shot.

I wrote to both *The Writer* and *Writer's Digest*, monthly magazines that catered to professional writers by providing up-to-date information about markets, pay rates, mergers, news items, and so on. I explained in detail about the extreme difficulty that I encountered in collecting payment from Challenge Publications. I learned that I was not the only one to lodge a complaint against Schnepf. He had ripped off hundreds, perhaps thousands of writers.

Each issue of *Sea Classics* contained around ten articles. Each month, Challenge Publications published twenty-one magazines on various subjects. That added up to more than two hundred articles per month, equating to two to three thousand articles per year. There was a never-ending stream of amateur writers who were so eager to get published that if each submitted only one manuscript, got burned, and either quit writing or moved on to other markets, Schnepf would never run out of innocent lambs to fleece.

This operational strategy reduced production costs significantly. Continual theft was profitable, and crime clearly did pay.

Most people grumble when they get ripped off, but seldom do they do anything about it. Instead of taking an active stance, they complain to their friends where it doesn't do any good. Depending upon the situation, they should instead protest where they have some chance of correcting the problem: to government officials, elected representatives, law enforcement departments, affirmative action groups, collection agencies, attorneys, and so on. Most people are too lazy to follow up in this regard: they just steam and stew ineffectively. Unfortunately, that is human nature.

If Schnepf occasionally had to pay a hard-nosed writer like me – one who didn't give up when it came to collecting a balance due – then he was still ahead of the game. He was playing the odds and winning hands down. I was nothing more to him than a write-off or a business expense.

The situation became so bad that the writing magazines published notices to the effect that Challenge Publications could not be considered a professional market. Such euphemistic language was a cop-out. They should have been more blunt and bold. And they should have organized a class action suit for their members and subscribers.

The magazines circulated my letter to other victims. Some wrote to me; a few called. I told them how to get their money. They all bellyached, but none was willing to do anything other than to add me to their list of sympathetic listeners. Schnepf was still winning.

He had not broken copyright law because the writers had submitted their manuscripts to him on a voluntary basis – writing on "spec" as it is called in the business – on speculation – in the hope that a manuscript would be accepted for publication. If a publisher requests from a writer an article on a specific topic, then it is known as "writing for hire."

Schnepf could not be prosecuted for failure to pay his debts. Such a case could be tried only in a civil court when an aggrieved individual filed a complaint.

Then Schnepf made the biggest mistake of his life. In 1989, in a new magazine that Challenge Publications called *Shipwrecks!*, he reprinted my *Doria* article *again* – and again he used all sixteen of my photos to illustrate the text. Not only that, but prominently displayed on the cover was the same underwater photo that had been used on the cover of *Sea Classics*.

If he had been smart, he would have destroyed the plates that had proven to be so costly. This time he had not only infringed on my copyright, but he had violated a contractual agreement that was binding in perpetuity.

I was apoplectic. Peterson was ecstatic. This was a suit that he could not possibly lose because it demonstrated the kind of premeditated infringement that the courts truly frowned upon. It portended a case that Schnepf could not weasel out of as cheaply as he had weaseled out of the last one. There was no need to put Challenge Publications on the alert, or to ask for restitution. Schnepf had knowingly violated copyright law as well as the terms of a court-sanctioned contract that was on file in the courthouse.

The case was open and shut. There was no question that we would win the case. The only question was for how much.

Peterson wasted no time in filing a suit in the Philadelphia court system. A process server served papers on Schnepf in his place of business. If he still employed the secretary who had put my collect call through to him years before, I imagined that she was snickering at her desk – she had to know from all the complaints she fielded that Schnepf was swindling his writers big time.

I contacted those victims who had previously contacted me through the writing magazines. As long as I was taking Challenge Publications to court, I thought that I could help to collect their money by adding their names to the complaint. They all had their grievances, but none of them wanted to get involved in a legal action, even though it wouldn't cost them a penny. That pusillanimous attitude was precisely what made it so easy for career criminals like Schnepf to rip off the public. So I proceeded on my own.

I would like to state that the Philadelphia courts launched a rocket docket, but such was not the "case." The machinery of the so-called justice system crawls at a snaillike pace.

Schnepf hired a local attorney to fight the action. This attorney did everything in his power to prolong the inevitable outcome. He didn't have a leg to stand on, so he stalled for more time. He filed briefs and counter briefs. He raised objections. When all else failed, he demanded my appearance in order to give a deposition.

I met Peterson in the lobby of the building that had been selected for the deposition. He gave me only one sentence of advice: "Answer the questions truthfully." I did.

Schnepf's defense hinged on a single point: that I did not own the copyright of the article in question. But I had stolen a march on him there. Years before, I had grouped a bunch of articles and had submitted them to the Library of Congress for copyright registration. After that, I had incorporated the article in the first book that I published through my fledgling publishing business: *Andrea Doria: Dive to an Era*. Thus the article was copyrighted not just once, but twice. I provided photocopies of the copyright registration forms, which were stamped with official seals.

The judge who had been assigned to handle the case called for a meeting with the attorneys. Peterson had requested a jury trial, but the judge had what he considered to be more important cases to try, so he wanted the matter settled out of court. Otherwise, he intended to assign an adjudicator to study and settle the case. Peterson didn't want the case to go to adjudication because he thought that we could get more money from a jury. According to the law, I had the right to a trial by jury. Nonetheless, the judge arbitrarily took away that option.

The judge was spending what he thought was an inordinate amount of time in reading all the briefs, counter briefs, declarations, and orders to produce; and in ruling on procedure. He told Peterson, "I've got $5,000 worth of my time in this case."

The judge overruled Peterson's objections, and sent the case to adjudication. He even stipulated the amount of award: between $5,000 and $10,000. The adjudicator settled on $8,500. The judge issued a court ruling that found Challenge Publications guilty of copyright infringement. As part of the settlement, Schnepf was admonished by the court to never again reprint my *Doria* article. So far he hasn't. Darn!

Schnepf claimed that he didn't have the money to pay the settlement in one lump sum. He made a down payment, then paid the remainder a month or two later. I don't know if he ever paid his attorney.

Stinging from this financial punishment, Challenge Publications commenced to issue notices in its magazines that heretofore all published materials were copyrighted in the name of the author. This new policy was diametrically opposed to Challenge Publication's previous copyright notice, which had read, "All rights reserved. Nothing in whole or in part may be reproduced without the written permission of the publisher." Ironically, this same notice appeared in the issues in which my stolen articles appeared.

I gleamed with satisfaction about forcing such an important change in Challenge Publication's editorial policy. Whether Schnepf ever started paying his writers, I never ascertained.

I studied a great deal of copyright law during the course of my legal confrontations with Challenge Publications. I learned a lot more in conversation with Dwight Peterson. According to the law, a person who was convicted of copyright infringement could be fined an amount up to $10,000, could be sentenced to prison for as long as a year, or both. I asked why the judge didn't pass sentence on Schnepf; or, barring that, why we didn't push to have these sentences imposed.

Peterson had been practicing copyright law for over twenty years. He told me that in his experience, no one – not a single person – had ever been fined or sent to jail for copyright infringement. And he had handled cases that resulted in multimillion-dollar settlements (mostly against record companies, where copyright infringement ran rampant). Nor could he recall ever reading or hearing about any case on record in which an infringer had been punished by the law. The courts let such matters fall into the realm of civil suit.

SDX in Retrospect

Copyright Infringement Case Number Two

By now my faithful readers are probably wondering how this subplot relates to Bret Gilliam.

In 1992, I wrote and published the first book on technical diving: the *Ultimate Wreck Diving Guide*. At that time, technical diving was just coming into vogue. Because it was the only book on the market that dealt with such esoteric subjects as nitrox and helium blends, the book became an overnight bestseller in the diving community. A lot of people wanted to know what technical diving was all about.

In light of my book's tremendous success, Gilliam jumped on the technical diving bandwagon by co-authoring another book on subject, called *Mixed Gas Diving*. When I saw Gilliam's book, I was astonished to see that three of my photos illustrated the text.

Only one of my photos was credited to me. One was uncredited, and one was credited to Ken Clayton. At first I wondered how Gilliam had obtained copies of my photos. When I examined his book more closely, I saw that all three photos had appeared previously in the *Ultimate Wreck Diving Guide*.

So there is no misunderstanding among my readers, I took all three photos with my camera. The picture that was credited to Ken Clayton, I took by setting the camera in place, stepping into the frame, and directing Nike Seamans when to press the shutter release button as I took different poses. All three photos were credited to me on the verso page of the *Ultimate Wreck Diving Guide*. All three photos are copyrighted in my name by the Register of Copyrights at the Library of Congress. The copyright registration is still in my possession. The original images are still in my possession, in their original mounts, which are dated. These photos left my possession only once: when I sent them to my printer in Hong Kong via Federal Express; the printer returned them to me directly via Federal Express.

I published the photos in color. *Mixed Gas Diving* printed them in black and white. When I checked my original color slides, I saw cropping marks on the cardboard mounts where I had cropped each image. None of the uncropped image area appears in the black and white reprints. I had my suspicions about how Gilliam had obtained the images, but my faithful readers can draw their own conclusions.

I contacted Gilliam immediately about this serious breach of ethics.

Instead of apologizing, he gave me the runaround. He claimed that I had sent the slides to him. I countered by saying that I had no recollection of having done so, and that if I had done so, I would have some kind of written record of the job. I kept records of all my business activities, for my own edification as well as for income tax purposes.

Professional photography is a business that requires strict attention to detail. I don't simply stuff a bunch of pictures into an envelope and mail them, hoping that they won't get lost in transit, or that the publisher will be conscientious enough to return them.

I sent only duplicates. Whenever I had a slide duplicated, I assigned a control number to the image. This control number doubled as a caption number. The control number was printed in red ink on the original slide, and in black or blue ink on the duplicate. This system enabled me to quickly distinguish an original slide from a duplicate, so that I did not accidentally submit an original to a publisher. My name was stamped on the mount of the duplicate.

None of the three images in question had a control number. Ergo, I had never duplicated the slides that Gilliam used in his book.

Lest you think that I invented this seemingly cumbersome system of organization, I did not. It is standard business practice that is promoted by the American Society of Media Photographers (ASMP).

I maintained a master caption log with a sequential numbering system. I wrote a caption for each image on the master list, copied that portion of the list that applied to the images that I was submitting for a job, then printed a job-specific caption sheet along with a work order that reflected the agreed-upon rate of pay - either a flat fee per photo, or a space-rate that depended upon the percentage of the page that the published image filled. My master list did not have captions for either of the three images. And I certainly would not have given credit to Clayton for a photo he didn't take.

Even if my memory were remiss, I still had all these other means of ascertaining that I did *not* send the images to Gilliam: my files contained no written request, no work order, no caption in my master log, no shipping receipt, and no control numbers on the original slide mounts.

I called Gilliam's bluff by demanding that he return my slides at once. He then claimed that he couldn't find them. I gave him time to look for them. Several months later, he claimed that he must have thrown them out.

When he began to suspect that I might sue him for copyright infringement, he wrote "You have not been slighted, injured or monetarily harmed in any way . . . *Where are your damages?*" (Gilliam's italics.) He thought that my claim had no "legal validity," and repeated himself: "You have no damages." He then threatened me with reprisals if I persisted in pursuing the matter.

Gilliam missed the point entirely. He seemed to believe that if I hadn't been damaged in some material or nonmaterial way, then I had no legal standing and it was okay for him to use my photos. The laws relating to copyright infringement contain no such caveat.

I didn't expect to receive any commiseration from Watersports owner Ken Loyst, who published *Mixed Gas Diving*, and I didn't. No one offered to pay for the use of my images.

I had already been ripped off by another Watersports project when editor Robert von Maier commissioned me to write a chapter for a proposed book called *Solo Diving*. After I wrote the piece and submitted it along with a bill, he informed me that he had no intention of paying for it. I withdrew the chapter from consideration. I later included it in the *Ultimate Wreck Div-*

ing Guide.

Watersports also used some of my photos in *Deep Diving*, and never paid me for them.

I discussed the situation with Victor Perlman, legal advisor to the ASMP. It was not worth suing over these simple cases of infringement. Yet it galled me that people were so flagrant in violating intellectual property rights. So I took a different tack – or rather, two tacks. This two-tack maneuver would not earn any money (or make friends), but as a professional photojournalist it was necessary for my livelihood and for my future in the business to take affirmative action to establish a resolute position with regard to copyright infringement.

By not contesting infringements, infringers might infer that I was condoning them; or, chronic infringers might come to believe that I was an easy mark, and that they could continually get away with breaking the law. The lack of protest sends the wrong message, and this was a reputation that I could not afford to incur.

In a business that is fraught with thieves and cutthroats, a photographer must take a firm stance to protect his stock in trade, because no one is likely to take that stance for him; and other lawbreakers are waiting around the corner.

For tack one, I served notice by drafting a document and submitting it to both Loyst and Gilliam. Although my grievance was primarily with Gilliam, who produced the book and may not have informed Loyst how he did so, I had to include the publisher as a matter of course. The document stated, in part:

> <u>Notice to cease copyright infringement</u>
> Demand is made that the above mentioned photographs be deleted immediately and forever from the current work in print, or that the book be withdrawn from circulation since the continued sale of infringed upon materials constitutes continued and knowing infringement.
>
> Demand is further made that no more copies of "Mixed Gas Diving" be printed unless

the infringed upon photographs are deleted, that these photographs be omitted from revised editions of "Mixed Gas Diving," and that these or any other photographs copyrighted in the name of Gary Gentile not be infringed upon in any other way, by the publisher and/or the authors, forever.

<u>Damages</u>

Gary Gentile's reputation has been irrevocably damaged because the infringed upon photographs, which are copyright in his name, have been published in "Mixed Gas Diving," a work which competes with Gary Gentile's work, "Ultimate Wreck Diving Guide," in which the photographs originally appeared, thus diluting the value of the photographs when their publication was unique to "Ultimate Wreck Diving Guide."

Gary Gentile's reputation has been further irrevocably damaged because two of the infringed upon photographs published in "Mixed Gas Diving," as well as one of Gary Gentile's photographs published in "Deep Diving," by Gilliam, Von Maier, Crea, and Webb, and published by Watersports Publishing, and which competes with Gary Gentile's book "Advanced Wreck Diving Guide," in which the one image originally appeared, have been erroneously credited to fictitious photographers, which casts doubt on the credibility of Gary Gentile personally, as well as his books, "Ultimate Wreck Diving Guide" and "Advanced Wreck Diving Guide," in which the infringed upon photographs were credited to Gary Gentile. Thus readers are misled into believing that Gary Gentile did not take the photographs which are copyrighted in his name.

Gary Gentile's reputation as a photographer has also been damaged by the poor reproduction quality of the photographs appearing in "Mixed Gas Diving" and "Deep Diving," in which his color photographs appeared in black and white, and in which his photographs were printed on poor quality rag paper, which made the resultant images appear indistinct.

Payment demand for lost photographic materials

According to accepted practice between photographers and publishers, and in accordance to guidelines suggested by the American Society of Magazine Photographers, photographers must be reimbursed for lost photographic materials at a rate of between $1,000 and $1,500 per image.

The last demand put Loyst and Gilliam on the spot. If, as Gilliam claimed, I sent the slides to him and he lost them, then by Gilliam's own admission, he and the publisher were ethically bound to reimburse me for their loss. He was trapped no matter which way he turned.

I did not expect to receive any money, and I didn't.

Criminal Investigation

Everyone knows from watching videotapes and DVD's that the Federal Bureau of Investigation posts a warning against copying the contents for commercial gain. As noted above, Dwight Peterson had advised me that copyright infringers were never indicted or prosecuted. Even so, that didn't mean that a victim shouldn't file a report with the appropriate authority, so that a complaint existed on record.

After all, when someone steals your car, you report it to the police. If a civic-minded citizen witnesses the commission of a crime, he alerts the law enforcement agency that is responsible for investigating that particular brand of crime.

For tack two, I filed a grievance with the FBI. Here is what I wrote:

> I have read with interest the new hard

stance which the FBI is taking against copyright infringement [not true, but I wanted to flatter them and give them the benefit of the doubt]: not just making empty threats like the warnings at the beginning of commercial videos, but taking action which needs to be taken if the common practice of infringement is ever to be brought under control. Here is another case which needs your attention, else scofflaws who have gotten away with their offenses all too easily in the past will continue to infringe upon the rights of others.

Briefly, the situation is this: photographs which I took and published in a book which I wrote, were copied out of my book and published without my knowledge or permission in a competitive book written by Bret Gilliam and published by Watersports Publications. Some of these photographs were credited fictitiously.

I have alerted both the publisher and the author about my knowledge of the infringement, explained that such infringement constitutes a violation of my copyright, and ordered them to cease infringing upon my copyright.

Not only does the publisher flagrantly continue to infringe upon my copyright, but the author avowed that there is nothing I can do about the situation, and he has twice threatened me (by mail) if I keep pursuing my claim with the publisher, and has stated that because I have pressed my complaint he now plans to victimize me further in the future.

Given the lackadaisical manner in which this federal offense has been dealt with by the law enforcement agencies in the past, their cavalier attitude is understandable. It is also regrettable, because the lack of legal indictment is tantamount to encouraging infringement, since offenders know that they can get away with it.

I should not have to suffer threats and continued copyright infringement, nor should I be forced through judicial inaction to take matters into my own hands. If the FBI investigates clear cases of copyright infringement, the threat of investigation alone will help curb the practice in the future.

I have copies of all correspondence between me and the publisher and the author.

I simply tasked the FBI with performing the job that the agency was federally mandated to perform, and which it always threatened to perform. As expected, the FBI completely ignored my letter. After several months I resubmitted my letter. This time an agent called me on the phone. He explained that the FBI had initiated an investigation, but after reviewing the circumstances, decided upon reflection not to proceed with prosecution. He did not specifically state why they would not proceed, but he implied that the case wasn't big enough: that is, either it didn't involve enough money, or it didn't involve enough notoriety for the FBI.. He suggested that I seek remedy in civil court.

I wasn't satisfied with this, so I complained to Bob Borski of the attitude and inaction of the FBI. My congressmen was always attentive to the needs of his constituents.

Borski's intervention forced a written reply from John Collingwood, FBI Inspector in Charge, Office of Public and Congressional Affairs. He confirmed what the previous agent had implied on the phone: "Since civil remedies are available to victims of copyright infringement, the Department of Justice will entertain prosecution of only the most egregious criminal violations of the copyright statutes. I can understand your constituent's concerns, our resources and manpower are such that prioritization is necessary in deciding which cases to accept for investigation. Based upon the information furnished by Mr. Gentile to date, there is no indication that his circumstances meet the level necessary for investigation. Since civil remedies are available to Mr. Gentile, he may wish to contact an attorney of his choice for legal guidance, if he has not already done so."

Dwight Peterson's presumption of FBI indifference was vindicated.

Imagine, if you will, that you return home and recognize a neighbor running out of your house with your money and jewelry. You call the sheriff or police. You are told: "We're not investigating burglaries or break-ins unless more than ten thousand dollars was stolen. Since you saw the face of the burglar, we recommend that you file a civil suit against him."

President Theodore Roosevelt said a mouthful when he stated, "Speak softly, but carry a big stick." The FBI speaks softly but carries no stick. Remember that the next time you see the FBI copyright warning on a videotape or DVD.

Be that as it may, my action at the very least put Loyst and Gilliam on notice that I was serious about protecting my copyrights.

Gilliam responded to me by writing, "I will remove the offending photos from all future editions of *Mixed Gas*. I will also delete all references to you and your books. I will do the same for the revision to *Deep Diving* which is now ongoing and will be released in early 1994. I will publish no more articles or features that refer to you in any way."

To remove my photos and references from *Mixed Gas Diving* would have meant completely rewriting and retypesetting the book. In the event, this threat proved impotent because *Mixed Gas Diving* did not see a revised edition.

This sordid affair explains Gilliam's intimate knowledge of the *Ultimate Wreck Diving Guide*, as well as his antipathy toward me. He was not so much *for* Chatterton as he was *against* me. He simply used the Chatterton interview as a vehicle to verbalize his stewing hatred for me - this despite his promise not to refer to me in any way in future articles or features.

Kill the Messenger

Some Internet posters who read, or who claimed to have read, *SDX* did not like being disabused of the dribble that *Shadow Divers* publicized as truth. Instead of checking my sources and researching the obvious historical inaccuracies that ran rampant throughout *Shadow Divers*, they blamed me for bringing the obvious fabrications to their attention. Here are some of their various and sundry justifications for maligning *SDX*.

The most oft posted negative criticism was that *SDX* was a case of "sour grapes." A bunch of other agitators then picked the phrase off the chat room vine and spit similar seeds into their invective. Sour grapes about what? I had no stake in the *U-869*. I did not claim to have discovered or identified the wreck.

If these ranters had actually read *SDX*, they would have known that I had no personal motive for writing the book. I didn't even *want* to write the book. In the Introduction, I explained that the diving community was up in arms about the pure fictions and gross embellishments that were replete in the pages of *Shadow Divers*. Some of these divers actually did the things that Chatterton and Kohler took credit for. It was this latter group of divers who pleaded with me to set the record straight.

All my life I have stuck up for the underdog. Because these particular underdogs were my close friends and peers, it didn't take much pleading for me champion their cause.

I knew that I was going to suffer unearned abuse for writing *SDX*. But the truth had to be told, and the book had to be written. Throughout my life I have been not only a writer of books but a righter of wrongs. Galileo was persecuted for speaking the truth, and other people were burned at the stake, but we live in a free country in which the truth cannot be treated in such a lethal manner. Today we have a different way to crucify heretics: the Internet.

Let's examine the ridicule and illogical fallacies that

have been heaped upon me for being the bringer of bad news.

Disaffected Cyber Critics
To paraphrase George Bernard Shaw: "Those who can, do. Those who can't, post."

"L. Haskell" wrote, "This book is not worth the effort." Whose effort?

"C. Engler" thought that *SDX* was "much like a first grader telling on a classmate." I wonder if he thinks the same about a witness who takes the stand and swears an oath to tell the truth about a person who is accused of misdoing. *SDX* was not a tattletale; it was a correction of falsehoods and overstatements.

"PS" wrote, "Gary Gentile cries on page 17 on what a better author he is, with 30 written shipwreck books and that is supposed to make him a better author." "PS" is deliberately mistaken. Nowhere in *SDX* did I write that I was a better author than Robert Kurson. I stated that I had more of a professional background in diving and shipwreck history than Kurson. I possessed research credentials that Kurson sadly lacked. This made me a more experienced historian and shipwreck researcher, and better acquainted with the facts.

Several cyber critics claimed that *SDX* was boring, one going so far as to compare the book with a scene from *Shadow Divers* in which Kurson made "going out for pizza exciting." Kurson made the pizza scene exciting by knitting it from whole cloth. Chatterton and Kohler *never* got together after work in the evening to discuss the *U-Who?* in a pizza shop: they lived an hour and a half away from each other, not around the block as Kurson implied.

Any time his fictional story sagged, Kurson spiced it up by making up scenes and incidents that never happened. I was constrained by the bald facts because I was writing a history book.

"Paul Ketseas" thought that my "frequent jabs toward the German people were distasteful and betrays a complete lack of understanding of the controlling dynamics and propaganda employed by the ruling Party of the era." Because he neglected to annotate any pages on which these putative jabs occurred, his accusation cannot be confirmed without rereading the entire book. I suspect that "Paul Ketseas" misread "Nazis" or the Nazi regime in Germany as "the German people," perhaps because of his insecurities about the subject matter: he may have a German heritage and therefore identifies himself with the German people. I certainly did take jabs at the Nazis – the greatest mass murderers in the history of the world – and I make no bones about having done so.

One anonymous poster admonished me by exclaiming that I should have written sooner about the *U-869*: "So what does he do? He writes a book on wilderness canoeing." At first blush this comment appears to be merely stupid, but let's analyze it in depth.

I started writing fulltime in 1979. Between then and 2005 I wrote forty books, with *Wilderness Canoeing: the Adventure and the Art* being my fortieth. Thus in twenty-six years of professional writing, I completed a book on the average of every 7.8 months: approximately one and a half books per year.

What exactly is this anonymous poster suggesting? That I should not have written *Wilderness Canoeing* at all? That I should have written about the *U-869* eight months before I wrote *Wilderness Canoeing*? That I should have written about the *U-869* as soon Mark McKellar identified it in 1993? Let's treat these possible implications one at a time.

The subject matter of *Wilderness Canoeing* far exceeds in adventure and excitement the discovery of yet another U-boat – one of seven that had been found in an eight-year period. Just because this anonymous poster is not interested in wilderness canoeing does not invalidate the book. Is he so selfish and self-indulgent that he believes that I should write about only those subjects that are of interest him, and him alone? *Wilderness Canoeing* appeals to a huge contingent of canoeists: a group of people who are much more active in canoeing than most cyber divers are in diving.

This anonymous poster was obviously ignorant of the fact that I *had* written about the *U-869*. I wrote an entire chapter about the wreck in *Shipwrecks of New Jersey: Central*, which was published in 2001 (before the appearance of *Shadow Divers*). Quite frankly, a chapter was all the subject matter was worth. The only way that Kurson could make a book out of an otherwise article-length topic was by padding it extensively with fictitious events and fake characterizations.

Why doesn't this anonymous poster castigate Kurson for writing two books about the Three Stooges (his only previously published books) before he wrote *Shadow Divers* eleven years after McKellar identified it?

I discovered four U-boats, but didn't write a book about any of them. Instead, I wrote a book about a U-boat that Bill Nagle discovered and that Mark McKellar identified.

In summation, this poster's comment is totally illogical and makes no sense on any level.

"Dean810" wrote, "Gentile goes so far as to accuse the reader who does not end up sharing his views as having a personality disorder." This is a lie; I made no such statement. It is worth noting, however, that to a psychiatrist, a person who cannot distinguish fantasy from reality, or one who chooses to ignore reality in favor of fantasy, suffers from a mental aberration – autism for example.

According to "Mike S", someone put a Trojan virus on my website that would transfer to visitors. I was never aware of it, so either it was a glitch in his computer, something that appeared on the Internet irrelevant of my website, or someone hacked into my website in a failed attempt to disable it or to punish visitors for contacting me.

Grudging Concessions

Some readers grudgingly conceded that *SDX* did indeed address mistakes that were made in *Shadow Divers*, but made light of those corrections.

"Brian J. Kirkwood" wrote, "He brings out a few interesting points and good facts(i have no reason to doubt his findings and research)but he seems to be more inline to get some revenge on Chatterton and Kohler here." The only revenge I wanted was on the fictions that they concocted.

"CC Ibsen" wrote, "Most of the points he brings up are, at best, minor details and some of the discrepancies [sic] are simply different recollections of stressful matters."

Steve McDougall's videotape footage was not a "different recollection." Videotape does not lie.

"Ben B" wrote, "In summation, there is really no new information worth mentioning from the original book, possibly a minor correction of an event, or a difference of opinion on a certain item from another." *SDX* contained literally thousands of undeniable facts, most of which were of major importance and all of which were fully documented and supported. I expressed no opinions.

These postings are so vague and incomprehensible that it does not seem possible that these cyber critics actually read *SDX*. They may have been shills acting in behalf of the authors.

"Patrick Heraghty" did not "dispute any of the facts," yet he had a bone to pick that was irrelevant to *SDX*. He had never researched a shipwreck, so he contacted me about a wreck that I covered in my Popular Dive Guide Series, asking for a list of sources so he could delve farther into the history of the wreck. I told him that I did not have a "list" as such because all my sources were primary archival documents straight from the National Archives. Apparently, he thought that I wrote my books the way a high school student writes an essay or term paper: by appending a list of books, articles, and other secondary sources from which the information was copied. The books in the Popular Dive Guide Series were written for the general public: readers for whom the origination of the facts is unimportant.

SDX in Retrospect

Because "Patrick Heraghty" didn't like my answer, he ridiculed *SDX* by claiming that I did not annotate my sources. In reality, *SDX* is thoroughly documented and supported, either by reference to archival documents or by the testimony of witnesses whose names I provided. *SDX* was a different kind of book that required supporting documentation, in order to contradict the unsupported bunkum in *Shadow Divers*.

In short, "Patrick Heraghty" applied what he didn't like about my Popular Dive Guide Series to *SDX*, so he could have justification for maligning it:, despite the fact that he couldn't disprove anything in my books.

The above cited cyber critics must have turned a blind eye toward the truth. The only "minor" mistakes and errors that I indicated in *SDX* were appropriately grouped in the fifth and final Appendix, which was called "Niggling Inaccuracies and Misconceptions." *Shadow Divers* contained not just scores, but hundreds of items that fell into those categories.

Most of *SDX* covered distortions of major significance: gross exaggerations and obviously fictitious events that were portrayed in *Shadow Divers* as actual occurrences.

One anonymous cyber critic objected to the way I advertised *SDX* with the sentence, "Now, for the first time, the real saga of the *U-869* can be told in full." He wanted to know why the "real saga" could not be told until "now." The answer was obvious to anyone who read *SDX*: because the "real saga" wasn't known "in full" until Harold Moyers' archival research unearthed the true circumstances surrounding the U-boat's loss. Neither Chatterton nor Kohler found the supporting documentation; instead, they invented a make-believe story to account for the presence and condition of the wreck. They presented wild and unsupportable speculation that fooled much of the public into believing that the so-called "detectives" were experts and based their conclusions on evidence that was found at the scene.

Fat, Dumb, and Happy

Some people did not want to be confused by the facts; they wanted to be entertained by fables.

"Blondie59" wrote, "Kurson's book Shadow Diver's was much better written and a more enjoyable read that actually developed and told a story, whether the two protagonists exaggerated their exploits or not. The fact was, I read Shadow Divers to hear the story of the history and discovery of the U-869, what she's like now, what the diver's saw, etc. I don't give a rip about who performed CPR on who or who performed the primary research at the Naval Archives or who created the gate idea on the Andrea Doria."

Shadow Divers would have been just as exciting if it had given credit to Tom Packer for performing CPR on Chris Rouse, instead of giving the credit to Chatterton. But then, if the authors had told the truth, Packer's dedication would have detracted from the book's mock heroism.

"Papa Charlie 'Pete'" wrote, "Even if Shadow Divers is as inaccurate as the author says, it was a GREAT read. . . . I have no reason to question the authenticity of the facts he presents, but after pages of his verbal assaults on and disparging [sic] references to various people, I really didn't care WHAT the facts were."

"O. Krag" wrote, "The book is way too expensive. . he critiques 'Shadow Divers' as an expert, but the writing is boring, and who cares. 'Shadow Divers' was a fun read."

"Colliam7" wrote, "I don't know (and don't care) which account, if either, is 'true'."

I suppose these cyber critics would be just as blindly gladsome if Chatterton and Kohler told them in their *Titanic* episode that the reason for the liner's collision was that Captain Smith had to leave port early because she was docked at a pier that was equipped with parking meters, and he had run out of dimes.

The fact of the matter is that some people are comforted by lies and would rather not know the truth. Or, if they know the truth, would rather not accept it so they can continue to live in their fantasy world. Like Peter Pan, these people are afraid to grow up, because then they would have to face the world the way it really is.

As L. Sprague de Camp wrote in *Lovecraft: a Biography*, "The public will pay vast sums to be bunked but practically nothing to be debunked."

Cavilers

Some cyber critics totally ignored the paramount issues that constituted the bulk of *SDX*, and instead raised trivial objections which were incidental to the theme of the book.

"Cameron Williams" wrote, "The appendix detailing "niggling inaccuracies" is just embarassing [sic]. Does anyone really care if it's grapple or grapnel, or if Kurson uses "man" instead of "diver" or "person"?"

If the only blunder in *Shadow Divers* was the misuse of a single word, this would be a fair aspersion. But my mention of this misapplication was twofold. First, incorrect usage contradicts the book's contention that Chatterton and Kohler were experts in the fields of diving and shipwrecks, else they would not have made such a simple and stupid mistake. Second, this instance was only one of a large number of similar misusages, the cumulative effect of which must be taken as an aggregate that further establishes their ignorance. "Cameron Williams" mentioned only one niggling inaccuracy, while the appendix was chock full of them.

Another poster parroted the "niggling inaccuracies" comment of "Cameron Williams," and argued that *SDX* insinuated that *everything* that Chatterton and Kohler did was sloppy. *SDX* made no insinuations; it stated facts. If this anonymous poster inferred that everything that the dynamic duo did was sloppy, then the facts are what led him to reach such a conclusion. Far be it for me to contradict an accurate inference.

Factual errors and mistaken conclusions run rampant throughout *Shadow Divers* and episodes of *Deep Sea Detectives*. *SDX* did not make those errors or reach those conclusions; it merely pointed them out to my faithful readers.

In this regard, it is enlightening to note a comment made by Vinnie Kralyevich, the producer of *Deep Sea Detectives*. On November 8, 2008, he gave a presentation at Metro West Dive Club's annual symposium called Wrecks, during which he frankly admitted to the audience that the television show was largely contrived, both to appease television executives and to create audience appeal. Lest there be any misunderstanding, he used the word in context with the meaning "to invent or fabricate, especially by improvisation; to plan with evil intent; scheme." Kralyevich made no bones about the fictional intent and content of the show.

As for the second part of the "Cameron Williams" posting, I do not expect everyone to find sexist attitudes objectionable. In a free democratic country, both Kurson and "Cameron Williams" are entitled to discriminate against women, just as I am entitled to call attention to their caveman attitudes.

A poster who signed himself as "David" also called attention to me as "a nitpicker for accuracy," then added, "Gary also rubbed the author of Deep Descent . . . the wrong way . . . as Gary charged the author for interviewing him!"

"David" is obviously unaware that consulting work is an ordinary part of my business. I have been researching shipwrecks for more than thirty-five years. I possess an enormous collection of shipwreck information, not only as a result of primary research but from personal experience in diving on wrecks around the world. As a result, I am besieged with phone calls from reporters who want facts or opinions about shipwrecks and/or about diving on them. I have granted as many as three interviews in a single day.

I have done consulting work for newspapers, magazines, television, the movie industry, treasure salvors, and individuals. I charge hourly and daily rates for conducting historical research and artifact appraisals. I have served as an expert witness in a number of civil suits involving injury or death in the underwater environment. Once I served as Special Master to the Court in a federal case involving the *Brother Jonathan.*

Kevin McMurray, author of *Deep Descent*, must not have been rubbed too far the wrong way, for he consulted with me again for a subsequent book, *Dark Descent.* I have provided background information to many other authors. Usually my work goes uncredited, but that is the nature of the business. A consultant generally works behind the scenes.

"JFM" wrote, "He at times takes to attacking minor generalities. For example, he attacks a narrator in a tv program for saying "fifty years ago ..." when in reality it was 48 years."

The instance in question was in an episode of *Deep-Sea Detectives* in which Chatterton told the viewers that the *Andrea Doria* sank fifty years before the broadcast date of 2004. Simple calculation therefore gives the year of the *Doria's* loss as 1954, when in fact she sank in 1956. This is misleading to viewers who don't know any better.

This inaccuracy does not stand alone. "JFM" plucked it out of a large number of errors of fact and perception that I annotated in *SDX*. Factual distortions, inattention to detail, and a cavalier attitude of "Who cares anyway?" permeated the television series. The series operated on the vanity that they could force-feed the viewer with fallacies and sophisms, as long as the show was entertaining. They expected the viewer to swallow it wholesale and go away happy. This conceit was conspicuous in every episode I saw.

History is set in time. It cannot be rounded off. Chatterton did not say "nearly fifty years" or "almost fifty years." He said "fifty years." I submit that if Chatterton had taken an arithmetic quiz in grade school, had been asked to subtract 1,956 from 2,004, and had given his answer as 50, the teacher would have marked him wrong.

This was only one of a plethora of generalizations that the so-called detectives fobbed off as history.

The Bitter Truth

The above-mentioned cyber critics assassinated my character, disparaged *SDX* without just cause or supporting documentation, blamed me for bursting their bubble of a fool's paradise, used it as a pretext to ventilate personal grudges, or made inane comments that were either highly opinionated or not founded on evidence. But, there is one thing that none of them ever did . . .

No one – not a single person – furnished counterevidence of any kind that would tend to dispute the case of *SDX* against *Shadow Divers*. No one even *attempted* to do so, or suggested that such counterevidence might exist. These avoidance maneuvers – these failures to address the actual issues at stake – speak volumes.

These circuitous critiques were as empty-headed and lacking in substance as *Shadow Divers*. These artless cyber critics attacked my person, my motives, my writing style – but they never attacked my facts.

The general consensus of disparagement appears to be one of discontent, perhaps even hatred, over the fact that *SDX* annihilated their fairyland image of *Shadow Divers* and the book's mythological heroes.

First Blood

Complaints were lodged against *Shadow Divers* long before the publication of *SDX*.

The first person to offer first-hand criticism was John Yurga. He was a central figure in *Shadow Divers*, having been on the so-called "discovery" dive and having accompanied Chatterton to Germany shortly afterward. I interviewed Yurga at length about his participation in subsequent events and about the way those events were related in *Shadow Divers*.

Yurga told me that Kurson asked him to proofread the manuscript of *Shadow Divers*. Yurga annotated the manuscript every time he read something that was wrong, misleading, or fictitious. By the time he was done, the manuscript was so marked up that it was barely legible. There was hardly a page that was not covered with redlines, corrections, and long annotations.

Kurson ignored all of Yurga's objections, claiming that he was trying to tell a story that was both exciting and vividly portrayed. He altered facts for dramatic presentation. Yurga threw up his hands in disgust at such a perversion of actual events.

Gary Gilligan cornered Kohler at a dive symposium, and asked him why he wrote that he (Kohler) had recovered the "Closed for Inventory" sign that the *Seeker's* gatekeepers had hung on the gate across the *Andrea Doria's* Second Class Dining Room, when he (Kohler) knew that Gilligan and I had recovered the sign. Kohler admitted the truth in private, but explained it away by claiming that "they" (Chatterton, Kohler, and Kurson) sacrificed facts in order to tell a dramatic story.

Soon after the appearance of *Shadow Divers*, Robert Louis Stevenson III wrote a scathing critique about an event in which he participated, and which *Shadow Divers* grossly misrepresented: "I was one of the divers who searched for Steve Feldman on the recovery mission Steve Bielenda organized in 1991. In Robert Kurson's *Shadow Divers* you will see this recovery mission portrayed as a thinly veiled attempt to 'claim jump' the *U-869*. This assertion is only one of Kurson's many errors of fact.

"In the several hours it took to reach the *U-869* aboard the *Eagle's Nest* that astringently cool morning, nobody talked about going inside the wreck to recover china. What we talked about, mainly, were the conditions we might encounter on the wreck and the various ways of pulling off an effective search. A month had passed since Feldman's death, and the currents over the wreck were reportedly strong. We all knew that our chances of recovering Feldman were slim. Yet, the night before, I had received a call from a friend, a former Special Forces Combat Swimmer who now specializes in search and recovery. 'A drowning victim's lungs will often fill with water and weigh the body down,' he had told me. 'If that happened to Feldman, he'll still be near the U-boat, despite the current.'

"Aboard the *Eagle's Nest*, Bielenda assigned each dive team a quadrant to search. These quadrants lay outside the wreck. Hank Garvin and I made the first dive and set the hook, lifting it off the sand at 230 feet and shackling it to the pressure hull forward of the hole where the conning tower had stood. In the grey light we swam thirty feet beyond the starboard hull and began our partial circumnavigation of the wreck. We moved forward, not examining the U-Boat, as we were tempted to do, but keeping our vision focused on the outlying sand. We rounded the bow and searched a short section along the port hull. Then, low on air and having found no trace of Feldman, we headed up the anchor line. Back on board the *Eagle's Nest*, we were debriefed to insure that the next dive team covered new territory. This debriefing was captured on videotape. In successive debriefings not a single diver said anything about venturing inside the *U-869*. What they said was that all ambient light around the wreck had disappeared, making a dangerous search even more difficult in dark water.

"After the dive, I wanted nothing more to do with the *U-869*, well aware, as we all were, of the frightful desecration taking place inside another German submarine, the *U-853*. No bone left unturned there. I felt at the time, as I feel today, that the *Seeker's* claim to the *U-869* was morally indefensible. As with the *Titanic*, *Lusitania*, *Empress of Ireland*, *U-853*, and other shipwrecks where loss of life has been vast and catastrophic and where the wrecks themselves serve as tombs that should not be disturbed for any reason, the *U-869* belongs only to the dead.

"The motivation behind this recovery mission was to provide solace to Feldman's family, who dearly wanted his body back. What kind of person would quarrel with that? That this humane effort aroused such ire among the *Seeker's* crew proves only how easy it is, for even brave and honorable men, to succumb to the twin seductions of glory and loot – a complex truth Kurson misses."

The Myth Buster

After the publication of *SDX*, one person who was appalled by the falsities on which *Shadow Divers* was based, was Mike de Camp. He was in a position to know the truth because he has been an active wreck-diver since the 1960's. De Camp called Kurson on the telephone and berated him for the nonsense that he wrote in his book. Instead of arguing in his defense, Kurson hung up on him.

A few minutes later, de Camp received a phone call from Chatterton. Kurson had called him and told him about de Camp's irate accusations. Chatterton did not defend *Shadow Divers* either. Instead, he told de Camp that "those guys" were jealous. He did not define "those guys," but I presume that he meant those who had taken a stance in telling the truth about events that were falsely described in *Shadow Divers*, and who had performed the actions for which Chatterton and Kohler took credit.

"Those guys" includes primarily Harold Moyers (who located the attack report which recounted the circumstances surrounding the incident in which the U.S. destroyer escorts *Howard D. Crow* and *Koiner* dropped hedgehogs and depth charges on a German U-boat), and this author.

Chatterton was wrong. No one in the wreck-diving community coveted Chatterton's ill-gotten reputation as a promulgator of lies, deceits, and twisters of truth. "Those guys" merely wanted to set the record straight so that future generations would not be misguided by the fictional events that were recounted in *Shadow Divers*.

Another Myth Busted

When *Deep Sea Detectives* aired its *Andrea Doria* episode in 2004, Chatterton told an innocent audience that Carrie Bisetti "just became the thirteenth woman to dive on the *Andrea Doria*." I noted in *SDX* that the thirty-seventh woman would have been closer to the truth. I hit closer to the head of the nail than I realized.

Since I brought this considerable underestimation to the attention of the world, the diving community took it upon itself to ascertain the truth that contradicted Chatterton's false statement. After an initial list was compiled offline, the list was circulated via e-mail to people who might know other women who had taken the deep plunge to the Grand Dame of the Sea. The list grew until the number reached its current total of forty-one (although one woman, Marcie Bilinski, did not dive on the *Doria* until after the show was broadcast). The list may not yet be complete.

Chatterton has remained mute on this point, but Kohler apologized to the diving community in Chatterton's behalf. At first blush it seems that at least one of them was willing to admit culpability in light of a public outcry for correction. Yet Kohler's wording absolved himself from blame, and placed the burden of guilt solely on Chatterton. Nice cop-out.

The Adult Pacifier

One person who took exception to *Deep Sea Detectives* was "2_dive_4@cox.net", who signed his messages as "Brent." He was a sailor who had spent twenty years in the Navy. His service at sea lent credibility to his comments. He shared his disappointment with Chatterton "when you tried to describe how men 'had to endure the stench' inside a submarine. Do you not think there may be folks out there with some better information? As a submariner I can tell you first hand that any smell inside a submarine builds up slowly, more slowly so than does the human nose perceive the change, so much so that only when the boat ventilates do you even sense 'fresh air.' I consider this a basic fact that your show seems rife with missing and reporting wrong and in some sensational way to make the story better. . . . Is it entertainment or education that you are after? I . . . cannot understand how a minimally-repudiated educational channel would so carelessly engender its viewing public with stupidity. My only recommendation is to stick to the facts and let them speak for themselves. Not popular opinion or the most sensational segue to a good story, but fact."

Chatterton's reply: "We try to put the shows we do into a mystery format, and some fit better than others. If there is no inherent mystery, then we try to reveal the story in a mysterious way."

When "Brent" viewed the episode about the scuttling of the interned German fleet at Scapa Flow, he wrote, "Your show has the word detectives in it, but I remember, I think from 7th grade history, nearly all the conclusions you spent an hour on TV declaring you discovered. And that was 25 years ago."

"Brent's" declaration adds yet another corroboration to the point that I made in *SDX*: that when Chatterton and Kohler presented their so-called findings to the viewing public, they took credit for reaching conclusions that had been reached long ago by their predecessors.

The Real-life Detective?

Linda Riley wrote an article about me and my underwater exploits in the Winter 1994 issue of *A to Z*, the quarterly journal of the Zoological Society of Philadelphia and the Thomas H. Kean New Jersey State Aquarium in Camden. Her description of me, and the title of the article, was "Detective of the Deep." I wonder if that was where they got the idea and title for *Deep Sea Detectives*.

Other Experts Speak out

Kimm Stabelfeldt had a background that enabled him to spot a serious distortion in *Shadow Divers*. After reading *SDX*, he wrote to me, "One thing jumped out to me was your input on John's military experience, as an ex-Army Platoon Sergeant E-7 in charge of 42 men myself. When I first read *Shadow Divers* I was surprised by John always being in front of his patrols. I have talked with John a number of times over the last year or so and like me he does not talk bout his service experience but once he found out my rank, he went to great distance to not talk about it."

Captain Lewis E. Davis, Jr. was the commanding officer of the *Howard D. Crow* when she was recommissioned for the Korean War, on July 5, 1951. Thus he had a strong interest in his vessel's war record. He read *Shadow Divers*, *SDX*, and Harold Moyers' analysis of the circumstances leading to the loss of the *U-869*.

Chatterton, Kohler, and *Shadow Divers* have consistently ignored the presence of a damage hole over the aft torpedo room. Davis assessed this hole as a result of "*Crow's* hedgehog attack."

Against overwhelming evidence to the contrary, the so-called detectives claim that the *U-869* sank as a result of her own circling torpedo. Almost no one else believes this to have been the case. In *SDX*, I went to great lengths to explain how this was impossible for the *U-869* given the condition of the wreck.

Davis wrote to me to present additional insights that were based upon his vast naval experience. "Following the hedgehog attack at 1653 hours and the follow-up depth charge attack at 1717 hours, *Crow's* target was described as moving 'slowly.' This apparent movement is more acceptable as mis-interpretation and translation of the effect of set and drift on *Crow*, i.e., current and wind, as the vessel maneuvered to hold contact. The ship's DIRT plotter accepts no other input than own ship's course and speed. Anchored to the bottom of the sea, *U-869* could not possibly be underway in these circumstances. Currents about *U-869* sunken position were frequently mentioned as impediments to the divers efforts while investigating the wreck site.

"Immediately following 1653 hours there are indications that the German crewmen were attempting to escape. At some point in time a depth charge laid alongside destroyed the remaining watertight integrity of the boat and dooming its crew.

"There are a number of clues that point to attempts to abandon *U-869* by crewmen. The first of these is the discovery of at least two open hatches by the divers, one the torpedo loading hatch in the forward torpedo room, and the second abaft the conning tower position over the engine room. This hatch provided access to the anti-aircraft gun aft by gunners. These hatches had to be opened by human hands following procedures to purposely flood the boat to equalize sea pressure so that the hatches could be opened. Diver Kohler describes an escape trunk blocking access to the motor through the engine room. This would be the escape trunk associated with the hatch used to access the anti-aircraft gun station aft of the conning tower position.

"American submarines had such an escape system wherein an escape trunk was lowered to near deck level, and the compartment purposely flooded to equalize the pressure in the boat to that of the sea. Crewmen used escape lungs, ducking under the trunk below the water level, to access the hatch now opened by a crewman.

"During WW II, USS *Tang* torpedoed itself while on the surface during an attack on a Japanese convoy. The boat bottomed quickly. Using the above procedure, surviving crewmen escaped to the surface but few were rescued. These procedures are limited by depth and attending problems while surfacing. This escape system to be used at shallow depths were known to submarine builders prior to the war. That *U-869* had a similar system can be verified by an inspection of *U-505*, also a Type IXC submarine.

"The population of many human remains found in the forward compartments of *U-869* also suggests that crewmen were mustered for a purpose. Rescue lungs were found among the debris. Had any crewmen escaped *U-869*, the perils of rising from an extreme depth 230 feet by free ascent without decompression into darkness on the surface precluded little chance of being rescued alive. But there was little choice.

"The finding of the conning tower abreast of the control room is suspect. Had *U-869* torpedoed itself, as some ordnance experts suggested lacking any other information, the vessel had to have way-on to maintain trim, if submerged, and usually with way-on when surfaced, when torpedoes are fired. Had the torpedo struck *U-869* as [*Shadow Divers*] envisioned, the debris field would have been aft of the boat's final resting place. After 50 years, a rusted and weakened conning tower structure could have been pulled off by draggers fishing the bottom, or currents, in time, to lay the structure alongside."

Davis' analysis corroborates that of Harold Moyers.

The Myth Purveyors Sing a Different Tune

In November 2006, when the Bay Area Divers held their annual dinner conference in Sandusky, Ohio, Erik Petkovic bought a booth at which to sell books that were related to the underwater realm. He used to sell *Shadow Divers* on his website (wreckdivingbooks.com), until he read *SDX*. He realized at once how much of a disservice *Shadow Divers* was to the public in general and to the diving community in particular. He immediately quit offering *Shadow Divers* for sale, and he informed his visitors and potential buyers why he had deleted the title from his assortment.

Chatterton and Kohler had a nearby booth. Several booths separated their booth from Petkovic's. According to Petkovic, they continually gave him "dirty looks." The reason was obvious: Petkovic had a complete set of my diving titles for sale, including *SDX*. In a strange bit of irony, people were buying *SDX* from Petkovic, and then showing it to other divers in front of the booth at which Chatterton and Kohler were selling their one and only book, *Shadow Divers*. Some people even asked Chatterton and Kohler to autograph *SDX*!

Maggie Bailey boldly asked Chatterton and Kohler if they had read *SDX*. Chatterton responded, "I have a copy but I haven't read it." Chatterton's statement is hard to believe but, given his established propensity for false pretense, it is in keeping with his character.

Kohler replied, "You can always tell a pioneer from the arrows in his back." Kohler's reply is doubly telling. First, it demonstrates his egotistical perception of himself as a trailblazer in a field in which he was very much a laggard and a latecomer (traits that I described in detail in *SDX*). He was certainly no technical diving advocate when the term came into general usage. He didn't even embrace the concept until long after others were breathing trimix on deep dives. Now he undoubtedly wishes the case were otherwise, and goes to great lengths to promote himself as a wreck-diving innovator, but it just isn't so (except in his mind).

Second, his comment was a direct quote from *SDX*. On page 130, I credited Mike Menduno with writing that sentence in an article in the first technical diving magazine, *AquaCorps: the Journal for Experienced Divers*, which Menduno started publishing in 1989. In *SDX*, I tried not to mention my contributions to the field unless they related directly to something in *Shadow Divers*. I did this so as to curb anticipated objections that *SDX* was a self-promotional scheme. Thus I left out many instances in which hostile or nonobjective readers might have misconstrued my priority, actual as it was, as a demonstration of vainglory. I kept myself as much as possible in the background of the controversy, and more in the vein of a disinterested historian.

In this regard, I refrained from mentioning in *SDX* that when Menduno wrote that sentence, he was referring to *me*. He was describing my groundbreaking dives on the *Monitor* and *Ostfriesland* – dives that I made in 1990, before the so-called "discovery" of the *U-Who?*. He wrote this biographical piece in the third issue of *Aqua-Corps*, dated Winter 1991. (See *Shipwreck Sagas* for a transcript of the interview that accompanied his summation of my achievements in the field of deep diving: achievements that preceded Chatterton's and Kohler's entry into technical diving.)

In adopting Menduno's sentiment for himself, Kohler was in essence identifying himself with me and my accomplishments – the same as he did in *Shadow Divers* when he took credit for recovering the "Closed for Inventory" sign that Gilligan and I recovered. Kohler's statement makes it seem as if he is suffering from a bizarre behavioral syndrome: a misidentity crisis, so to speak.

It is interesting to note that Menduno published his "pioneer" declaration long before Chatterton and Kohler contemplated diving on mixed-gas. Neither Menduno nor *AquaCorps* are mentioned in *Shadow Divers*, as if Chatterton and Kohler were unaware of their existence. This ignorance shows how far away from the field of technical diving they were at that time. Not only were they not pioneers, they didn't appear to know that thousands of divers were already employing technical diving techniques that Chatterton and Kohler claim to have invented.

Chatterton suffers from the same syndrome that Kohler suffers from. In a similar vein, he paraphrased one of my statements and took credit for coining a concept. In the Gilliam interview that is noted above, he said, "We used to say we would go to the *Andrea Doria* to tune up for diving in the Mud Hole. Conversely, when you were picking up a lot of dives in the Mud Hole, by the time you got to the *Andrea Doria*, you were ready to go."

Compare this with what I wrote in *Shipwrecks of New Jersey: North* (which was published in 2000): "If you can dive the *Choapa* you can dive the *Doria*. But just because you've dived the *Doria* doesn't mean you're ready for the *Choapa*."

Although Chatterton claimed not to have read *SDX*, subsequent admissions prove otherwise. Elsewhere in the Gilliam interview, Chatterton adjusted some of the *Shadow Divers* fabrications to reflect challenges that I made in *SDX*. For example, in *Shadow Divers*, everyone but Chatterton and Kohler hid in the cabin of the *Seeker* when the Rouses surfaced without decompressing; Chatterton and Kohler were alone in effecting their rescue. Now he said, "We put a man on either side of the ladder to help him and he said, 'I can't make my legs work.' We quite literally dragged him up." Chatterton then contradicted himself and fell back on his *Shadow Divers* exaggeration by claiming that he "basically did a fireman's carry."

In *Shadow Divers*, Chatterton sent Kohler for the "crash kit" to aid in treatment of the Rouses, then performed solo CPR. As far as I know, there is no such thing as a crash kit, and in my experience the *Seeker* never carried one. The author invented the item, perhaps because the alliteration sounded macho. In the interview, Gilliam suggested to Chatterton, "The only tools you had out there were oxygen and basic CPR." (No crash kit.) Strictly speaking, cardiopulmonary resuscitation is not a tool, but a method of treatment. Chatterton did not correct Gilliam's mistake, but replied, "We were doing CPR on him."

Now "we" were doing CPR instead of "I." In actual fact, Tom Packer performed solo CPR for an hour and a half, not Chatterton.

In *Shadow Divers*, the Coast Guard rescue swimmer tossed his medical bag into the water next to the *Seeker*, then jumped in after it and swam to the boat with the bag in tow. In the Gilliam interview, Chatterton recounted the event differently: "The Coast Guard swimmer comes down with the rescue basket." This was the way I described the incident in *SDX*, based upon the recollections of four other witnesses.

When Chatterton received a letter from British U-boat authority Robert Coppock, *Shadow Divers* implied that the letter was a reply to a query from Chatterton. In fact, the letter was addressed to Mark McKellar in response to *his* letter in which he *informed* Coppock about his discovery of Ultra decrypts that made it clear that the Tenth Fleet was tracking the *U-869* across the Atlantic Ocean, and dispatched a hunter-killer group to intercept it. Mark McKellar was never mentioned in *Shadow Divers*. Yet in response to a challenge that was posted by "tonka97," Chatterton admitted, "Bob Coppock sent me a copy of a letter to Mark McKellar."

Chatterton consistently claims – in *Shadow Divers* and in postings – that the U-Who? was not identified until he recovered the tag on August 31, 1997. Yet he sang a different tune in an interview on page 21 of

AquaCorps Number 9, which was published in January 1995. In answer to the question, "I understand you recently made a positive I.D. on the U-Who? That sounds exciting," Chatterton replied, "I believe we have positively identified the wreck as the *U-869*." Thus he claimed publicly that he knew the identity of the *U-869* (courtesy of McKellar's research) two and a half years before he recovered the tag that merely confirmed what he already knew.

A couple of paragraphs later, Chatterton said, "History isn't always what you've been told." That is a mouthful of prescience.

The fact that Chatterton continues to change his stories is proof that *Shadow Divers* was not a "true adventure" as the cover blurb claims, or as Chatterton and Kohler would like their readers to believe. If you are going to make false claims, you need to be consistent.

In the Gilliam interview, Chatterton alleges that Kurson told him, "Trust me. I can make this story a bestseller."

So Chatterton and Kohler cooked up a fantastic story, and Kurson overcooked it.

The Doubtful Redoubt

On page 194 of *Shadow Divers,* it was written that an anonymous "group of cutting-edge warm-water divers" introduced trimix to Chatterton. I commented on this on pages 129 and 130 of *SDX*. In order not to draw attention to myself, I declined to mention that when Chatterton took his mixed-gas diving course, my *Ultimate Wreck Diving Guide* was the only technical diving book on the market, and that instructors used it as a textbook.

Furthermore, *AquaCorps* had been published periodically since 1989. Yet *Shadow Divers* makes no mention of this seminal magazine that introduced the concepts of technical diving to the world.

Instead of acknowledging his roots, in *Shadow Divers* Chatterton makes it seem as if he invented technical diving all by himself. This attempt at misdirection might be overlooked by readers who have no background in scuba, but the diving community in general and the technical diving community in particular are eminently aware that such is not the case. It is just another concoction to patronize the public with placebos.

Imagery without Substance

In the April 2008 edition of *Northeast & Midwest Dive News*, Kohler placed an advertisement in which he claimed that he and his wife had "more than 40 years of diving experience and qualifications in technical diving, wreck diving and advanced rebreather diving."

One might ask: How did a person who was still in his forties derive such a fantastic amount of cumulative "experience and qualifications" in disciplines that usually required many years to attain? The answer is simple: creative addition.

In *Shadow Divers* he claimed that his father once took him underwater at the age of 9. Despite the fact that he didn't obtain a junior certification until the age of 15, didn't become trimix certified until the late 1990's, had been diving on a rebreather for only a year or two at the time he placed the ad, he took this sole shallow plunge as a starting point and added the five or so years since his wife earned her basic scuba certification.

Presto! Forty years of "technical diving, wreck diving and advanced rebreather diving."

If this new kind of math sounds somewhat shifty, or like arithmetical prestidigitation, perhaps that is because it is.

The Binnacle Caper

Joe Mazraati saw a side of Kohler that is cleverly hidden by Kohler's false persona and media hype. Mazraati discovered a compass binnacle lying loose on an unidentified shipwreck. On the boat after the dive, he announced what he had found and precisely where he had found it. According to the wreck-diver's unwritten code of ethics, Mazraati had dibs on the artifact because he was the finder. He followed the code by calling attention to his find, thus laying his claim to it.

Kohler pleaded with Mazraati to leave the binnacle alone so that Dan Crowell could videotape it in place. Mazraati could recover it later. Mazraati agreed. Kohler dived on the wreck shortly afterward, and recovered the binnacle without informing Crowell of the discovery.

Mazraati learned of Kohler's double-cross almost immediately, as he happened to see Kohler and the binnacle on the boat as it was returning to port from the offshore trip.

When I asked Kohler to confirm his recovery of this binnacle, he readily admitted to the deed, but would provide no additional details. I waited for him to mention that Mazraati had found the binnacle, but he did not. When I asked him pointblank what dive boat he was aboard, he refused to tell me. Instead, he said that he promised not to reveal the name of the boat in order to protect the identity of the skipper.

I already knew from Mazraati that the boat was the *Independence*, Captain Dan Bartone.

Politically Correct – the New Stance

In 2005, at the annual event of the Boston Sea Rovers, Chatterton and Kohler presented their version of the *U-869*. Afterward they solicited questions from the audience.

Peter Hess asked, "John, would you use your high profile status to speak out against current laws which would make it illegal today, to do what you did to identify the U-boat?"

Among others, Evelyn Dudas, Harold Moyers, Tom Packer, Pat Rooney, and Brad Sheard were flabbergasted by Chatterton's immediate reply: "Well, I guess if a law keeps wreck-divers from sucking the bones out of war graves, I think I'm in favor of a law like that."

Kohler added, "Yeah, imagine if Japanese tourists airlifted the bones from the USS *Arizona* so they could get a Navy dish."

Do What I Say, Not What I Do

John Yurga told me that during a visit to the museum at the Washington Navy Yard, Kohler stole a gauge that was not secured. Yurga had to shame Kohler into replacing it. Pat Rooney told me a similar story about Kohler's attempted theft of a chronometer from the museum ship *Olympia*.

According to an article that was posted on the Cyber Diver News Network (dated May 8, 2008), Kohler led an expedition on the dive boat *Trident* to the Gulf of Thailand for the express purpose of recovering artifacts from local shipwrecks. One of these wrecks was the *Tottori Maru*, a freighter that was operated by the Japanese Imperial Navy during World War Two. The *Tottori Maru* was known by Americans as the "Hell Ship," because she transported thousands of Allied prisoners of war to concentration camps, where most of them died in captivity. The Hell Ship was torpedoed by the U.S. submarine *Hammerhead* on May 15, 1945. No POW's were on board at the time of her loss.

The article reported that Kohler and his group had "taken numerous artifacts from the wreck, including one of the ship's telegraphs." I called Dan Bartone after reading the article. He was one of the divers on the trip. He confirmed that the group did indeed recover the telegraph. He also told me that they recovered so many other artifacts that they had to freight them home by ship at a cost of $600 per person. As far as he was concerned, the trip was unabashedly successful in achieving its goal.

The article then cited the opinion of self-styled Canadian archaeologist Rob Rondeau. He accused Kohler and the charter boat company that owned the *Trident* of "looting" shipwrecks.

Let's stop for a moment for clarification. I define a "shipwreck looter" as "someone who took something from a shipwreck that the accuser would have taken if he had gotten there first." Thus Kohler and his group were castigated as looters because they rescued relics that someone else wanted; or relics which, without their efforts, may have lain on the seabed and been lost forever.

Rondeau wanted the *Trident* company "investigated for looting and violating international maritime law." He accused the *Trident* of taking recreational divers to other wrecks as well, from which her tourists recovered numerous artifacts. It developed that Rondeau was planning an exploratory trip that was similar to the *Trident's*, for October of that year, the purpose being to locate "the wrecks of several Hell Ships in South East Asia." Rondeau earns his living by organizing so-called "archaeological expeditions." In this case the *Trident* pre-empted his search plans.

Rondeau's accusation was based upon the "law" that military vessels, warships, and "everything aboard the ship still belongs to its flag country." It is somewhat of a stretch to claim that the *Tottori Maru* fell into either of these categories. She was not a commissioned vessel, any more than was a Liberty ship that was chartered by the U.S. War Shipping Administration to deliver cargoes for the war effort.

These points are moot to the present discussion. It is not my purpose to make a case against Rondeau's self-serving allegations, and his misinterpretations of the terms of the International Law of the Sea Convention.

I am not concerned that Kohler recovered artifacts from abandoned shipwrecks. I am not even concerned that Kohler recovered artifacts from military vessels or warships. The U.S. law that forbids the disturbance of sunken vessels of war was wrongfully passed, and is therefore objectionable and invalid with respect to democratic principles.

I *am* concerned that Kohler has consistently taken artifacts from known warships, but takes the moral high ground by presenting a public persona that is not in keeping with his activities.

Kohler readily admits that he scavenged the German U-boat *U-869* for artifacts, especially those that were stamped with a Nazi emblem. He also admits to having removed artifacts from the U.S. destroyer *Murphy* after he learned the wreck's identity. He has consistently been taking artifacts from the armored cruiser *San Diego* since his very first dive on the wreck, in the 1980's.

Again, lest I be misunderstood, I am not lodging a complaint against these recoveries. To repeat, my complaint lies in the fact that in public he berates others who recover relics from warships, while he continues to do so himself. His public persona is one of political correctness, which contradicts his personal philosophy and activities. In public he presents an appearance of respectability, and always says what is politically correct.

Either Kohler should practice what he preaches, or he should stop preaching against his practices.

Revealing Statistics

A poll of the American public ascertained that in the previous year, only 3% of the people had so much as entered a bookstore to buy a book. Of those who did, only 2% had purchased more than one book during the entire year.

The current population of the United States is approximately 300 million people. If 3% of them purchased a single book in any given year, then they bought a total of 9 million books (presumably, 9 million different titles, as most people do not buy duplicates).

However, of those 300 million people who make up the population, 25% are children, 18% do not speak English, and 1% are illiterate. From these statistics I can infer that the book-buying public consists of approximately 56% of the population, or 168 million people, of which 3% equals 5,040,000 (5 million 40 thousand).

Corporate book sales are a closely guarded secret. In the Gilliam interview, Chatterton claimed that "somewhere just south of a million copies in hard bound and paperback" of *Shadow Divers* were sold. This figure amounts to one copy for every 300 people in the country (including children, illiterates, and those who do not speak, read, or write English). Viewed another way, of all the potential book buyers who bought a solitary book in the year following publication, approximately one out of five must have bought *Shadow Divers* (according to Chatterton's puffery).

This is remarkable. I won't state categorically that Chatterton was lying, but I believe that his estimate was "somewhere just south" of the truth. Not even the *Bible* sold as many copies as Chatterton claimed *Shadow Divers* sold.

A *Titanic* Sham

In the Gilliam interview that is noted above, Chatterton claimed, "Richie and I put together a project on the *Titanic*. We went out, we chartered the Russian support ship *Keldysh*, took the submersibles, we did the whole thing on our own dime, made our own preparations, and then went to The History Channel and sold it as the executive producers."

This statement is not entirely true. In fact, the expedition organizer and leader was Dave Concannon. Chatterton and Kohler were initially invited to tag along on an expedition that Concannon was putting together with Mike Harris, with whom he had worked on the 2000 salvage expedition to the *Titanic*. When the Harris expedition looked like it was not going to happen, Concannon pulled out. It was then that Chatterton asked Concannon if he could put together an expedition for a new production company that Chatterton and Kohler were putting together.

Concannon is an attorney and explorer who had already participated in several prior expeditions in various capacities. By 2005, Concannon had organized and led an expedition to Mt. Kilimanjaro, he had served as a legal and logistical advisor to two expeditions to Mt. Everest, and he had served as the General Counsel to The Explorers Club, X-Prize Foundation, and the Professional Shipwreck Explorers Association. More important, Concannon had already served as a legal and logistical advisor to six deep diving expeditions, including five *Titanic* expeditions and another expedition that had discovered the world's deepest wooden shipwreck, in the heart of the Bermuda Triangle. Concannon had participated in four of these expeditions, and he had already made three dives to explore a vast portion of the *Titanic* wreck site, and another record setting dive to a depth of 16,109 feet.

Organizing international expeditions of such great cost, complexity, and logistical magnitude was not an easy task, nor one to be taken lightly. An incredible amount of paperwork was involved. Because the support vessel *Keldysh* and the *Mir* submersibles were Russian owned, language difficulties were complicated by political considerations. But the primary ingredient necessary to organize these expeditions, particularly expeditions to the *Titanic*, was the existence of personal relationships. One does not simply call the Russian Academy of Sciences and hire the *Keldysh* and *Mir* submersibles. The Russians do not and will not work with just anyone. Instead, they will work only with a few select individuals they know and trust from prior expeditions. By 2005, Concannon had already spent months aboard the *Keldysh* and days in the *Mirs*. More importantly, he had developed close personal and professional relationships with the *Keldysh* and *Mir* crews, and within the Russian Academy of Sciences. This background experience made Concannon the prime candidate to lead the 2005 expedition, and to oversee onsite operations.

The primary goal of the 2005 expedition was to explore a new area of the *Titanic* wreck site that Concannon had discovered on his last dive in 2000, and to shoot high-definition footage of this previously unknown area of the wreck site. There is a common misconception that the *Titanic* wreck site has been thoroughly explored since the wreck's discovery in 1985. In fact, most expeditions to the wreck have focused on photographing and recovering artifacts from small areas surrounding the bow and stern sections.

There are vast areas of the wreck site, covering more than three square miles on the bottom, which have never been explored. This new area was located far to the south of what was previously believed to be the edge of the *Titanic* wreck site, and it held tantalizing clues to the ship's contents and final moments.

When the Harris expedition stumbled, Chatterton asked Concannon if they could put together their own expedition. Concannon agreed to organize and lead the expedition while Chatterton and Kohler would organize and produce a documentary of the expedition. For the next several months, Concannon organized the logistics of the expedition through his company, Explorer Consulting, LLC, while Chatterton and Kohler produced the documentary through their new company, On the Bottom Productions, which they established at a meeting in Concannon's office.

It was Concannon, not Chatterton and Kohler, who chartered the *Keldysh* and *Mirs*, and he was personally liable for the cost of the charter if the expedition fell through. It is true that Chatterton and Kohler paid for much of the expedition. However, some of the costs of the expedition, including Concannon's fees and expenses, were paid out of funds received from a corporate sponsor that Concannon brought in to defray the costs of the expedition. Concannon organized the same expedition he would have organized with Harris, and he was designated as the official expedition leader by both the Russians and On the Bottom Productions. Nothing much changed for Chatterton and Kohler. They simply joined an existing expedition that was already planned, but they were able to do more and stay on site longer because they had the *Keldysh* and *Mirs* at their complete disposal, rather than having to share them with the other participants in the Harris expedition.

Concannon told me that when Chatterton and Kohler boarded the *Keldysh*, they had a television episode already laid out, and they had already worked out a "hook" for the show: some new and incredible piece of evidence on which to focus their deductive powers. The so-called "detectives" already knew what they wanted their camera crew to videotape: pieces of the *Titanic's* double-bottom hull that lay in the debris field. The show would focus on investigating a "grounding theory" which had been postulated by two Titanic historians, David Brown and Parks Stephenson, in a white paper presented to the Marine Forensic Panel of the Society of Naval Architects and Marine Engineers, in 2001.

The theme of the show revolved around finding pieces of the *Titanic's* double-bottom hull in the new debris field that Concannon had discovered in 2000, and either proving or disproving the "grounding theory."

Concannon, who had seen what he described as "ribbons of steel" – that is, sections of the side plating from the *Titanic's* hull – in the debris field in 2000, was instructed to find and film sections of the *Titanic's* double-bottom hull in the new debris field on the expedition's first dive, so the investigation of the grounding theory, now dubbed "David Concannon's Grounding Theory," could proceed accordingly.

The problem was that Concannon had not seen pieces of the double-bottom hull in the limited area of the new debris field that he had stumbled onto in 2000; he had never heard of the grounding theory; and it was extremely unlikely that the expedition would discover the proverbial "needle in a haystack" in a new and unexplored area of unknown size.

Whether Concannon actually found pieces of the *Titanic's* double-bottom hull in the new debris field was not important to the outcome of the story for the "detectives," or for their reputations. If the double-bottom hull pieces were not present, Concannon's theory could be debunked by the "detectives" as just another wild goose chase. If the pieces were present, however, the "detectives" could investigate the hull sections and see where these clues led.

On the first dive of the expedition, Concannon led Chatterton back to a spot on the bottom that was well to the south of the commonly accepted edge of the *Titanic* wreck site. There, nearly one kilometer "off the grid" that surrounds the known area of the wreck site, lay a stream of *Titanic* artifacts and debris leading away from the wreck to the southwest. Concannon and Chatterton followed the trail of debris, which contained pieces of metal, numerous shoes, tile, plumbing, cooking utensils, and other light debris, until it petered out nearly two kilometers away from the southern edge of the wreck. Although the two divers had redrawn the map around the *Titanic* by a wide margin, they had not found pieces of the *Titanic's* double-bottom hull. Nor did they find the "ribbons of steel" that Concannon had seen on his previous dive. But this was not surprising, given that these side pieces were located farther to the north, and the *Mir* had traveled to the map coordinates that Concannon had recorded on his previous dive, using a path that was several hundred meters to the east of the path that Concannon had taken in 2000.

Despite finding and exploring a new area of the *Titanic* wreck site, Chatterton and Kohler's frustration at not having found pieces of the *Titanic's* double-bottom hull was profound. The script of their documentary, which was written around obtaining footage of these elusive hull pieces, would have to be rewritten in mid-expedition. Chatterton and Kohler were so frustrated that they pulled themselves out of the submersibles on the second dive day, and held closed-door meetings with the production staff, which continued throughout the day.

As they customarily did on all of their expeditions aboard the *Keldysh*, Concannon and Anatoly Sagalevitch, the designer of the *Mirs* and "Head of Expedition" for the Russians, met privately in the late afternoon to discuss the plans for the next day's dives. It was obvious to both men that the production crew was unhappy with not finding pieces of the double-bottom hull on the first day's dives. Both men knew there were large pieces of the *Titanic's* hull located just to the east of the propellers. Concannon had personally seen these hull pieces on a dive with Sagalevitch in 2000.

These hull pieces had been discovered at least as early as the Discovery Channel expedition to the *Titanic* in 1993, and possibly on the IMAX expedition in 1991. Both pieces were well known to the Russians, and they had been videotaped and side-scanned on several subsequent expeditions. In 1997, Susan Wels wrote a Time-Life book about the Discovery Channel expedition entitled, *Titanic: Legacy of the World's Greatest Ocean Liner*. The book included a site plan that clearly showed the hull pieces and their location in the debris field. Anyone can obtain a copy of her book to confirm this. Although Chatterton and Kohler are neither skilled researchers nor shipwreck experts, it would not have taken much asking around to learn about the existence of these hull pieces, even if they had not read the book. Any *Titanic* aficionado could have told them.

Although the existence of the hull pieces was well known, nobody had really studied them before. Consequently, Concannon and Sagalevitch decided to send the *Mir* submersibles to the east on the third and final dive day, so that Chatterton and Kohler could film and examine these sections of the hull. Maybe this would pacify them and save their show. Concannon discussed the plan with Bill Lange, a veteran of several *Titanic* expeditions, and who was on board to oversee filming with high-definition television equipment on loan from Woods Hole Oceanographic Institute. Lange agreed that the hull sections and area to the east held the most promise for additional exploration. The plan was then discussed with Chatterton and Kohler in a scene that was filmed for inclusion in the documentary.

On the third and final dive day, Chatterton and Kohler were taken directly to the spot that Sagalevitch had visited many times before, in order to film and examine the large hull pieces. These hull pieces were, in fact, large sections of the *Titanic's* double-bottom hull, nearly ninety feet in length. They were exactly what the "detectives" had hoped to find. Ironically, despite warnings from several veterans of earlier expeditions that the hull pieces were well known, Chatterton and Kohler later claimed on television, and in the publicity surrounding their show, to have discovered them.

It is difficult for a knowledgeable person to accept their on-screen tripe about "discovering" anything. The resulting television show was standard *Deep-Sea Detectives* fare: the premise of a mystery that they set out to solve, a couple of token dives to establish for the audience that they had actually visited the site, and a solution that they concocted after only a few minutes of observation.

As usual, the "detection" took place in a studio editing room, where the evidence was fabricated for viewer appeal.

When the broadcast was aired, Concannon was shocked to learn that he had been demoted from his role as Expedition Leader to a mere onlooker, and mischaracterized as a "Titanic enthusiast" in the description given to him on screen in the television program. Quite the contrary, he is not a "Titaniac" or "rivet counter," as armchair *Titanic* explorers are known among the veterans of *Titanic* expeditions. He was an experienced expedition specialist whose involvement in the *Titanic* was undertaken on a strictly professional basis.

Chatterton and Kohler took credit for Concannon's leadership, took credit for a discovery that had been made by others, and invented a storyline that was designed to bamboozle a naïve audience.

As long as Chatterton and Kohler continue to tell perpetrate hoaxes, I will continue to write exposés. This may very well become a full-time job.

Pièce de Résistance

In 1988, Bill Nagle took a boatload of divers to an offshore wreck site aboard the *Seeker*. After making two dives, everyone settled down for the long ride home.

Nagle took time to veer off the direct course to port in order to confirm a set of numbers that had been given to him by the Bogans: a family of head boat operators who had been running fishing charters since the 1930's. One of the Bogans had learned to dive, and had struck up a friendship with Nagle. He wanted to see for himself some of the wrecks that he had been fishing on for years. But the wreck that Nagle steered for this day was too deep for Bogan. The wreck lay in an area where the water was deeper than 200 feet. Bogan was not experienced enough to dive to such a depth, so he gave the numbers to Nagle to investigate some time when he found himself in the vicinity.

As Nagle cruised over the spot that was indicated by the loran numbers, a spike jumped up on the depth recorder. The wreck beneath the boat was large: a couple of hundred feet in length with a vertical profile of fifteen feet. Once again the Bogans had not let him down.

Nagle informed the divers about the newfound wreck. He asked if anyone was willing to make a bounce dive to check it out. Wreck-divers are always eager to explore a previously undived site. There is no telling what kind of wreck might be waiting at the bottom of the anchor line. But this time there was a problem. Everyone had already made two deep dives, so their tissues were still saturated with nitrogen. The surface interval after the previous dive was short. This meant that even on a bounce dive, one would incur a significant decompression penalty.

Those were the days when northeast wreck-divers had only air to breathe, and when the concept of accelerating decompression by breathing nitrox blends or oxygen had not yet been fully realized. Technical diving, as the innovation of breathing helium mixes and enriched air came to be called, was then in the developing stages.

There were only two volunteers who were willing to take the risk: Chuck Wine and Bart Malone.

The pair donned their gear and prepared for the plunge. They jumped over the side wearing double tanks. They descended the white nylon anchor line into the depths.

Malone had a low tolerance to nitrogen narcosis; he was particularly prone to getting narced at depths at which many divers barely felt the effects. At 150 feet he encountered a fishing net that was hung onto the wreck. Between the net and narcosis, he felt that he had gone far enough. He signaled to Wine that he was turning back.

Wine continued down the line. Gradually he saw the wreck come into view: much like a ghost that took on form from a wisp of smoke. By the time he alighted on the sandy seabed, his vision and his mind were blurred somewhat from narcosis. But he was not so narced that he didn't recognize the hull as that of a submarine. Nor was he so narced that he couldn't grab a couple of lobsters and put them into his mesh bag.

Wine *thought* that he had reached a depth of 245 feet. But those were the pre-digital days of analogue depth gauges that were prone to inaccuracy when their depth limitation was exceeded.

When Wine returned to the boat and told everyone what he had discovered, no one believed him. Gene Peterson was on the boat that day. He recalled, "Bart was narced and returned after running into a net at 150 feet, but Chuck kept going until he reached the wreck. He came up from the bounce dive declaring he had dived a sub. He recovered a couple lobsters and we on board considered his report incredulous thinking he was narced too. Nagle took him seriously and noted it. The rest of us just blew it off knowing that there were no submarines off the Jersey Coast except for the *S-5* and that was somewhere supposedly off Cape May."

Chuck Wine had dived into history: he became the first person to see the *U-869* since those dreadful days of World War Two.

The incident faded out of wreck-diving memory. Wine quit diving the following year, after a decade and a half of avid activity. He got divorced, moved away, found another occupation, suffered a serious bout with cancer, and lost contact with everyone in the diving community.

He resurfaced in March 2008, after an absence of nearly two decades, when he strolled into Gene Peterson's dive shop in Pleasantville, New Jersey. Wine and Peterson used to work together for Norm Lichtman at The Dive Shop of New Jersey, before Peterson had opened his own shop, Atlantic Divers. During their reunion, they reminisced about the old days. The dive on the submarine came up in conversation when Peterson told Wine about the controversy that *Shadow Divers* had created by making wild and wildly fictitious claims about the *U-869*.

I contacted Wine as soon as I heard that he was back in the fold. He and I had always been good friends. Malone and I had been dive masters for eleven years for The Dive Shop of New Jersey, when Wine worked there as a scuba instructor. After we caught up on current events, he repeated for me the details of that history-making dive on what turned out to be a German U-boat.

I then called Malone and confirmed the story from his side. All three of them – Chuck Wine, Bart Malone, and Gene Peterson – concurred in their recollection of the events of that historic day.

Peterson said, "I believe Chuck was the first one to dive the *U-869* and Bart the first to be narced over it."

The Real Deal

There is no need for additional evidence to prove that *Shadow Divers* was a humbug. The proof is overwhelming. But it is satisfying to add confirmation to my contention that Nagle got the location of the German U-boat from the Bogans, and not from a fictitious character named Skeets only days before the so-called discovery dive, as *Shadow Divers* wanted its ingenuous readers to believe.

When Nagle took the *Seeker* to the *U-869* in 1991, he wasn't going there to discover an undived wreck. He was going *back* to a site that he had visited three years earlier. That was why he could organize a trip to go specifically to that spot in 1991: he already knew the location, and he knew that a wreck was there. He also knew that it was a submarine. He just didn't know that it was a U-boat.

That was also why, when Nagle organized the trip, he could tell the customers how deep they should be prepared to dive.

The 1991 dive was not a discovery dive, but a confirmation dive. In the process of confirming that the wreck was indeed that of a submarine, the divers pooled their observations and were eventually able to determine that the submarine was German.

Dealing with Denial

As I demonstrated above, some people will believe anything from the ridiculous to the absurd. Instead of accepting the fully supported truth against unsupported lies, they rationalize a way to make falsification appear believable. These people are not to be blamed for their weakness, but pitied. These are the kind of people who believe that the *Apollo* Moon missions were faked, that alien abductions are real, that ghosts inhabit the netherworld, that it is possible to communicate with spirits on the "other side," and that trolls live under bridges (when in fact they live in caves).

Shadow Divers perpetrated the greatest literary hoax of the century, perhaps of the millennia, perhaps since Johann Gutenberg invented moveable type for his printing press. The *Shadow Divers* canard is even greater than Edgar Allen Poe's spurious newspaper story that came to be known as "The Balloon Hoax." In 1844, he wrote "Astounding News by Express" for *The New York Sun*, in which he claimed that a group of men had crossed the Atlantic Ocean in a balloon after a passage of seventy-five hours. He wrote it as truth to play on people's gullibility. That *Shadow Divers* played a similar gambit doesn't say much for the evolving sophistication of human intelligence in more than a hundred sixty years.

To a certain extent, gullibility is based on ignorance. But a person who later learns the truth, and still falls prey to his original gullibility, is far worse than simply credulous. Such a person is intentionally self-deluded. Such a person knowingly and willingly accepts quackery and imposture, perhaps even craves them, because the fantasies that he has chosen to believe are more satisfying to his nature than inescapable reality.

Shadow Divers preyed upon naive minds the way hallucinogenic drugs prey upon addicts who believe that drug-induced hallucinations are real. For a person who repudiates the existence that is perceived by his five natural senses, and who lives instead in an altered state of consciousness, his imaginary world replaces reality. When this fixation goes too far, the external world seems to lack materiality.

Spoon-fed Delusions

No matter how many copies of *Shadow Divers* were sold, no matter how many people were duped into believing the book's inventive elements, the fact remains that the facts remain. Flummery may change the perception of a devoted few, but it cannot change actuality. A person who believes that he can defy the law of gravity will nonetheless be killed when he hits the ground after leaping off a thousand-foot-high cliff.

Shadow Divers was rife with boastful exaggerations, theatrical embellishments, and unnecessary historical inaccuracies, many of which I addressed in my exposé so that the actual facts would be available to the public. Some witnesses were ignored altogether so that dissenting views of events did not contradict the self-glorifying plot. The testimony of others was altered, resulting in accounts that are at variance with the truth. *Shadow Divers* painted all divers as bickerers and subservient to its two chosen heroes. The exposé showed the teamwork and camaraderie that are essential facets of the technical diving community.

The egos of Chatterton and Kohler are nourished by the adulation of their sycophants, whose numbers are startlingly few: the couple of baker's dozens that are noted above. For every hate mail or bad review that *SDX* received, there were scores of people who sent thanks, commendations, and votes of confidence. *SDX* was not written for the vocal minority of Chatterton-Kohler sycophants, but for future generations who will not have been indoctrinated by fictitious accounts of mock-heroics.

Real heroes earn their reputations through their accomplishments, not through ambitious lies and deceit. Shameless hype and promotion through endless repetition may sell an unworthy product, like a patent medicine that consists of phony ingredients, but it cannot heal the sick or alter reality.

A lie is like a house of cards: only the barest puff of truth is needed to knock it down. Chatterton and Kohler have been silent about *SDX* because there is no defense against the truth. But the truth won't go away simply because they have ignored it. Witness the statements that I noted above, in which they have changed their stories to fit closer to the facts than the way the were represented in *Shadow Divers*.

The repetition of a lie may create an urban legend, but it can never change a lie to reality. Not matter how many times a lie is reiterated, it remains a lie that is defied by actual events.

The truth never changes. Facts are eternal. Reality is immutable.

The Final Word

Authors are always being asked to write blurbs and forewords for the books of other authors. I've done some myself (see *Shipwreck Sagas*). It goes with the job description. I could do no better than to end this chapter with the words of an author who wrote a blurb for *Shadow Divers*, then repented having done so after reading *SDX*:

> Dear Gary,
>   I suppose you think I'm the prize horse's ass.

Stupid me, I was suckered into the *Shadow Divers*, believing the hype the editor laid on me when asking for a quote. I thought it was pretty fantastic and unbelievable, but had no reason at that time to realize Chatterton and Kohler were the two blithering assholes on *Deep Sea Detectives*. God, I can't stand their BS and I only watch the program to see what ludicrous venture they're up to next. The last segment I watched on the lost tribes of the Dominican Republic was so idiotic words fail me. I should not bother to watch their antics since they send my blood pressure through the roof.

Anyway, please accept my apologies for my ignorance. I should have studied the book more carefully before I ran off half-cocked with a quote.

My compliments on *Shadow Divers Exposed*. You have done the diving world a true service.

All the best.
Your friend, I hope,
Clive Cussler

Books by the Author

The Popular Dive Guide Series
Shipwrecks of Massachusetts: North
Shipwrecks of Massachusetts: South
Shipwrecks of Rhode Island and Connecticut
Shipwrecks of New York
Shipwrecks of New Jersey (1988)
Shipwrecks of New Jersey: North
Shipwrecks of New Jersey: Central
Shipwrecks of New Jersey: South
Shipwrecks of Delaware and Maryland (1990 Edition)
Shipwrecks of Delaware and Maryland (2002 Edition)
Shipwrecks of Virginia
Shipwrecks of North Carolina: Diamond Shoals North
Shipwrecks of North Carolina: Hatteras Inlet South
Shipwrecks of South Carolina and Georgia

Shipwreck and Nautical History
Andrea Doria: Dive to an Era
Deep, Dark, and Dangerous: Adventures and Reflections on the Andrea Doria
Great Lakes Shipwrecks: a Photographic Odyssey
The Fuhrer's U-boats in American Waters
Ironclad Legacy: Battles of the USS Monitor
The Lusitania Controversies (Book One):
    Atrocity of War and a Wreck-Diving History
The Lusitania Controversies: (Book Two)
    Dangerous Descents into Shipwrecks and Law
The Nautical Cyclopedia
Shadow Divers Exposed: the Real Saga of the U-869
Shipwreck Heresies
The Shipwreck Research Handbook
Shipwreck Sagas
Stolen Heritage: Grand Theft of Hamilton and Scourge
Track of the Gray Wolf
USS San Diego: the Last Armored Cruiser
Wreck Diving Adventures

Books by the Author

Dive Training
Primary Wreck Diving Guide
Advanced Wreck Diving Guide
Ultimate Wreck Diving Guide
The Advanced Wreck Diving Handbook
The Technical Diving Handbook

Nonfiction
Wilderness Canoeing

Science Fiction
A Different Universe
A Different Dimension
A Different Continuum
Entropy (a novel of conceptual breakthrough)
A Journey to the Center of the Earth
The Mold
Return to Mars
Silent Autumn
The Time Dragons Trilogy
   A Time for Dragons
   Dragons Past
   No Future for Dragons

Sci-Fi Action/Adventure Novels
Memory Lane
Mind Set
The Peking Papers

Supernatural Horror Novel
The Lurking: Curse of the Jersey Devil

Vietnam Novel
Lonely Conflict

Videotape or DVD
The Battle for the USS Monitor

Visit the GGP website for availability of titles:
http://www.ggentile.com

Of the thousands of decompression dives that Gary has made, over 190 of them were on the Grand Dame of the Sea: the *Andrea Doria*. He was the first scuba diver to enter the First Class Dining Room, from which he recovered many items of elegant china. He also recovered and restored hundreds of items of jewelry and souvenirs from the Gift Shop, located at a depth of 220 feet. More important, he discovered and recovered a number of ceramic panels that once adorned the walls of the First Class Bar. These colorful panels were the work of famed Italian artist Romano Rui.

In the early 1990's, Gary was instrumental in merging mixed-gas diving technology with wreck-diving. His 1990 dive on the German battleship *Ostfriesland*, at a depth of 380 feet, triggered an unprecedented expansion in the exploration of deep-water shipwrecks, and the advent of helium mixes as a breathing medium. He wrote the first book on technical diving. In 1994, he participated in a mixed-gas diving expedition to the *Lusitania*, which lies at a depth of 300 feet.

Gary has specialized in wreck-diving and shipwreck research, concentrating his efforts on wrecks along the eastern seaboard, from Newfoundland to Key West, and in the Great Lakes. In addition to diving on hundreds of known shipwreck sites, he has been on more than forty discovery dive trips.

He has compiled an extensive library of books, photographs, drawings, plans, and original source materials on ships and shipwrecks. He has conducted surveys on numerous wrecks, some of which have been drawn in the form of large-sized prints that are suitable for framing.

Over the years, he has rescued many thousands of shipwreck artifacts from the ravages of the sea, making him a leading authority in recovery techniques. He has gone to great lengths to preserve and restore these relics from the deep, and to display them to thousands of interested people, divers and nondivers alike. Throughout the years, these artifacts have been displayed at various museums, symposiums, and club-oriented exhibitions.

Author's Biography

Gary has written scores of magazine articles, and has published more than three thousand photographs in books, periodicals, newspapers, brochures, advertisements, corporate reports, museum displays, postcards, film, and television. He lectures extensively on underwater topics, and conducts seminars on advanced wreck-diving techniques, high-tech diving equipment, and shipwreck photography.

He is the author of 52 books: primarily novels of science fiction adventure and nonfiction books on wreck-diving and on nautical and shipwreck history. The Popular Dive Guide Series will eventually cover every major shipwreck along the East Coast of the United States.

There is also another side of Gary's life: that of an outdoor adventurer. In this guise he has climbed rock and mountains, backpacked through country high and low, bivouacked in the snow, and paddled his canoe through rapids and down untamed wilderness rivers - often for weeks at a time. His longest trip lasted a month, when he and five companions paddled 380 miles down the George River in Labrador. For three weeks straight they did not encounter another human being, or see signs of civilization. Gary embraces total self-sufficiency in the wilderness.

He has captured on film all of these wonderful outdoor adventures, as well as the splendor of nature's colorful scenery. He has given slide presentations to dive clubs, hiking clubs, canoe clubs, elder hostels, church groups, cub scouts, power squadrons, Naval associations, Civil War societies, Masonic lodges, Mensa, corporate functions, scientific organizations, and many, many other groups too numerous to mention.

In 1989, after a five-year battle with the National Oceanic and Atmospheric Administration, Gary won a suit which forced the hostile government agency to issue him a permit to dive on the USS *Monitor*, a protected National Marine Sanctuary. Media attention that was focused on Gary's triumphant victory resulted in nationwide coverage of his 1990 photographic expedition to the Civil War ironclad. Gary continues to fight for the right of access to all shipwreck sites.

www.ingramcontent.com/pod-product-compliance
Lightning Source LLC
Chambersburg PA
CBHW051042160426
43193CB00010B/1039